THE SPIRES STILL POINT TO HEAVEN

In the series *Urban Life, Landscape, and Policy,*
edited by David Stradling, Larry Bennett, and Davarian Baldwin.
Founding editor, Zane L. Miller.

THE SPIRES STILL POINT TO HEAVEN

Cincinnati's Religious Landscape,
1788–1873

MATTHEW SMITH

TEMPLE UNIVERSITY PRESS
Philadelphia • Rome • Tokyo

TEMPLE UNIVERSITY PRESS
Philadelphia, Pennsylvania 19122
tupress.temple.edu

Library of Congress Cataloging-in-Publication Data

Names: Smith, Matthew, 1977– author.
Title: The spires still point to heaven : Cincinnati's religious landscape,
1788–1873 / Matthew Smith.
Other titles: Urban life, landscape, and policy.
Description: Philadelphia : Temple University Press, 2023. | Series: Urban
life, landscape, and policy | Includes bibliographical references and
index. | Summary: "Explores how Cincinnati became a cultural focal point
of the early American republic, highlighting questions of religion,
ethnicity, and immigration in the context of specific issues such as
epidemic disease, temperance reform, slavery, and education"— Provided
by publisher.
Identifiers: LCCN 2022017979 (print) | LCCN 2022017980 (ebook) | ISBN
9781439922941 (cloth) | ISBN 9781439922958 (paperback) | ISBN
9781439922965 (pdf)
Subjects: LCSH: Religious pluralism—Ohio—Cincinnati. | Cincinnati
(Ohio)—History—18th century | Cincinnati (Ohio)—History—19th century
| Cincinnati (Ohio)—Religion—18th century | Cincinnati
(Ohio)—Religion—19th century | Cincinnati (Ohio)—Social
conditions—18th century | Cincinnati (Ohio)—Social conditions—19th
century | United States—Territorial expansion—History—18th century. |
United States—Territorial expansion—History—19th century.
Classification: LCC F499.C557 S66 2023 (print) | LCC F499.C557 (ebook) |
DDC 977.1/78—dc23/eng/20220706
LC record available at https://lccn.loc.gov/2022017979
LC ebook record available at https://lccn.loc.gov/2022017980

Printed in the United States of America

9 8 7 6 5 4 3 2 1

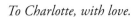

To Charlotte, with love.

Contents

Acknowledgments

My thanks begin with Zane L. Miller, professor emeritus of urban history at the University of Cincinnati (U.C.), who encouraged me to write for the Urban Life, Landscape, and Policy series. Though I regret never having met Zane in person, I enjoyed corresponding with him for some time before his death in March 2016. His good-humored wisdom was in my thoughts as I wrote this book.

David Stradling, Zane L. Miller Professor of Urban History at U.C., has advised me since the outset, stepping into the breach left by Zane's passing. I could not have asked for a more supportive editor, and I have enjoyed our lunches at Izen's Drunken Bento and Ruth's Parkside Café. Thanks also to Aaron Javsicas at Temple University Press for steering this book to completion.

Although there are too many to be thanked individually, my thanks go to the staff and librarians at the following institutions: the Amistad Research Center at Tulane University; University of Chicago Library, Special Collections; the Filson Historical Society in Louisville, Kentucky; the Kentucky Historical Society; the Presbyterian Historical Society, Philadelphia; St. Mary's Seminary and University, Baltimore; and the University of Notre Dame Archives, South Bend, Indiana. Also, thanks to all at the Cincinnati Historical Library, a Queen City treasure.

Thanks to colleagues past and present at Miami for their mentorship, including Carla Pestana, Mary Cayton, Peter Williams, Katharine Gillespie, David Fahey, and Curt Ellison. I regret Drew Cayton is no longer with us.

His insight and passion informed my interest in Cincinnati and Midwest history.

Thanks to *Ohio Valley History* for granting use of my article, "The Specter of Cholera in Nineteenth Century Cincinnati," *Ohio Valley History* 16, no. 2 (Summer 2016): 21–40, sections of which appear in Chapter 2 of this book.

Thanks to Kelli Lyon Johnson, Henry Claxton Binford, and Rob Schorman for feedback on the manuscript at earlier stages. Thanks also to Julie Turner at the Mount Healthy Historical Society and James Bratt at Calvin College for sharing their time and knowledge.

Friends who kept me steady on the road include Will Taylor and the triumvirate of Martin Johnson, Tom Flanigan, and Anthony Miller. Thanks also to the staff at El Comal in Hamilton for some excellent lunches.

Special thanks to my mother, Dinah Smith, for her keen interest and support. Both she and my late father, Patrick Smith, nurtured my love of history.

Finally, thanks to Whitney and Charlotte for putting up with my whims, moods, and enthusiasms, with love.

Note on Usage

In the interests of consistency, I distinguish between the capitalized "Native" to describe American Indian people and civilization and lowercase "native" or "nativist" to describe anti-immigrant activism and activists of the nineteenth century. Since anti-immigrant nativists of this period often referred to themselves as "Native Americans," I additionally use the term "American Indians" when referring to indigenous populations and society in order to avoid confusion. And in the interests of accuracy, where possible, I favor the particular over the generic, referring to American Indians by their specific tribal demonyms.

THE SPIRES STILL POINT TO HEAVEN

Introduction

So shall they fear the name of the LORD from the west, and his glory from the rising of the sun, when the enemy shall come in like a flood, the Spirit of the LORD shall lift up a standard against him.

—Isaiah 59:19 (Authorized King James Bible)

The humorist Mark Twain allegedly remarked that when the world ended, he wanted to be in Cincinnati, "because it's always twenty years behind the times."[1] Whether or not Twain ever spoke those words, Cincinnatians have long cultivated his gibe as an in-joke. Such indulgence obscures more than it enlightens, for although Twain's reference to the end times poked fun at the millenarian hopes and anxieties of evangelicals, Cincinnati was no mere backwater awaiting the apocalypse. Instead, it was a thriving, entrepreneurial, cosmopolitan city, its various nicknames attesting to its unique influence and vivid hold on the national imagination. Henry Wadsworth Longfellow dubbed Cincinnati "the Queen of the West" in his famous poem extolling the sweet Catawba wine cultivated along the banks of the Ohio. To some, the Queen City was the "Athens of the West," a commercial center destined to rival Philadelphia and even the cities of Europe in cultural and intellectual sophistication. Others, more vulgarly, referred to the hog-slaughtering center of the United States as "Porkopolis." Immigrant manuals described "a compact, well built, and bustling city, extending rapidly in all directions . . . the great inland commercial town of the West."[2] Anticipating later urban historians' preoccupation with central metropolitan hubs, Cincinnati boosters projected the growth of their city beyond the hinterlands of the Ohio Valley, one writer venturing to predict "that within one hundred years from this time, Cincinnati will be the greatest city in America; and by the year of our lord two thousand, the greatest city in the world."[3]

This book presents a case study in the formation of American pluralism and religious liberty. It explores why—and, importantly, *how*—Cincinnati became a focus of culture in the United States. Questions of citizenship, education, and public health loomed large, as competition between Protestant denominations and the Catholic Church intensified within the commercial emporium of the Ohio Valley. By the mid-nineteenth century, networks of domestic missionary enterprise extended Cincinnati's influence beyond the frontier, even as Eastern Seaboard cities such as Boston, Philadelphia, and New York shaped America's religious landscape. In relation to such urban geography, this book asks several key questions, among them: How did Cincinnati's status as a center of commerce, culture, and missionary influence shape relations with other major cities? How did Cincinnati address the challenges of sectarianism and nativism compared to these major cities? How did sectarian dialogue and conflict manifest in the Queen City's religious landscape?

Cincinnati occupied a crossroads between free soil and slave soil, eastern influence and western development. As historian Daniel Aaron put it, the city "was a kind of American primer. . . . Geographically and culturally [it] symbolized America."[4] Even those factors that made Cincinnati unique—"the first completely *new* big city developed by the United States," as Henry Binford noted—made it remarkably representative.[5] Thus, Cincinnati was not only quintessentially American but key to understanding the urban development of the nation. Shedding comparative light on Cincinnati's history, studies such as Dominic Pacyga's *Chicago: A Biography* (2011), Adam Arenson's *The Great Heart of the Republic* (2011), Tyler Anbinder's *City of Dreams* (2016), and Andrew Heath's *In Union There Is Strength* (2019) explore the political, cultural, and religious landscapes of Chicago, St. Louis, New York, and Philadelphia respectively. Several parallels suggest themselves between these cities and Cincinnati during its nineteenth-century heyday, including political geography, economic growth, and immigration. Placing Philadelphia in the context of urban consolidation, national growth, and empire, Heath identifies how Philadelphians explained the growth of their city in terms of "Manifest Destiny"—a tendency more literally manifested in Chicago, where the "iron bands" of rail infrastructure connected the nation from the Great Lakes to the Gulf of Mexico.[6] As Arenson noted, the phrase "Manifest Destiny" was coined in New York and rationalized national expansion during the Mexican-American War in the 1840s. But the idea of America's mission to the world was older, dating back to the Puritan "errand into the wilderness."[7]

While Cincinnati was geographically blessed by its foundations on the Ohio River, its good luck did not last forever. Rival cities such as St. Louis and Chicago flourished with railroad expansion as the Queen City struggled to expand commerce to prairie towns such as Alton, Quincy, and Peoria in Illinois and Davenport in Iowa.[8] While it is tempting to depict Cincinnati as the city Manifest Destiny left behind, its early prospects were altogether more promising. In contrast to eastern ports of entry, especially New York, where immigrants clustered in poorer neighborhoods, Cincinnati offered enticing opportunities for those with the resources to relocate, including German immigrants who dominated the Queen City's immigrant population.[9] And although Cincinnati experienced outbreaks of ethnic and sectarian violence, such bloodshed was comparatively deadlier in eastern cities like Philadelphia, where anti-Catholic rioting in 1844 inspired talk of "civil war" and weeks of martial law.[10]

Despite Cincinnati's nineteenth-century prominence, scholars have overlooked its distinct religious and ethnic landscape. At the beginning of the nineteenth century, for example, Cincinnati emerged apparently unscathed from firestorms of evangelical religion blazing through the Ohio Valley and Kentucky. But Cincinnati was more susceptible to revival enthusiasm than many historians assumed. Although what historians subsequently termed the Great Revival (1797–c. 1805) was mostly considered an agrarian frontier precursor of the Second Great Awakening, the urbanization of the Ohio Valley absorbed and diffused evangelical enthusiasm.[11] As the region developed, transportation, commerce, and migration wove the Queen City into its hinterlands. Pioneer physician Daniel Drake, an influential booster, recognized as much in his 1815 guide, *Natural and Statistical View, or Picture of Cincinnati and the Miami Country*, noting: "The relations of a town with its surrounding country are an essential part of its history, and cannot be understood without studying both."[12]

Fascination with landscape was no mere antiquarian preserve. Many Americans equated the opening of the West with the opening of the gospel, heralding the thousand-year reign of Christ and the salvation of mankind. From the Errand into the Wilderness through Manifest Destiny, the dynamic was familiar. With American Indians driven from Ohio by the turn of the nineteenth century, frontier preachers concentrated on churching outlying settlers, exhorting against irreligion and infidelity. The vanguard of these missionaries hailed from the northeastern United States. Steeped in a tradition that identified the American nation with Mosaic Israel, they viewed the frontier as an abode of struggle, "a deep valley or thick forest," haunted by Satan.[13] For New Englanders, above all, theology and history justified sowing the gospel in the wilderness. "In the discovery and settlement of this country," enthused one Maine pastor in 1820, "God had some great end in view . . . so this land may be favored with the dawn of the millennial sun, which may return to the east, shining with glowing brightness."[14] Such zeal impressed many observers of early America. Among the most notable was French author Alexis de Tocqueville, who was surprised to encounter graduates of elite eastern colleges like Yale and Andover embarking for the prairies of Illinois and Missouri.[15]

As Tocqueville marveled at wealthy New Englanders evangelizing the rural Midwest, his travels demonstrated the urbanization of the young republic. In December 1831, Tocqueville and his friend Gustave de Beaumont spent three days in Cincinnati, their tour of the United States encompassing the fastest-growing inland river city of this time. Preachers evoked biblical metaphors of wilderness, but the Ohio Valley frontier was long since domesticated. Signs of urbanization arose amid the Great Revival, which swept the agrarian heartlands and manifested on the streets of Cincinnati. This forerunner of the Second Great Awakening divided mainline Protestant clergy into pro- and anti-revival factions while antagonizing critics ranging from frontier Catholics to deists. Even those who approved of the revival frequently decried the extemporaneous preaching, exhortation, shouting, stamping, dancing, singing, swooning, and ecstatic visions that became its unwonted hallmarks and threatened the orderly urban settlement of the frontier.

Alarmed by popular enthusiasm, the national leadership of the Presbyterian and Congregationalist churches announced a Plan of Union in 1801, reasserting their authority while pooling resources in the Ohio Valley. With deep pockets and cultural cachet, the Congregationalists dominated New England yet struggled to influence the frontier. By contrast, the Presbyterians had greater numbers in the West but wrestled with sectarian competition. Both churches hoped to extend mutual influence. Since Congregationalists and Presbyterians drew upon similar Calvinist heritage and similar educational standards for the ministry, in theory the union was sound. In practice, the scheme harbored seeds of division. The partnership resulted in eastern funds and Congregationalist ministers pouring into the Presbyterian pulpits of Cincinnati and the Ohio Valley. But since the confessional standards of the Congregationalist ministry were more liberal than those of the Presbyterians (who held fast to the 1646 Westminster Confession of Faith), many conservative Presbyterians resented this influx of New Englanders.[16]

Notwithstanding its limitations, the 1801 Plan of Union had profound consequences for the development of Cincinnati. In the short term, union strengthened the Congregationalist and Presbyterian clergy in the Ohio Valley. Moreover, it widened channels of missionary enterprise, enabling unprecedented levels of voluntaristic organization led by the laity as much as the clergy. Protestant agencies such as the American Bible Society (established 1816), the American Tract Society (1825), and the American Home Missionary Society (1826) flourished in the Queen City. Nationalistic in name and mission, such associations orchestrated missionary effort in the Ohio Valley and beyond. Their success rendered more traditional church-led forms of organization all but obsolete, with one notable exception. While the Catholic Church was barely evident on Cincinnati's religious landscape at the turn of the nineteenth century, immigration and institutional growth made Catholicism a formidable rival to Protestantism within a few short decades.

Cincinnati became the western headquarters of the so-called Evangelical United Front, or Benevolent Empire, which in the wake of disestablishment became what historian Daniel Walker Howe termed the "functional equivalent of an established church."[17] Influenced by the New Divinity theology of the Great Awakening, agencies such as the American Home Missionary Society and the American Bible Society emphasized a philanthropy of "disinterested benevolence," although later historians read their influence more in terms of social control.[18] Supported by private subscription rather than taxation, and funded by businessmen such as Arthur and Lewis Tappan, the Benevolent Empire exerted influence beyond the pulpit in matters ranging from poor relief to the curriculum of public schools. Its activities wove Cincinnati into the urban fabric of the United States, connecting its western hinterlands to organizational headquarters in the eastern metropolises of New York City, Boston, and Philadelphia. Yet power ran both ways, and Cincinnati emerged as an important center in its own right.

Lane Theological Seminary (1832), designed to educate young preachers for the West, demonstrated the ambition of the Benevolent Empire. Lane's Presbyterian and Congregationalist trustees wooed one of America's leading evangelical spokesmen, Rev. Lyman Beecher, as their first president, bolstering the institution's claims to religious leadership while underlining Cincinnati's strategic importance. Through his presidency of Lane and as minister of Cincinnati's Second Presbyterian Church, this preacher from Connecticut played an energetic role in the life of the city. But anxiety clouded evangelical confidence. In welcoming Beecher, Lane's trustees sounded a familiar tune, warning of "the combined powers of darkness coming in . . . like a flood."[19] From his western vantage, Beecher likewise expressed foreboding. His anti-immigration tract *A Plea for the West* (1835) warned that "mighty causes, like floods from distant mountains, are rushing with accumulating power, to their consummation of good or evil, and soon our character and destiny will be stereotyped forever."[20]

Defying nativist fears, Cincinnati boomed on the back of economic migration, becoming the sixth-largest city in the nation by 1840.[21] The change was remarkable, even by American standards. By 1850 foreign-born people made up 46 percent of Cincinnati's population, not including growing numbers of first-generation children. Ethnic Germans were nearly one-third of the city's population, with immigrants from Ireland the next-largest minority at roughly 12 percent. An estimated two-thirds of the city's Germans and most Irish were Roman Catholics. German-speaking immigrants also included significant numbers of Jews and anticlerical freethinkers, complicating the mix.[22]

While Cincinnati's Catholic immigrants provided a bright splash of variegation, Protestant revival culture endured long after the Great Revival. By 1830, one-quarter of Ohio's nearly one million inhabitants clustered in the state's southwestern corner, only sparsely inhabited at the turn of the century. This diverse population concentrated in the Queen City and northward into the rich farmlands of the Miami Valley.[23] These hinterlands furnished Cincinnati with essential markets and raw materials, including herds of semi-feral pigs that fed its slaughterhouses and surplus corn for distilleries. They also proved fertile ground for religion. In the 1820s, for example, English-born Cincinnati resident Frances "Fanny" Trollope described how her "curiosity was excited by hearing the 'revival' talked of by everyone we met throughout the town. 'The revival will be very full'—'We shall be constantly engaged during the revival'—were the phrases we constantly heard repeated."[24] To Trollope, it appeared as if the enthusiasm of the surrounding hinterlands had erupted into Cincinnati's streets.

This book echoes Trollope's perception of the porous boundaries between urban and rural and Daniel Drake's holistic view of the landscape, but, while extending beyond Cincinnati, it remains emphatically a work of urban history. Why this should be so is no mystery. In his classic 1957 study, *Revivalism and Social Reform*, historian Timothy L. Smith asserted: "The vital center of American Protestantism was in the cities rather than the rural West."[25] In a similar vein, Richard Wade's *The Urban Frontier* (1959) claimed: "The towns were the spearheads of the frontier."[26] Such complementary understanding of the central importance of American cities eclipsed the fading orthodoxy of Frederick Jackson Turner's "frontier thesis." Turner explained American national development in terms of "the existence of an area of free land, its continuous recession, and the advance of American settlement westward." The most influential American historian of the twentieth century, Turner relegated religion to the margins of his vision, but historians who followed him in seeing the frontier as "the line of most rapid and effective Americanization" adopted his framework to describe the religious landscape.[27] One manifestation of frontier worship—the camp meeting revival—became synonymous with the rural antebellum West. In the words of one Turnerian scholar, "the camp meeting itself simply 'grew up' with the frontier."[28] Persistent religious revival in nineteenth-century Cincinnati and the adaptation of camp meeting measures in an urban environment, however, complicates such dichotomy between the city and its surrounding countryside.

Recent studies of the United States emphasize the "market revolution," a transitional phase that developed the agrarian economy of the early republic into full-blown capitalism. New methods of agriculture, manufacturing, and marketing advanced with communications and transportation, internal and overseas immigration, and consumer culture, transforming everyday life from the most bustling urban metropolis to the farthest frontier community. The metaphor of the market extended into every aspect of early American life, including religion. One tendency of this shift has been to boil down the "religious economy" to "the characteristics of winners and losers in a free market religious environment that exposed religious organizations to relentless competition."[29] Market forces admittedly explained many transformations in Cincinnati, including networks of religious publishing and domestic missionary enterprise, the voluntaristic growth of organized religion, and the ostentation of religious architecture. According to one recent study, the Queen City "became nothing less than an urban marketplace for religion."[30] But religion in Cincinnati was more than the sum of its marketable parts. For many Cincinnatians, especially women, black people, and immigrants, it opened the door to unprecedented engagement in the public sphere. Salvation of souls and communities might have lead the way, but civic participation left an indelible legacy.

This book's chapters take the form of interlocking essays, following a broadly chronological and logical sequence and written in order of appearance. Chapter 1 takes a broad view of the Ohio Valley's religious landscape, from the foundation of Cincinnati in 1788 through the antebellum period. The Queen City's relations with its region are explored within the context of the Great Revival, with particular focus on the urban dimension. This chapter explores how the city transformed the revival, absorbing its enthusiasm, while laying the foundations of a sophisticated, voluntaristic network of evangelical Protestant missionary enterprise connecting Cincinnati to national centers of organized religion including New York City, Boston, and Philadelphia.

Chapter 2 explores disease, public health reform, and temperance activism. It considers how Cincinnati's waterways and slums became battlegrounds during the global cholera pandemics in 1832 and 1849, amid death and suffering, anti-immigrant sentiment, and struggles to assert moral authority. Chapter 2 also examines controversies surrounding temperance reform, which mounted in the wake of cholera. Temperance was ambivalent, hardening sentiment around issues of vice, consumption, and religion while providing a template for grassroots organization. Although overlapping with the rise of xenophobic, nativist politics, temperance broadened democracy in the Queen City, opening the door for women and working-class and immigrant Cincinnatians to enter the public sphere. And the emergence of Catholic temperance was a potent reminder that citizens defined themselves, culturally and politically, as much by shared struggles as by sectarian stereotypes.

Chapter 3 again takes a broader geographical view, exploring competition between the Catholic Archdiocese of Cincinnati and the American Home Missionary Society in the Ohio Valley. Founded in 1826, the A.H.M.S. was America's largest Protestant domestic missionary organization; it was headquartered in New York City but had a western base of operations in Cincinnati. Its missionaries rode the same circuits and often preached to the same communities as Cincinnati's Catholic outriders. Comparison of the extensive records of both organizations reveals similarities in the methodology and influence of these itinerants, emphasizing the logistical importance of Cincinnati as a missionary hub for Catholics and Protestants alike.

The final two chapters address nativist backlash to Catholic immigration in Cincinnati, concluding with one strand of its resolution in the post–Civil War Reconstruction era. Chapter 4 explores the convergence of anti-Catholicism and political nativism that led the anti-immigrant American Party to within a hair's breadth of the Cincinnati mayoralty in the 1850s. Even as the United States slid toward Civil War over the question of slavery, Cincinnatians subscribed to wild sectarian conspiracies. Some even feared the Vatican might relocate to the Queen City. In the end, however, Cincinnati's anti-Catholicism was as much political as religious. While Catholic immigration roused Protestant prejudice, the most virulent opposition came from anticlerical German immigrants, who identified Catholicism with political reaction in the United States and Europe. Chapter 4 explores such nativism in Cincinnati; its overlapping religious, political, and ethnic dimensions; and the unlikely bedfellows it produced.

Finally, Chapter 5 focuses on education and the Bible War, a struggle over the teaching of scripture in Cincinnati public schools. This chapter spans the period of the Civil War, culminating in 1873 when the Ohio Supreme Court overturned a lower court ruling that protected Protestant instruction in the public curriculum. Cincinnati's Bible War was constitutionally significant, a test case in landmark legal battles throughout the nation. These included the 1963 United States Supreme Court case, *Abington School District v. Schempp*, that finally ruled against public schools sponsoring Bible readings and recitation of the Lord's Prayer. Chapter 5 explores how the separation of church and state in the context of public education galvanized evangelicals and secularists, Jews, Catholics, and others. The same issues of freedom and conscience contested in nineteenth-century Cincinnati remain contested in today's United States. Understanding the Bible War as a case study rooted in the political and sectarian landscape of the Queen City highlights the evolution of American pluralism and the historical boundaries of religious tolerance and liberty.

1

—————

Beyond the Frontier

The Religious Landscape

No person, demeaning himself in a peaceful and orderly manner, shall ever be molested on account of his mode of worship, or religious sentiments, in the said territory.

—THE NORTHWEST ORDINANCE (1787)

This whole valley is covered, to a vast depth, with the ruins of a former world.

—ATWATER, *A History of the State of Ohio*

The Northwest Ordinance of 1787[1] paved the way for Cincinnati's foundation, providing a uniquely American framework for the new territory north of the Ohio River. The characteristic township system, with its orderly grid of surveyors' lots, avoided the land grab that entangled frontier Kentucky with an overlapping patchwork of "shingled" claims. At the same time, the Northwest Ordinance extinguished American Indian land rights, ensuring rich pickings for ambitious speculators. Moreover, its principle of religious toleration, designed to encourage immigration, emphasized principles of order as much as freedom while erasing the Native culture whose beliefs shaped the land.[2]

This chapter explores the foundation of Cincinnati's religious landscape, emphasizing its regional and cultural interdependency. By the second decade of the nineteenth century, Cincinnati was the powerhouse of the Ohio Valley. Its prosperity, however, depended on the slave economy of the South, fueling tensions that led the United States into the Civil War. Culturally, as well as economically, the city was complex. Evangelical revivalism in the Ohio Valley, especially, shaped Cincinnati's development, forcing religious leaders to absorb, contain, and diffuse popular enthusiasm. In this regard, the Benevolent Empire, or Evangelical United Front, was significant. This Protestant connection of voluntaristic associations arose during the Second Great Awakening (1790s–early 1800s). Though the Benevolent Empire developed in the urban northeastern United States, Cincinnati became its western hub. This chapter also considers the Queen City's transformation by European immigrants, who by the 1830s lent a distinctly Catholic cast to the religious landscape.

"The Touch of a Feather"

In December 1788, when Israel Ludlow, Matthias Denman, and Robert Patterson chose the future site of Cincinnati on a broad bend of the Ohio River, its prospects for survival were doubtful. Even the town's original name of "Losantiville" was ungainly—a portmanteau of English, French, Greek, and Latin roots concocted by surveyor John Filson.[3] Since the early 1770s, settlers and speculators had coveted the rich soil of the Miami Valley in southwest Ohio. As the death toll mounted, however, even "the dark and bloody ground" of Kentucky to the south seemed more welcoming than what became notorious as the "Miami slaughterhouse."[4] Some seventy thousand American settlers had already pushed west of the Appalachians, occupying the tribal hunting grounds of the future Bluegrass State. North of the Ohio River, bloodshed intensified in lands fiercely defended by the Shawnee, Miami, Wyandot, and other nations. Ohio settlers looked to the nascent authority of the Northwest Territory for military support against their Native adversaries. Despite construction of the nearby federal garrison of Fort Washington the following summer, conquest of Losantiville's hinterlands seemed far from imminent.

Euphoniously renamed in 1790 after the Society of the Cincinnati—an elite fraternity of Continental army officers—the frontier city clung to the banks of the Ohio between two other settlements destined to be absorbed by its eventual growth: Columbia (1788) to the east, founded by New Jersey–born Benjamin Stites by the mouth of the Miami River, and North Bend (1789) to the west, established by land speculator and fellow New Jersey native John Cleves Symmes. These settlements endured flooding, economic hardship, and ever-present threats of warfare, challenges that at first seemed overwhelming. To Symmes, the lack of federal government support seemed almost as dire as the threat posed by the Shawnees and other tribes. "I am mortified to see people running away from these settlements," he wrote in 1789, "merely because no care is taken by their superiors to save them and their families from the rage of the savages . . . they feel themselves abandoned to destruction, and whether the danger they apprehend is real or imaginary, 'tis the same to them."[5]

Given its brutish struggles, Cincinnati seemed an unlikely place to usher in the kingdom of heaven. Few could imagine its transformation, within a generation, into a metropolis of culture and religion—a city that evoked "gilded spires gleaming among gardens and shrubbery."[6] Frontier violence discouraged, if it did not preclude, all but the necessities of survival, leaving politics and religion in apparent neglect. Settlers who might never have prayed to the Almighty lobbied the central government, betraying bitter anxiety when aid and assistance failed to materialize. As Symmes complained, the garrison at Fort Washington was composed of "one ensign and twelve soldiers in a little block-house badly constructed." With American Indians armed and supplied by the British, who retained designs on the Northwest Territory, Ohio settlers received "not an axe, hoe, spade, or even tomahawk" from their government. "Not a swivel is afforded us, when . . . each village should have two or three field pieces at least. I have indeed lost sight of any succor from the United States," Symmes lamented.[7]

The grievances of Symmes and his fellow settlers looked ominous from an American perspective, as the Northwest Territory exhibited frailties reminiscent of earlier intrigue in neighboring Kentucky. The Ohio Valley was the cornerstone of the early republic, but western discontent led Thomas Jefferson to warn as early as 1785 that Kentucky might "separate[e] . . . from the confederacy."[8] Between the French and Indian War and the War of 1812—"the Long War for the West"—the United States risked much against the British and their Native allies, not to mention the empires of France and Spain.[9] The inaccessibility of the Mississippi River was a particular grievance. Spanish authorities in Louisiana embargoed American commerce along the river that marked the border with the United States. The reluctance of the federal government to press the issue dismayed western farmers for whom Mississippi commerce was a matter of survival, given parlous overland routes and the need to bring goods to market.

Matters came to a head. The ensuing intrigue, known as the Spanish Conspiracy, embroiled a cabal of leading Kentuckians pledging allegiance to the Spanish crown, rumors of secession, and a freebooting expedition to capture New Orleans. While these plots fizzled out, the conspiracy's broad outline became an open secret, its audacity eclipsed only by the Burr Conspiracy of the early 1800s. Perhaps its most shocking implication was the thought of American citizens pledging allegiance to a foreign, Catholic monarch. In any event, Symmes never sank to the depths of his Kentucky acquaintance James Wilkinson, who in 1787 wrote: "I hope that no one can say of me with justice that I break any law of nature or of nations, of conscience or of honor, in transferring my allegiance, from the United States to his Catholic Majesty."[10] The caginess of Wilkinson's clandestine pledge hinted at likely conflicts between Kentucky and Catholic Spain; most Kentuckians were nominally

Protestant, and many regarded the pope as the Antichrist. Had his betrayal become public, Wilkinson might well have been hanged. Instead, he served many more years in uniform, including command at Fort Washington. But as George Washington himself acknowledged, these were strange times: "The Western settlers . . . stand as it were upon a pivot—the touch of a feather would turn them any way."[11]

Washington's fears of western secession were unfounded, but for Ohio Valley tribes, American expansion was cataclysmic. Despite Native victories, mounting pressure from the United States Army combined with the influx of settlers set a template for conquest that endured through the century. The consequence was not just the slaughter and dispossession of indigenous people but the obliteration of a prosperous, sedentary civilization established some three thousand years before. Arriving at Fort Washington as a young officer, future United States president William Henry Harrison later recalled: "When I first saw the upper plain on which [Cincinnati] stands, it was literally covered with low lines of embankments. . . . The number and variety of figures in which these lines were drawn, was almost endless, and, as I have said, almost covered the plain."[12]

Like the ruins of Stonehenge or the Pyramids, the region's monuments were objects of wonder and speculation. Debate centered as much on *who* constructed the mounds as why, as well as what their decline indicated for civilization in the region. For some settlers, the prospects were sobering. Early Cincinnati Methodist preacher John Kobler reflected, "The justice of God and the downfall of nations are recorded here in a most fearful manner."[13] Rev. Manasseh Cutler, a western land speculator, wryly noted in 1789: "It struck me as rather curious that military gentlemen should contend that they were constructed for religious purposes, and that a clergyman that they were works of defense—opinions so contradictory to their professional prejudices."[14] A map of Cincinnati in Daniel Drake's 1815 *Natural and Statistical View* brought such "Remains of Antient [sic] works" to wider attention. Most prominent was an ovoid mound stretching east to west between Fourth and Fifth Streets, transected by Vine Street. "These vestiges consist of mounds, excavations, and embankments or walls, of various forms and dimensions," wrote Drake. Sadly, they were soon gone. The central mound was leveled in 1794 to make way for a watchtower, and the whole structure was eradicated in 1841. Such destruction, ironically, yielded archaeological treasures, illustrating historical trade routes between the Ohio Valley and Mesoamerica centuries before European contact. As Drake noted, comparing the mound builders of Ohio with the Aztecs: "The bigotry of Spain in the 16th century seems not to have been more destructive to the historical paintings of Mexico, than the indifference, negligence or idle curiosity of many of our citizens are to these interesting relics."[15]

Controversy still surrounds the significance of the mounds constructed by the pre-Columbian Adena culture (fl. 1000 B.C.E.–200 C.E.), but for Ohio tribes, fighting for their survival, such speculation was moot. Matters came to a head in November 1791, when a coalition led by Little Turtle of the Miamis waylaid United States forces led by Arthur St. Clair, the military governor of the Northwest Territory. Leading a force some one thousand strong deep into the Ohio country, St. Clair suffered the loss of some six hundred men near the Wabash River and narrowly escaped with his own life. As remnants of his ragtag army stumbled back into Cincinnati, only the encouragements of Presbyterian minister James Kemper prevented an exodus of panicked civilian inhabitants.[16]

Though failing to stem the tide of American conquest, Little Turtle's triumph remains the single greatest indigenous victory over the United States Army, his forces inflicting over twice the casualties borne by Custer at Little Bighorn (1876). Ultimately, however, a revamped American force under Revolutionary War veteran "Mad" Anthony Wayne erased the failures of St. Clair and his equally hapless predecessor, Josiah Harmar. Fighting alongside Kentucky militia forces in August 1794, Wayne's troops scored a decisive blow at the Battle of Fallen Timbers near present-day Toledo, Ohio. The Treaty of Greenville, imposed on Native leaders the following year, effectively ended the Northwest Indian War, enforcing United States claims over most of Ohio and reducing the indigenous population to the northwestern corner of the future state.

Notwithstanding his victory at Fallen Timbers, Wayne's strategy was ultimately impersonal, averting the blundering confrontation of previous commanders. Instead of reckless pursuit, Wayne extended a series of roads and fortifications deep into tribal country to ensure "the tranquility of the frontiers."[17] Such measures reinforced the military presence so deprecated by Symmes and other settlers. They capitalized on the sparse American Indian population in the Northwest Territory, reduced over generations by smallpox and other diseases. The train of garrisons radiating north from Cincinnati projected United States power on a beleaguered landscape. Forts Washington, Hamilton, St. Clair, and Jefferson comprised a spur of military and political authority, ensuring further settlements in their shadow. Not until the advent of the Miami and Erie Canal a generation later were such dramatic inroads made toward the urbanization of the Ohio Valley.

Even as military occupation ensured the growth of Cincinnati, the garrison at Fort Washington brought conflict with civilian settlers, reflecting the aggravations associated with bored young men in uniform. The city's earliest recorded riot—the first of many punctuating its violent history—erupted in 1792 after soldiers attacked a local merchant. Blame was not one sided, however. One Cincinnatian decried his fellow citizens the year before as "very licentious and too great a portion indolent and debauched."[18] Arthur St. Clair, combining the roles of garrison commander and civil magistrate, introduced Ohio's Blue Laws in 1788. Predating statehood, they targeted "idle, vain and obscene conversation, profane cursing and swearing," and "set apart the first day of the week, as a day of rest from common labors and pursuits," so that "all servile labor, works of necessity and charity only accepted, be wholly abstained from on said day."[19] Although such statutes made only a modest impact, St. Clair's dour Sabbatarianism foreshadowed tensions between reformism and civil liberty in early Cincinnati.

Despite Cincinnati's uncertain start, the future Queen City kindled great expectations. Coinciding with the Spanish-American Treaty of San Lorenzo (1795), which finally secured Mississippi navigation rights, the Treaty of Greenville was a milestone for the growth of the city. "Prior to the Treaty of Greenville," recalled businessman Jacob Burnet, "but few improvements had been made, of any description, and scarcely one of a permanent character."[20] But as pioneer Baptist preacher John Gano recalled, once "hostilities ceased, and the settlements began to increase rapidly every thing relating to them put on a new aspect." Settlers vied to "open the most Land for cultivation get the first fruit and raise the most grain pork and Beef" while development accelerated with technologies such as the steamboat and the canal.[21]

Cincinnati's growth accelerated in the first decades of the new century, although few Cincinnatians reflected on its bloody foundations. In an 1815 editorial, pioneer journalist Joseph Charless recalled how the city's hinterlands were "a dreary wilderness, the haunt of ruthless savages" in the 1790s. But within twenty years, the valley was remarkably "sprinkled with towns . . . spinning and weaving establishments, steam mills, manufactures in various metals, leather, wool, cotton, and flax," not to mention "seminaries of learning conducted by excellent teachers." By dramatizing the terrors of the wilderness, boosters contrasted rapid material change with the primordial horrors of frontier warfare. Charless even ventured into doggerel:

> *Here where so late the appalling sound*
> *Of savage yells, the woods resound*
> *Now smiling Ceres waves her sheaf*
> *And cities rise in bold relief.*[22]

Charless's verse reflected prevailing dogma, but Cincinnati's expansion blurred the purportedly orderly processes of civilization. One English visitor in 1797, for example, described a city of "about three or four hundred houses, mostly frame-built. The inhabitants are chiefly employed in some way of business, of which there is a great deal here transacted, the town being (if I may so call it) the metropolis of the north-western territory."[23]

Organized religion in the city grew relatively slowly, but some glimmers of religiosity shone from the outset. Cincinnati's development as a garrison town shaped its rowdy character, marked by outbreaks of binge drinking, street brawling, and petty larceny.[24] In spite of its notoriety, however, Cincinnati was no worse than most frontier settlements. One Scottish visitor describing the city's religious services noted "the attention and gravity which becomes the worship" and "many persons, who go to church three times on the same day."[25] Though Cincinnati boasted just two houses of worship by the turn of the nineteenth century, both were constructed shortly after the first settlement, pointing to fundamental demand. The first was the Baptist Church built in 1790 at the site of Columbia. Then, in October that year, Rev. David Rice, an influential Kentucky Presbyterian, founded "an organized church composed of six males and two females in Columbia and Cincinnati."[26] This conjoined congregation grew steadily but made do without a roof over its head for two years. In 1792, Rice's protégé, James Kemper, arrived, overseeing construction of the first Presbyterian church in Cincinnati, "an utterly plain and bare frame building" some 1,200 square feet in area.[27]

Among the appeals of organized religion was the settlement of ministers like Kemper, men who were identified with the schoolroom as much as the pulpit. Indeed, the Northwest Ordinance of 1787, which laid the foundation for Ohio to join the Union, presumed the supply of an educated clergy as the nation expanded. "Religion, morality, and knowledge, being necessary to good government and the happiness of mankind," it declared, "schools and the means of education shall forever be encouraged." The ordinance's toleration for all "mode[s] of worship" and "religious sentiments" (albeit for persons of "peaceful and orderly" behavior) anticipated religious diversity while foreshadowing the federal constitution's prohibition of religious establishment.[28] Nevertheless, churches and settled clergy were few and far between in early Cincinnati. Itinerant preachers, on the other hand, prevailed on the city's streets as late as the 1830s, among "all persuasions . . . except the Episcopalian, Catholic, Unitarian, and Quaker."[29]

Itinerant missionaries produced some of the earliest, most critical descriptions of Cincinnati. Among the first of these missionaries was Johann

Heckewelder. A member of the pietist Moravian sect, Heckewelder migrated to Ohio from Pennsylvania in 1773 to minister to the Delaware Indians at Gnadenhutten, near present-day Canton. The earliest permanent settlement in the future state founded by Europeans, Gnadenhutten suffered tragedy in 1782 when Pennsylvania militia attacked the mission, murdering nearly one hundred pacifist Native converts. "Destitute of both honour and humanity," Heckewelder wrote, such men maintained "that to kill an Indian, was the same as killing a bear or a buffalo."[30] Despite revulsion at such vigilantism, by 1792 Heckewelder was an agent for the United States, his language skills making him a valuable intermediary in negotiations with tribal leaders. Accompanying Brigadier General Rufus Putnam to the Indiana frontier settlement of Vincennes, Heckewelder dreaded the violence of westward expansion. He described Cincinnati with the scruples of a seasoned evangelist, but the burden of his diplomatic mission leached into his anxiety.

Heckewelder's journal contains the earliest extant description of Cincinnati by a preacher. He portrayed a coarse settlement corrupted with avarice, foreshadowing later critiques by mainline Protestant clergy, not to mention early Catholic itinerants. The town was "overrun with merchants and traders and overstocked with merchandise; there are already over 30 stores and warehouses." Criminality was rife, religion ridiculed: "Idlers are plentiful here, according to the assertion of the respectable people a multitude like the Sodomites." Nevertheless, he hoped that "this bad element" would be cleared out, "for experience teaches, that as soon as they are brought under the hands of the law, they seek the shores of Kentucky (which lies directly across the Ohio), and if they are caught there, they escape to the extreme borders of the Clinch or Cumberland river, or even to [New] Orleans."[31]

Depictions of Cincinnati as a frontier Sodom should be read cautiously. Itinerants emphasized citizens' love of whiskey, cards, and chewing tobacco decades before the English travel writer Fanny Trollope described "the total and universal want of good, or even pleasing, manners, both in males and females."[32] The city's rough edges endured between Heckewelder's first visit in 1792 and 1803, when Methodist bishop Francis Asbury preached on one of his many tours of the region. Stung by missionary frustration, Asbury left a bitter impression in his journal. "My mind is greatly engaged with God in public and in private," he wrote, "but I feel the power of Satan in those little, wicked, western trading towns."[33]

Other pioneer preachers echoed Asbury's complaints, buttressing the image of the godless frontier. Fellow Methodist John Kobler visited the city from Kentucky in 1798, finding the surrounding region "very spare indeed," with "only now and then a solitary family." Cincinnati remained forbidding, despite the peace dividends of Greenville. The adjacent Fort Washington appeared as "a declining, time-stricken, God-forsaken place," already decaying. The city, such as it was, was composed of "a few long buildings extra of the fortress, and a few families residing together." Kobler complained that there was "no opening or reception of any kind whatever" for his preaching. Intriguingly, he observed "a small printing office just put into operation, and a small store opened by a gentleman named Snodgrass."[34] Frontier cities such as Cincinnati evolved around such amenities, with commerce the backdrop against which preachers ventured their moral authority. Not surprisingly, many of them perceived the marketplace as a threat to the gospel, deploring its excesses to the point of exaggeration.

As the Methodist circuit system developed, Roman Catholics maintained a small but tenacious presence on the frontier. Cincinnati had no recorded Catholic population at the beginning of the nineteenth century, but the city was familiar to early preachers (among them Dominican friar Edward Fenwick, later bishop of Cincinnati) traveling from Kentucky to scattered communities in Ohio. Local settlers viewed these priests as "singular and unearthly," despite their plain suits of "cloth manufactured in the country," which enabled them to blend in with the population.[35] For all their alleged strangeness, Catholic preachers seldom complained of hostility from frontier Protestants, with whom they often got on better than their own congregations.

Among the earliest Catholic preachers in Cincinnati was Stephen Badin, an émigré from revolutionary France and the first Catholic ordained in the United States. Badin was cut from the same tough cloth as Asbury and his fellow circuit riders, and he shared their concerns about frontier conditions. In 1797, he wrote John Carroll of Baltimore, archbishop of the only Catholic diocese in the nation at that time. Badin implored him to pray for "Divine Providence to raise up a new generation of faithful; for the youth . . . appear to be almost strangers to faith and good morals."[36] Badin's puritanical reputation was established by the time fellow laborers joined him in the field. Samuel Wilson, a Dominican colleague, complained in 1806 that the French Sulpician and his Belgian assistant, Charles Nerinckx, rode roughshod, trampling the amusements of their scattered congregations: "Young people are not admitted without a solemn promise of not dancing *on any occasion whatever*, which few will promise & fewer still can keep. All priests that allow of any dancing are publicly condemned to Hell!"[37] As Wilson suggested, relations between Catholic priests and their flocks were often contentious. More to the point, friction between the clergy and the laity colored the development of Catholicism in the Queen City.

North of the Ohio River, one redeeming grace shone out: Ohio was free from the curse of slavery. In neighboring Kentucky, slavery's legality was contested in statehood conventions, but when Virginia's westernmost territory became the fifteenth state of the Union in 1792, plantation elites enshrined the peculiar institution in the state constitution.[38] The strongest antislavery voice in Kentucky was Rev. David Rice, later founder of Cincinnati's First Presbyterian Church. In the run-up to Kentucky statehood, Rice published a pamphlet entitled *Slavery Inconsistent with Justice and Good Policy* (1792). He argued for abolition on moral, political, and religious grounds, linking the birth of Kentucky to the principle of grace: "Slavery is the national vice of Virginia; and while a part of that State, we were partakers of that guilt. As a separate State, we are just now come to the birth, and it depends upon our free choice, whether we shall be born in this sin, or innocent of it."[39] In the end, Rice's appeal fell on deaf ears, leaving many Kentuckians, evangelical and otherwise, looking elsewhere for settlement.

One of many antislavery Kentuckians who emigrated to Ohio, the Virginia-born Baptist preacher David Barrow came north in 1795 hoping to relocate with his family. He extolled Cincinnati as "a thriving town on the north bank of the Ohio. . . . Business of almost every kind is going on rapidly in this place." Crossing the river, he "felt rejoiced that I had once the privilege to set my foot on a land where hereditary slavery . . . should never come."[40] Many shared Barrow's relief at leaving slave soil behind, including speculators who sought to profit from Kentucky's exodus. Self-interest qualified John Cleves Symmes's opposition to slavery. "The case is already decided that you must settle on this side of the Ohio," he wrote his grandsons. "You cannot live comfortably in Kentucky without negroes." In the Northwest Territory, he assured them, "you will need none." By contrast, Kentuckians who sought an honest living from the land, "owing their bread to their *own* labor," were forced to endure "the haughty manners of their opulent neighbors the slaveholders."[41]

Like the river Jordan, the Ohio divided free soil from slave soil, but this separation was somewhat illusory. On the face of things, the differences were substantial. Most significantly, the Northwest Ordinance of 1787—the instrument by which Ohio became the seventeenth state in 1803—asserted that "neither slavery nor involuntary servitude" was legal in the Northwest Territory.[42] Thanks in part to the abolition of unfree labor (excepting lawful criminal conviction), and to a more rational and orderly system of land title, Ohio's population surpassed that of Kentucky by 1820.[43] But the new state was never the bastion of freedom that might be inferred, despite Cincinnati's later reputation as a haven of Underground Railroad activity. Even as Ohio's founding constitution confirmed the state's free-soil status, for example, it tore away the franchise from free blacks, restricting citizenship to "white male inhabitants, above twenty-one years of age."[44] As historian Nikki Taylor has shown, municipal Black Laws in 1804 and 1807, followed by race riots in 1829, defined the Queen City's racial legacy, just as its trade in agricultural produce bound farms in the Miami Valley to plantations in the Deep South. Such relations cast a long shadow. As one citizen commented, "Cincinnati was located on the 'Frontiers of Freedom,' and the dark ramparts of slavery, with towering walls and stormy battlements, overshadowed the 'Queen' and cast a gloom over her mental prosperity."[45]

Such was the plight of the antebellum city, grown wealthy on trade (and trade with the slave states, in particular) but divided by slavery and racism. Such problems cut deep among Cincinnati evangelicals, for whom issues of labor, liberty, and freedom were rooted in hopes for the millennial reign of Christ. Presbyterian Lyman Beecher declared it "the design of heaven to establish a powerful nation in the full enjoyment of civil and religious liberty," established "by one great successful experiment of what man is capable" to inspire "revolutions and overturnings until the world is free."[46] Given such prophetic utterances and the tendency to view the nineteenth century through the lens of the Civil War, the fact that Beecher and other Cincinnatians were equally exercised by other issues, including immigration, can easily be overlooked.[47] Yet from the late 1820s, political and religious nativists, including many evangelicals, revived slumbering fears of popish power and influence, identifying Roman Catholicism with chattel slavery and the erosion of republican sovereignty. Such ghosts would not be quietly exorcised.

In the first decades of United States settlement, revival of a different kind awakened in the Ohio Valley, redefining the religious landscape. What historian Paul Conkin dubbed "America's Pentecost" spread far and wide, inspiring a plethora of sects and religious movements while accelerating the national growth of domestic missionary enterprise in the early American republic.[48]

The Great Revival

In the summer of 1797, Cincinnati settler Charlotte Ludlow penned a lively letter to her father, a retired Continental army general living in Pennsylvania. Relating how the city's "brilliant Fourth of July celebration was terminated by a sad accident," the newlywed wife of speculator Israel Ludlow described how a party of settlers, "glowing with all the heroism of 'Seventy-Six,' mounted a blunderbuss on the bank of the river, and . . . made its shores resound, rivaling in their imagination the ordnance of the garrison!" She went on to relate that as the settlers were encouraged by this result, "the load was increased in proportion to their enthusiasm; and when the 'Western Territory' was toasted, the gun summoned every power within it . . . and burst in pieces!" Concluding her anecdote with a terse casualty report, she recorded: "Wounded, four men. Killed, one gun!"[49]

Little in the humor of Charlotte Ludlow's anecdote suggested the woman revealed in letters over the next few years, save her disdain at the ridiculous escapade she witnessed. Yet burdened with worries for her salvation and those of her loved ones, her correspondence took a serious turn. While her husband was away surveying the frontier, she confided to her mother in 1797: "How empty and unsatisfactory are the pursuits of the worldly! When I take my seat among those whose joys are those of travelers seeking a better country . . . I feel as though the Millennium was begun!" Around the same period, she wrote her sister describing a public sermon delivered at her house by one "Mr. S.," an itinerant preacher, who "produced a powerful effect on the audience." Raised in a conservative Presbyterian household, Ludlow's letter hinted at family tensions. "You say that Methodist, and Enthusiast, are terms applied to me. The idea of being subjected to ridicule as unfashionable, and enthusiastic, has no terrors for me. I am not only willing to endure this, but 'bonds and death,' for the Lord Jesus! . . . As fidelity in friendship, constancy in love, modesty in woman, and filial affection, are worthy and respectable—so are ardor and zeal in religion!"[50]

Ludlow's enthusiasm pointed to dramatic changes in the religious landscape. Commencing two hundred miles south of Cincinnati, a seemingly unstoppable blaze of religious revival quickened the Ohio Valley. The first spark ignited in the spring of 1797 among Presbyterian communities along the Cumberland River between Kentucky and middle Tennessee. Worshipers were stirred by the fire-and-brimstone preaching of Rev. James McGready. McGready, in turn, attributed the spread of the revival to the exhortation of a young local woman "accompanied with divine blessing to the awakening of many."[51] From there, the revival hastened north into the farmlands of the Bluegrass and southwestern Ohio, like "fire in dry stubble driven by a strong wind."[52]

Remembered by historians as the Great Revival of the West, this western precursor of the Second Great Awakening surprised contemporaries with its heat and intensity. At its peak in August 1801 at Cane Ridge, Kentucky, an eight-day preaching marathon drew some ten to twenty-five thousand worshipers to a clearing in the woods: remarkable for such a relatively sparse, rural region.[53] Local Presbyterian minister Barton Warren Stone proclaimed a supernatural outpouring of the Holy Ghost. Impressed by the sights and sounds of awestruck, trembling worshipers falling by the dozens, as though "slain in battle," Stone noted, "The scene to me was new, and passing strange. It baffled description."[54]

Before the era of Catholic immigration, the Great Revival was the most seismic event in the religious landscape of the Ohio Valley. Though caricatured as a movement of "simple frontiersmen who wanted their whiskey straight and their religion red-hot," the revival radiated within a broader national context.[55] Other awakenings occurred in upstate New York and in New England, the latter sparked by the sermons of Timothy Dwight, president of Yale and grandson of famed evangelical Jonathan Edwards. Evangelical clergy and laity interpreted these regional revivals as signs of an outpouring of the Holy Ghost, presaging the millennium. They hungrily consumed news of awakenings elsewhere, supplied by such journals as the *New York Missionary Magazine* and the Pittsburgh-based *Western Missionary Magazine*, both of which circulated widely through the Ohio Valley. Narratives of revivals and miracles were read from the pulpit, in many cases triggering new outbreaks. A national epistolary circuit developed, fueled by grassroots revivals but filtered by the urban religious press. Accounts such as James McGready's "Narrative of the Commencement and Progress of the Great Revival of 1800," which chronicled the Great Revival's beginnings in Logan County, Kentucky, became staples of pietism.[56]

Subsequent developments supported historian Timothy L. Smith's assertion that "the vital center of American Protestantism was in the cities rather than the rural West," but distinctions between city and country, urban and rural, remained fluid at the time of the Great Revival.[57] These differences mattered less than the development of a regional agrarian economy, whose integration bound the orderly streets of the city to the log cabins of the hinterlands in the imagination of settlers.[58] Notably, among early Cincinnatians, Daniel Drake recognized the city's "*relations* . . . with the surrounding country" while acknowledging how much "their landscapes vary from each other."[59] In due course, the Great Revival transmuted the landscapes of both, as eyewitnesses attested.

The archetypal camp meeting of the Great Revival, Cane Ridge impressed contemporaries as a supernatural outpouring of grace, but its appearance was deceptive. One eyewitness romanticized the gathering as "awfully sublime," describing "ranges of tents, the fires, reflecting light amidst the branches of the towering trees; the candles and lamps illuminating the encampment." Just twenty miles outside the market town of Lexington, the swaying, torch-bearing crowds at Cane Ridge evoked "Gideon's army," but such comparisons also suggested the willful suspension of disbelief.[60] Far from being spontaneous, Cane Ridge was stage-managed, building upon rumors and anticipation that saturated the Ohio Valley, including Cincinnati, for three years. "From the commencement," remembered another participant, "the roads were literally crowded with wagons, carriages, horsemen, and people on foot; all pressing to the appointed place."[61] As enthusiasm spread, triggering "a self-perpetuating revival," such congestion only highlighted the logistical headaches that resulted.[62]

Nominally a "Holy Fair," or Presbyterian sacrament of the Lord's Supper, Cane Ridge stood out on account of its vast scale. The prevalence of "bodily agitations or exercises" was widely documented. Many worshipers exhibited strange falling, jerking, dancing, and laughing behaviors. A few even barked like dogs.[63] Just as problematic for some conservative clergy was unprecedented collaboration between Protestant denominations. Night and day, some eighteen Presbyterian ministers, four Methodist clergymen, and several Baptist preachers evoked visions of heaven and hell. One Presbyterian recalled "the surrounding forest, vocal with the cries of the distressed; sometimes to the distance of half a mile or a mile in circumference."[64] Methodist James B. Finley, a young boy at the time, recalled "a noise like the roar of Niagara" through the trees before seeing a "vast sea of human beings . . . agitated as if by a storm."[65]

Although its rural setting prompted naturalistic metaphors, contemporaries remarked on the density of attendance at Cane Ridge: "Since the days of Pentecost," wrote one, "there was hardly ever a greater revival of religion."[66] The nearby city of Lexington, dwarfed by the revival crowds, served as a rendezvous for those attending from far and wide, including Cincinnati and the Miami Valley. The multitude made Cane Ridge resemble a city emerging from the forest, the parked wagons alone covering an area equivalent to four city blocks.[67]

In February 1803, Kentucky Presbyterian Terah Templin reflected on the revival to Joshua Lacy Wilson, an austere Calvinist and later a leading minister in Cincinnati. Templin conceded that "the Lord . . . in mercy caused a refreshing shower to fall upon us" but warned, "I suppose with all revivals of religion so in this; while the good seed is sowing the wicked one is sowing his tares."[68] Such misgivings reflected ambiguity. Enthusiasts hailed the revival as an authentic work of God. Many supporters, including Charlotte Ludlow, predicted Christ's millennial reign on earth. At the same time, such emotion led others to hedge their bets, afraid of chasing delusion. Barton Stone, who eventually disavowed the extreme enthusiasm at Cane Ridge, recalled: "Many things transpired there, which were so much like miracles, that if they were not, they had the same effects as miracles on infidels and unbelievers; for many of them by these were convinced that Jesus was the Christ, and bowed in submission to him."[69]

The Great Revival's blending of the sacred and profane made it uniquely problematic. Critics worried less at the diversity of the camp meetings than their "promiscuity," implying undertones of dalliance and racial mixing. With opportunities for drunkenness and fornication as well as pious devotion, revivals attracted every walk of life: rich and poor, black and white, urban and rural. Before the revival, religion "was but very little attended little attended to," recalled Robert Breckenridge McAfee: "dancing, and the hustings constituted the general amusement of both young and old."[70] The Great Revival broke the ennui of frontier life, however, overshadowing the amusements of theater and tavern afforded by pioneer cities such as Lexington and Cincinnati.

Revivalists defended their movement against bourgeois concerns for respectability, elevating claims of supernatural agency. Among the notable worshipers at Cane Ridge, Colonel Robert Patterson, one of the founders of Cincinnati, described the revival to John King, a Presbyterian minister and former Continental army chaplain. "Of all ages," marveled Patterson:

> from 8 years and upwards; male and female; rich and poor; the blacks; and of every denomination; those in favor of it, as well as those, at the instant in opposition to it, have instantaneously laid motionless of the ground. Some feel the approaching symptoms by being under deep conviction; their heart swells, their nerves relax, and in an instant they become motionless and speechless, but generally retain their senses. It comes upon others like an electric shock, as if felt in the great arteries of the arms or thighs; closes quick into the heart, which swells, like to burst.

Despite such alarming symptoms, Patterson hailed it as "a miracle, that a wicked unthoughtful sinner . . . should rise out of one of those fits and continue for the space of two hours recommending religion and Jesus Christ to sinners."[71]

Not all Cincinnatians were so impressed by the Great Revival. Its cacophony wearied John Cleves Symmes. Describing the Miami Valley, Symmes wrote his daughter:

> The Methodists worship [God] by grunts and groans, stamping, raving and roaring like so many bulls and wolves and crying amen, at

every ten or twenty words of the preacher. Another sect, Newlights, worship him by screaming, clapping hands, crying hell fire and damnation, as loud as they can yell, tumbling down, lying on their backs.

Another sect, the Shakers, say they worship God best by singing merry tunes and dancing and hornpipes. They almost dance themselves to death, for they all look pale like so many ghosts.

Outlining a hierarchy from grunting Methodists to ghostly Shakers, Symmes cast aspersions on "old Presbyterians, Seceders . . . [and] Independents," as well as "Roman Catholics who have their sins pardoned by their priests." He counseled his daughter: "The best religion after all is to fear God and to do all the good we can to ourselves and families, our neighbors, our country and to mankind."[72]

Despite wealthy sympathizers like Charlotte Ludlow and Robert Patterson, the Great Revival troubled both local elites and the Presbyterian establishment. Rev. John Lyle, touring the Ohio Valley at the height of the revival, kept a diary on behalf of the Synod of Kentucky, which then extended into southwestern Ohio. He complained that colleagues included "illiterate exhorters . . . chiefly Arminians in sentiment . . . who ride in circuits after the manner of the Methodists." To conservative Presbyterians, nothing was more damning than the smear of Arminianism (a seventeenth-century tradition that rejected the predestinarian teachings of Calvinism) or, worse, the emulation of supposedly unlettered Methodists. Lyle recorded many irregularities, including "a baptist negro," who raved half an hour in the throes of the spirit, and lodging with a party of men and women "engaged in singing, conversation, leaping, and shouting," who seemed "much like a drinking party when heard from the other room." He concluded by entreating the synod: "My reason for wishing missionaries to spend some time in these congregations . . . is that I think there are many pious people here who are in a measure, deluded, that would receive the truth were it proposed in a plain affectionate manner."[73]

Foremost among Lyle's conservative Presbyterian colleagues was the "talented, intolerant, eccentric, and pious" Adam Rankin of Lexington's Mount Zion (First) Presbyterian Church, who orchestrated the regional backlash against the Great Revival.[74] Rankin's 1803 *Review of the Noted Revival in Kentucky* decried the "strange emotions & passions" of the awakened, listing their *"extravagant affliction, such a falling into dead fits, strong convulsions, fearful exertions, great swoonings, foamings, faintings, pedantic whimsical gesticulations, leaping, dancing without taking the least notice of any person or thing, imaginary sights, visionary representations, starting upwards, and reaching their hands toward*

heaven, as though they were apprehending some invisible object, extatic [sic] rap-
tures, bawling, screaming, yelling, bellowing, crying, laughing and wallowing, until
they have spent their strength in such ungovernable measures." Rankin lamented
this "motley crew" as a deafening wall of voices, exhorters as well as preachers,
among them women, children, and slaves.[75] His litany revealed fear of social
disintegration. The prospect of white settlers, free black people, and slaves
mingling in spiritual equality resonated through the Ohio Valley, forcing evangelicals like Robert Patterson to defend the integrity of the revival. "The most
inveterate," Patterson complained, "call it enthusiasm, hypocrisy, witchcraft,
possession of the devil, sympathy, in fine, every thing but what it really is."[76]

Though overlooked in studies of the Great Revival, the Ohio Valley's Catholic clergy expressed particular alarm at evangelical enthusiasm. Dominican
friar Edward Fenwick, the future Bishop of Cincinnati, compared the excitement at Cane Ridge to "the fanatical doings of the Anabaptists in Germany,"
calling it "one more sad commentary on the Protestant rule of faith."[77] His
colleague Stephen Badin, meanwhile, attributed "the pullulation of sin &
vicious habits among the American Catholics . . . to their intermixture in life
and connection in marriage with Protestants, Latitudinarians, Deists, Libertines &c."[78] Badin's anxiety verged upon bathos, but he consistently deplored
the excesses of the awakened, evoking a world turned upside down. "I have
been informed that 20,000 Presbyterians, Baptists, Methodists &c met from
all parts to an association in August in Bourbon County," he wrote, describing how "hundreds were knocked down by the Spirit at a time, as it were in
a state of death and then after remaining several hours without apparent ani-
mation."[79] Similarly, Fenwick wrote his superior in 1807: "Men and women
of every age, rank and color meet at certain seasons in the woods for nights,
days and whole weeks," he noted, "and call these assemblies Camp Meetings,
Castrametantium." Fenwick continued:

> There they preach or spout much, pray little, inebriate themselves, sing
> sacred and profane hymns, dance altogether, or rather jump and spring.
> . . . They sometimes when heated strip off part of their clothes, par-
> ticularly the sex, and during these buffooneries embrace on another,
> which they call the kiss of peace. These diabolical meetings are the
> real *Bacchanalia*, source of unbridled libertinism under the cloak of
> religion.[80]

Exaggerated as it was, Catholic critique of revivalism merited attention. Though
Fenwick and his colleagues channeled other anti-revivalist accounts, their

commentary at the time of Cane Ridge revealed not just the concerns of a marginalized group but those of a church that obtained numerical plurality over all other denominations both nationally and regionally by midcentury.

As the Great Revival blazed through the Ohio Valley, its most spectacular manifestations concentrated in the agrarian hinterlands, siphoning the more enthusiastic elements away from Cincinnati. The most otherworldly group to emerge was the United Society of Believers in Christ's Second Appearing, or the Shakers. Originating in eighteenth-century England under the charismatic "Mother" Ann Lee, this millenarian cult was confined to a scattering of rural communes in the northeastern United States at the time of Great Revival. Prompted by events in the Ohio Valley, however, the New York Shakers sent three church elders some 1,200 miles to the frontier, journeying three months along a "Wilderness of very tedious Mountains, lonesome rivers, & some disagreeable inhabitants."[81] Arriving in March 1805, these missionaries preached among the leading lights of the revival, including Barton Stone. At first, Stone found them "humble and interesting . . . plain and neat . . . grave and unassuming, very intelligent and ready in the Scriptures," and admired the "great boldness in their faith."[82] For many revivalists, Shakerism held strong appeal, offering "gifts of healing, prophecy, and tongues, their loud and joyful singing, their visions, their contact with departed spirits, and their perfectionism."[83]

Stone later recoiled from their overtures, but the Shakers converted several Presbyterian ministers and their congregations. Whole communities came into the Shaker fold by these means: four in Ohio, two in Kentucky, and one in Indiana. Most notable was Turtle Creek, a prosperous farming community thirty miles northeast of Cincinnati, which became the leading Shaker settlement in Ohio. By 1810, Shakerism boasted 1,200 converts in the West, yet numbers declined over subsequent years, hampered by an insistence on celibacy and rejection of family life, as well as the practice of sexually egalitarian but gender-segregated communalism, all of which aroused external hostility.[84]

Other sects and movements flourished with the Great Revival, but its splintering effects hit the Presbyterians hardest. The earliest schism occurred in 1803 when the Synod of Kentucky (which then oversaw Cincinnati and southwestern Ohio) arraigned Barton Stone and several other revivalists for heresy and other irregularities. Rather than submit to censure, Stone and his colleagues formed the breakaway Springfield Presbytery, an independent communion, which grew to fifteen congregations in Ohio and Kentucky. Stone and his colleagues had no ambition to found a rival denomination, however, and in June 1804, they published a remarkable declaration, *The Last Will and Testament of the Springfield Presbytery*, which willed "that this body die, be dissolved, and sink into union with the Body of Christ at large."[85] A more enduring schism occurred in 1810, when James McGready and his followers formed the Cumberland Presbytery, protesting the synod's attempt to enforce educational and confessional requirements on ministerial candidates. Though Cumberland Presbyterians flourished in Kentucky and Tennessee, they made limited inroads in Cincinnati, save the occasional itinerant, whose preaching style was apt to be conflated with Methodism.[86]

In Cincinnati, the effects of the Great Revival played out over generations. First Presbyterian Church, settled by James Kemper in 1792, kept the enthusiasm of Cane Ridge at arm's length, but Kemper's congregation split in 1828 because of revivalistic flare-ups. The rump of First Presbyterian remained under his conservative successor, Joshua Lacy Wilson, while a splinter group established the city's Third Presbyterian congregation.[87] Kemper himself remained in the orthodox fold of the Presbyterian Church. Appointed a commissioner of the General Assembly (the church's national governing body), he undertook extensive preaching tours, including an 1830 mission to northwest Ohio at seventy-seven years old. He served as the Cincinnati agent for the United Foreign Missionary Society from 1824 and helped found Lane Seminary in 1829, on the site of his family farm.[88]

Only long afterward was the Great Revival's impact in Cincinnati fully apparent. In the mid-1840s, Rev. George Lewis toured the United States on behalf of Scotland's Free Presbyterian Church, describing Cincinnati in a journal published as *Impressions of America and the American Church*. Lewis preached from the pulpit of Joshua Lacy Wilson, "the patriarch of the city." Wilson, in turn, gave Lewis a statistical summary of the city's houses of worship. Among thirty-eight Protestant congregations in Cincinnati, five New School Presbyterian congregations outnumbered three Old School congregations. The addition of two separatist Calvinist churches (one "Covenanting," the other "Associate Reformed") balanced the sectarian divisions of Presbyterianism in the Queen City. Alongside Presbyterians, the city also boasted eight Methodist churches (including a Welsh Methodist congregation) and three Regular Baptist meetinghouses. The inclusion of three "Campbellite" or Disciples of Christ churches and a "Restoration Church" indicated the inroads of the revival. A millenarian theology associated with both the Irish-born preacher Alexander Campbell and the followers of Barton Stone, evangelical primitivism looked back beyond the Great Revival to the purity of apostolic Christianity. As Cincinnati's religious landscape evolved, however, the growth of Jewish, Catholic, and other congregations indicated an emerging marketplace of religion, at once a consequence and catalyst of migration in the Ohio Valley.[89]

Unlike the fractious Presbyterians, or the predominantly rural Baptists, Methodists provided the vanguard of the Great Revival in Cincinnati. Although their first meetinghouse was not constructed until 1807, Methodists were active on the city's streets from at least the 1790s, lending the revival its most tangible presence. What they lacked in numbers, they made up for in enthusiasm, as Caleb Swann Walker recollected. Later a Methodist circuit rider and outspoken abolitionist, Walker attributed tremendous significance to the Great Revival. His unpublished diary recalled how "the holy fire of reformation spread in all directions and reached Cincinnati in 1802," just one year after Cane Ridge. Walker was a youth at the time but recalled life in the frontier Queen City in detail. The success of the gospel was more surprising, he argued, given the vices of early Cincinnatians, which included horse racing, gambling, drinking, and carousing. There was, he noted, "on the ground where the Sixth Street Market now is . . . a well made race track of one mile in circuit." The site boasted "sheds and shanties for the sale of eatables and various kinds of drinks, and many of them had a faro bank or some game of Chance in operation." The hustings as well as the racetrack provided much entertainment. The municipal elections of 1802, for example, were celebrated "with an ox roasted whole . . . at the Northwest Corner of Main and Fourth Streets . . . and the drinking of toasts."[90]

Though Walker recalled the licentiousness of Cincinnati with dismay, such scenes typified the festive democracy of the early republic. More surprising, in Walker's reckoning, was how many unchurched and often skeptical citizens fell miraculously before the Holy Ghost. Although itinerant preachers and lay exhorters were instrumental in the revival, its operation assumed an uncanny, supernatural agency in Walker's telling. One Cincinnatian was passing by a tavern on Sycamore Street when the owner, James Fithian, called out from the doorway: "Have you seen the 'Fall-Downs' [converts] yet?" He then called on his friend, "Let us take something to enliven our spirits and go over and see them." The next moment "Fithian fell helpless to the floor and the other fled with haste and trepidation." Walker likened Fithian's unlikely conversion to that of "Saul of Tarsus," although similar occurrences closer to home would have been familiar.[91]

While the trope of the converted infidel was commonplace in revival literature, narratives of the Great Revival reflected genuine evangelical fervor. In his diary, Walker provided the example of his Methodist neighbors. New England natives, the Carter family embodied the prayerful devotion of their fellow religionists, focused more on the family hearth than in the formal meetinghouse. They "sometimes continued their religious exercises most of the night," recalled Walker. One adolescent daughter, Mary Carter, once "lay for several hours in a state of trance or unconsciousness." Revivalists regarded such manifestations as signs of the Holy Spirit; anti-revivalists, meanwhile, denounced purported hysteria, especially in adolescent girls. Writing at a time when the formerly deprecated Methodist faith had attained mainline respectability, Walker recalled that the Carters "were included in the first class of Methodists that was formed in Cincinnati." In 1804, the Carter family hosted Methodist minister John Collins, who preached to a congregation of some dozen worshipers in an upper story of their house, reflecting the popular religiosity of the time. The pious Mary went on to become Mary Carter Denison, the mother of William Denison Jr., governor of Ohio at the outbreak of the Civil War and an outspoken opponent of slavery. Though Walker also described the activities of New Light Presbyterians in the vicinity of Cincinnati, he celebrated fellow Methodists like the Carter family as the embodiment of Christian perfection.[92]

The Benevolent Empire

In Cincinnati, the spirit of the Great Revival turned toward social reform and the institutional project of nation building as bourgeois Presbyterians and Congregationalists challenged the spiritual populism of Baptists and Methodists. Radiating from the northeastern United States, the gospel of the Benevolent Empire coalesced with the establishment of new domestic missionary institutions. Among the first was the Cincinnati Female Society for Charitable Purposes (1812), organized by local women, which fundraised "by annual subscription, by donations, and by charity sermons, preached quarterly, according to their appointment." The Cincinnati Miami Bible Society, an ecumenical Protestant charity, joined this grassroots organization in 1814. It aimed to distributed Bibles "among the poor of the Miami country; particularly those on the frontiers, who are . . . peculiarly embarrassed in their religious interests."[93]

The lay-oriented, interdenominational character of voluntary societies signaled the direction of Protestant philanthropy. Just as individualism flourished amid the market revolution, what contemporaries called a "United Evangelical Front," or Benevolent Empire, flourished amid upheavals of the early republic. "An epidemic of organization" heralded the growth of private evangelical agencies throughout the United States, whose collective expenditure by 1828 rivaled that of the federal government on internal improvements to national transportation and communications.[94] This Benevolent Empire addressed industrial society by fundraising, voluntaristic association, marketing, and appeals to nationalism, creating a modern, urban network that dwarfed the traditional capacities of ecclesiastical authority.

In transforming the religious landscape, the Benevolent Empire opened pathways into the public arena for women such as Charlotte Ludlow, a leading light among the female-led charitable organizations in Cincinnati. Since remarrying Presbyterian Rev. David Riske in 1808, the former Mrs. Ludlow's youthful enthusiasm had mellowed. "Religion," she confided in an 1816 letter, "is not the effect of excited passions, but of convinced reason." Later that year, she described her role in founding the Cincinnati women's auxiliary branch of the American Bible Society. She and two female friends "took upon ourselves the labor esteemed disagreeable—that of soliciting funds for its treasury." Despite initial resistance to their fundraising efforts, women like Charlotte Ludlow Riske assumed new influence in the Queen City, corresponding with voluntary societies across the nation and establishing Sunday schools "for the improvement of the African race," among other enterprises.[95]

Access to financial capital, urban orientation, and appeals to national identity shaped the Benevolent Empire through the early nineteenth century. Economic advantages tilted the religious landscape in its favor despite competition from other evangelical groups, notably the Methodists. Though both groups itinerated throughout the United States, the groundwork for the first national domestic missionary network was founded by urban associations like the Massachusetts Missionary Society, the Philadelphia Bible Society, and the Philadelphia Missionary Society. In 1813, these three bodies alone subscribed some $1,300 for two missionaries, John F. Schermerhorn and Samuel Mills, to spend nine months spreading the gospel west of Appalachia. By contrast, in 1815, the Methodist Ohio Conference (centered in Cincinnati) spent $914.19 to support seventy-three circuit riders and two bishops for the entire year. Though expenditure was not the only index of influence, this averaged out as a measly salary of $15.77 per Methodist preacher, per year, contrasting with Mills's and Schermerhorn's generous stipends of $650 each.[96]

Before emerging as the western hub of the Benevolent Empire, Cincinnati was a muddy frontier outpost, boasting barely one thousand people at the time of Cane Ridge. The city aspired to the laurels of rival Lexington (population fourteen thousand), located some one hundred miles south. The ensuing competition between the two cities left a rancorous legacy. Even as Cincinnati closed the gap in wealth and population, one writer could declare Lexington in 1815 to be "the Athens of the West" while sneering that Cincinnati was still "struggling to become its Corinth."[97] Yet the Benevolent Empire made Cincinnati the leading cultural city of the Ohio Valley just as its river trade brought commercial prominence.

The Plan of Union (1801)—itself a response to the popular enthusiasm of the Great Revivalism—anticipated the sort of ecumenical cooperation later embodied by the Benevolent Empire. This pact between the Congregationalist and Presbyterian churches integrated and disciplined unchurched congregations under the ministry of an orthodox, educated clergy. It capitalized on the similarities of the denominations while seeking to minimize disparities between Congregationalists on the Atlantic coast and Presbyterians on the frontier. Reciprocity allowed the Presbyterians to consolidate their influence in the Ohio Valley, establishing bastions such as Lane Theological Seminary (1829). The Congregationalists, in turn, benefited from settling ministers in western pulpits. Notably, Lyman Beecher took on Cincinnati's Second Presbyterian Church along with the presidency of Lane in 1832. Such arrangements anticipated national associations such as the American Bible Society (1816) and the United Domestic Missionary Society (1822), which flourished in the Queen City.

The Plan of Union enabled unprecedented cooperation between ministers of different stripes, but it unwittingly alienated traditionalist clergy. Recalcitrant Presbyterians, identified as the Old School faction, broke ranks with the New School of Beecher and other evangelical accommodationists. What became known as the Old School–New School Controversy fomented in Cincinnati, fueled by the antagonistic personality of Joshua Lacy Wilson, the Virginia-born, Old School Calvinist minister of First Presbyterian. Having initially supported Beecher's appointment to Lane Seminary, Wilson locked horns with Beecher, arraigning the New Englander before the Presbytery of Cincinnati in 1835. Charging him "with propagating doctrines contrary to the word of God and the standards of the Presbyterian church" on a variety of issues, including "Total Depravity and the work of the Holy Spirit in effectual calling," Wilson attempted to evict his ministerial colleague from the pulpit.[98] Beecher was acquitted of heresy, but the rancor was irreversible. Although Wilson's charges were narrowly theological, his determination in pursuing them reflected an ongoing struggle for prestige and legitimacy between the ministers of Cincinnati's leading Presbyterian congregations, whose meetinghouses sat just a couple of blocks apart on the city's Fourth Street.[99]

Wayfarers and Pilgrims

A generation after the Great Revival, Cincinnati came into its own as a commercial entrepôt, if not yet the great metropolis envisioned by its boosters. An auspicious year, 1819 saw the city's incorporation by Ohio's General Assembly. Awarded its own municipal charter, granting its mayoral government and city council formal powers of taxation, legislation, and law enforcement,

Cincinnati was increasingly recognized as the foremost city in Ohio. Other mileposts came that year. One of the city's leading citizens—physician, polymath, and urban reformer Daniel Drake—obtained a charter for the Medical College of Ohio, the forerunner to the present-day University of Cincinnati. Christ Church, the first Catholic congregation in Cincinnati, was also organized in 1819, laying the foundations for what became the largest denomination in the Queen City. Cincinnatians celebrated these signs of their city's vitality. Immigrants from every corner of the nation and beyond, from many faiths and none, abided in relative peace and harmony, quickly forgetting the turmoil of frontier conflict.

The *Cincinnati Directory* (1819) illustrated prodigious growth but scant presage of the national financial panic that engulfed the city toward the end of that year, causing credit to contract, banks to go bust, and reformers to denounce "the theatre and the circus, brokers and shavers, speculation, luxury, extravagance, effeminacy in dress and manners, auctions and pawn brokers, lotteries and lottery offices, insurance, [and] great and sudden changes in circumstances," as causing the decline of social and economic order.[100] Instead, the *Directory* listed foundries and blacksmiths, tinware and copper manufactories, silversmiths and cabinetmakers, coach makers and clockmakers, breweries and distilleries, soap makers and chandlers, and potters and hatters among the city's flourishing businesses.[101] An unofficial census the previous year counted some nine thousand residents, including some 367 "people of color." The author made no effort to disguise the city's "mixed" demographics, "composed of emigrants from almost every part of christendom" (Cincinnati soon housed a notable Jewish minority as well). In addition to native-born Americans, there were "many foreigners amongst us, and it is not uncommon to hear three or four different languages spoken in the streets at the same time." The editor described how such variety translated into economic and social life. Cincinnati suffered "but few of those traits of provincial character which are so visible in older settlements . . . every individual is obliged to sacrifice to the general opinion many of his prejudices and local peculiarities and to adopt a more liberal mode of acting and thinking." This melting pot extended to the influence of faith: "Great attention is paid to the institutions of religion, and the mass of the more respectable citizens are regular in their attendance on public worship." Belying depictions of the city as a godforsaken backwater, the city was solidly churched, even if its seventeen taverns outnumbered its ten "Places of Public Worship."[102]

The solidity of early Cincinnati was always conditional. Despite evidence of growth, for example, the city's religious fragility in the wake of the Great

Revival was as pronounced as its economic fragility on the eve of financial panic. Thus, in the spring of 1818, a ragged group of pilgrims known as the Mummyjums triggered alarm as they approached the city. For the previous eight months, these religious misfits had wended their way by foot from the hills of New England via New York, Pennsylvania, and across Ohio. Like medieval penitents, their disheveled appearance and peculiar behavior declared their sanctity, setting them apart from the world. Leading them was the red-bearded, self-proclaimed prophet Isaac Bullard. A strikingly foul individual, Bullard was notorious for imposing punishing acts of penitence and for refusing to wash his body, shave, or cut his hair—and for insisting his disciples follow suit. Though they numbered only forty-five individuals, including numerous children, word of this strange caravan preceded its arrival. The Vermont Pilgrims, as they styled themselves, had lodged the previous month among the Shakers at Union Village, twenty-five miles north of the city. In contrast to Bullard's noisome disciples, the Shakers were proverbial for cleanliness, celibacy, and contemplation. Bound in public imagination by their otherworldly piety and prophetic beliefs, however, the Shakers and the Mummyjums both labored under pejorative names: the Shakers shaking in the presence of the spirit and the Mummyjums mumbling wildly in tongues. Though both groups were outsiders, they differed broadly in practice as well as belief. Conflict set in, and the Shakers tired at last of the Mummyjums' antisocial behavior, not least Bullard and his male apostles' lodging "promiscuously with their women."[103] It was time for them to move on.

Evicted from the Shakers' communal Eden, the Mummyjums proceeded toward the Queen City. Rumors of sexual deviancy and abject behavior provoked a mixture of fascination and disgust. More alarmingly, reports emerged of disease among them, contracted shortly after their departure from Union Village. Cincinnati's mayor and city council, receiving "authentic information of their affliction by the small pox," sent a delegation imploring the Mummyjums "to pass by at as great a distance from the town, as convenience would permit." Amid fears for public health, civic intervention evidently had little effect. On Sunday, April 12, "columns of citizens" streamed out of the city and surrounding countryside to meet the "wayfaring pilgrims." The road "was almost literally choked with passengers," reported Cincinnati's leading newspaper, the *Western Spy*, "each with anxious eye, pressing forward for a peep at the seat of filth."[104] The pilgrims, having departed from Woodstock, Vermont, the previous year clad in fur caps and girdles, now sported a bizarre ensemble of mismatched rags and sewn-on patches, the change resulting from one of Bullard's erratic claims of revelation.[105]

Echoing widespread ridicule of these religious drifters, the *Western Spy* noted:

> Their theological reason for thus wandering about the country with- out a home, and without scarcely any of the necessities of life, was readily and willingly given: "it is imitating the practice of the ancient patriarchs and good men of old," they say. But the basis of their dirty religion they seem unwilling to disclose. Perhaps they have been sub- dued and are treacherously governed by a strong and natural inclina- tion to hate everything bordering upon industry. It may not be. We suspect it.[106]

In the editor's view, these "dirty" sectarians were both fanatical and alien: work-shy parasites besmirching the values of civilized, urban society.

The year 1818 was not the last time the city press stirred up hatred of an insanitary, fanatical, religious Other. The onset of Catholic immigration in the 1830s triggered the same reflexes. Channeling the nativist language of Lyman Beecher's *A Plea for the West*, for example, the Protestant *Home Missionary and American Pastor's Journal* (hereafter abbreviated as the *Home Missionary*) regarded Cincinnati as "the cause of the West—for there the great battle is to be fought between truth and error, between law and anarchy— between Christianity, with her Sabbaths, her ministry and her schools, on the one hand, and the combined forces of Infidelity and Popery on the other."[107] The anti-immigrant *Cincinnati Daily Times*, meanwhile, deplored Catholi- cism's "secrecy, in the confessional, in Jesuitism, in the silent dungeons and in the accursed precincts of the 'Holy Inquisition,' which echoed for centuries with the shrieks of tortured victims, and the groans of dying heretics!"[108] Such past horrors, readers were told, would again proliferate in the Queen City unless immigration was stanched.

No matter how alien their depiction, neither the Catholics nor the Mum- myjums arrived from another world. Their passage to Cincinnati followed established routes of transportation and migration. Despite nativist hostility, Catholics immigrants flourished in the Queen City, settling in its neighbor- hoods and shaping them in their own image. The Mummyjums, by contrast, were nomadic, striving for their Promised Land in the trans-Mississippi West. For them, Cincinnati was one stage on a longer pilgrimage. Over the protests of city council, Bullard and his followers pressed ahead and entered the city. Despite the city populace's fears of contagion, the Mummyjums succeeded in selling off their oxen, horses, and rolling stock and purchased a wooden flat- boat for their passage down the Ohio River. Having traveled eight hundred miles mostly by foot, the bustling river city offered them a welcome change in transportation. "They take water passage here, and it is very possible we will see them no more," foretold the *Western Spy*, adding this was "a source of no regret."[109]

The Mummyjums' exodus carried them deep into frontier territory, where they endured trials of starvation and disease for which they were unprepared. Many perished along the way. Others abandoned their increasingly unhinged and enfeebled prophet. In 1819, the New England writer and preacher Timothy Flint, itinerating on behalf of the Missionary Society of Connecticut, encountered "the wretched remains of that singular class of enthusiasts" on a river island near New Madrid, Missouri. Some half dozen followers remained, reduced to "mush and milk." Bullard himself was barely coherent, though Flint compiled a rough account of the Pilgrims' "austerities and privations" from the prophet's wife and scattered local eyewitnesses. A New England Congregationalist, Flint described how Bullard preached "in union with the Methodists"—a sure sign, he intimated, of Methodism's dubious orthodoxy. But the cost of the Mummyjums' enthusiasm needed no elaboration. "Emaciated with hunger," Flint warned, "and feverish from filth and the climate, many of them left their bones." These skeletal remains, "ordered by the prophet, from some direct revelation which he received, to lie unburied," lay "bleaching on the island."[110]

The ghoulish fate of Isaac Bullard and his followers concluded one of American history's murkiest horror stories, but their passage through Cincinnati was soon forgotten. As the Mummyjums' bones languished on an island far downriver, the Queen City prospered. For Timothy Flint, a Harvard-educated evangelical and Cincinnati booster, the Vermont Pilgrims were just one more cautionary tale in the moral drama of the Ohio Valley. Around the time of their unlikely sojourn, he noted, Cincinnati "was the only place that could properly be called a town, on the course of the Ohio and Mississippi, from Steubenville to Natchez, a distance of fifteen hundred miles." While lauding the benefits of urban civilization, Flint conceded, poverty and squalor were common, especially among new arrivals. One immigrant family was crowded into a single room, the father dying, the mother "sick in the same bed," and three children struck with fever. "It is gloomy to reflect," he noted, "that the cheering results of the settlement of our new states and territories, are not obtained without numberless accompaniments of wretchedness like this. No charitable associations are more needed than societies to aid emigrants . . . located at the great resorts of departure and embarkation."[111]

By 1840, Cincinnati was the sixth-largest city in the nation, a magnet for voluntary charitable associations, including immigrant aid societies. The

Vermont Pilgrims, in all their morbid fascination, faded from memory. More enduring concerns arose from the population of foreign immigrants, strangers whose wretchedness, poverty, and perceived uncleanliness struck closer to home.

Despite Richard Wade's observation that flourishing towns like Cincinnati were "the spearheads of the frontier," religion in the early American republic developed on the sectarian fringes as well as in urban centers. Thus, sects like the Vermont Pilgrims and the Shakers, lumped together as misfits and outsiders, were less outliers on the religious landscape than mirrors of the mainstream, albeit clouded and distorted in their reflections. The crowds that thronged the main road to greet Bullard and his disciples were motivated by curiosity and, like any freak show audience, sought to glimpse themselves in the spectacle. But something deeper than spiritual voyeurism struck home. Many of those gathered to greet the Pilgrims witnessed supernatural sights and sounds a generation before, during the revival. Their experiences combined with those of later immigrants, preachers, and reformers to lay the foundations of Cincinnati's religious landscape, a peculiar blend of skepticism, enthusiasm, and experimentation.[112]

Amid many depictions of antebellum Cincinnati, the experiences of one cultivated sojourner stand out. The daughter of a Church of England clergyman, Frances "Fanny" Trollope was among early Cincinnati's unlikeliest inhabitants. In her account of her residence in the city, published in 1832 as *Domestic Manners of the Americans*, she was also among its harshest critics. With three young children in tow, Trollope immigrated to the United States in 1827, abandoning an abusive husband and prevailing expectations of female dependence. Seeking financial as well as social self-sufficiency, Trollope settled in Cincinnati the following year, drawn by the city's renowned "beauty, wealth, and unequaled prosperity." Grasping opportunities, she commissioned a "strange edifice topped by an outlandish cupola" three blocks from the river. Her haberdashery store and emporium, "Trollope's Bazaar," ended in failure, like many businesses in that speculative age, but its distinctive architecture remained a familiar landmark until the late nineteenth century. Housing the Ohio Mechanics Institute and eventually a brothel, it stood out amid a cityscape of orderly public spaces and spired churches.[113] When Trollope returned to England in 1831, she had better luck with her pen than her ledger. *Domestic Manners of the Americans* was an unlikely bestseller, which, as one Victorian critic put it, "made the Old World laugh, and the New World howl with rage."[114]

For all her independence, Trollope exhibited a conservative streak, attributable to her traditional Anglican upbringing and evident in her condescen-

Figure 1.1 Frances "Fanny" Trollope (1779–1863), English sojourner in Cincinnati and author of *Domestic Manners of the Americans.* (Wikimedia Commons)

sion of the Ohio Valley. She described Cincinnati as "a triste little town," lacking amusements, but she acknowledged that "the churches and chapels of the town" furnished one of the few social backdrops for the city's confined womenfolk. "I am tempted to believe," she wrote, "that a stranger from the continent of Europe would be inclined, on first reconnoitering the city, to suppose that the places of worship were the theatres and cafes of the place." If church architecture and polite worship embodied the facade of religion, Trollope discovered its more rambunctious aspects as well. Evangelical fervor had long shaped the Ohio Valley, but it resonated loudly in Cincinnati's urban landscape. Such enthusiasm contrasted with Trollope's sober Anglican faith. Nowhere was the discordance more jarring than in the revival meeting, manifesting periodically amid the hubbub of the city's streets. "We had not been many months in Cincinnati," Trollope recalled, "when our curiosity was excited by hearing the 'revival' talked of by everyone we met throughout the town. 'The revival will be very full'—'We shall be constantly engaged during the revival'—were the phrases we constantly heard repeated." Trollope explained how "the most enthusiastic of the clergy travel the county, and enter the cities and towns by scores . . . and for a week or fortnight, or if the population be large, for a month; they preach and pray all day, and often for a considerable portion of the night, in the various churches and chapels of the place. This is called a Revival."[115]

As Trollope suggested, religious revivals were ubiquitous in Cincinnati, though often confusing to outsiders. Taken aback by the extent of evangelical culture, she noted that all persuasions in the region still relied on itinerant preachers, even in the city, save only Episcopalians, Catholics, Quakers, and Unitarians: "I heard of Presbyterians of all varieties; of Baptists of I know not how many divisions; and of Methodists of more denominations than I can remember." To her chagrin, Trollope was never invited to a revival meeting and had "nothing but hear-say evidence to offer." Though she apologized to her readers that "my information comes from an eye-witness, . . . [but] one on whom I believe I may depend," her ensuing account was liberally embroidered with familiar tropes: "trumpet-mouthed" preachers, "repeatedly mounted on the benches," while agonized worshipers were seized with "violent hysterics and convulsions," only to be drowned out by the tumultuous bellowing of the preacher. Her description was peculiarly gendered and sexualized: "by far the greater number" of the audience, she noted, were "very young women," whipped into a state of frenzied ecstasy by the male preachers. These "poor creatures" included "a young girl, apparently not more than fourteen . . . supported in the arms of another, some years older; her face was pale as death; her eyes wide open, and perfectly devoid of meaning; her chin and bosom wet with slaver; she had every appearance of idiotism."[116]

For all its sensationalism, *Domestic Manners* remains revealing. Trollope barely considered the motives of those attending the revival, and she threw in much rebuke for good measure. "Did the men of America value their women as men ought to value their wives and daughters," she demanded, "would such scenes be permitted among them?" Unwittingly, the limitations of Trollope's imagination revealed her exclusion from the subculture she described. Unlike earlier camp meetings in the Ohio Valley, urban revivals in Cincinnati were mostly closed-door affairs. Cincinnatians once traveled to hear the revival; now the revival came to them, as the city absorbed the enthusiasm of the frontier gospel within sharper physical, denominational, and social boundaries. And for all Fanny Trollope's distaste at revivalistic exuberance, her chagrin indicated her displeasure at being excluded.

Cincinnati's emergence as the leading city of the West ensured future revivalism assumed, or at least contended with, urban and national tendencies. The city became a hotbed not just for new churches but for domestic missionary societies, Sunday schools, orphanages, temperance societies, tract depositories, education and print culture, and a plethora of reforms reflecting the technological and cultural homogenization of the nation, even amid pockets of hard-shell sectarian eccentricity. At the same time, overseas immigration, especially from Germany and Ireland, transformed the city and its hinterlands, giving the landscape a new, less Protestant complexion. The combination of immigration with religious and other civic institutions transformed provincial Losantiville into the pluralistic Queen City within a few short generations, as Catholic, Protestant, and Jewish Cincinnatians shaped a diverse American region in the Ohio Valley.

2

Athens of the West?

Immigration, Cholera, and Alcohol

All that is solid melts into air, all that is holy is profaned, and man is at last compelled to face with sober senses his real conditions of life, and his relations with his kind.

—MARX AND ENGELS, *Communist Manifesto*

On the bright afternoon of September 24, 1848, photographers William S. Porter and Charles Fontayne mounted their camera on a Newport, Kentucky, rooftop, surveying across the Ohio River. The resulting daguerreotype panorama of eight glass plates revealed the fastest-growing city of the United States in spectacular detail. Marking the foreground was the Ohio River, the great artery of Western commerce emblazoned with steamboats such as the *Meteor* and *Ohio Belle*. Cincinnati itself rose from the muddy landing, its slope pell-mell with boiler yards and lumber. Brick warehouses advertised their contents to passing boatmen and their passengers, signs promising "FOREIGN WINES & LIQUOR" or "RECTIFIED WHISKEY." Set back from the river, church spires punctuated the horizon, receding against the tree-lined backdrop of the city's hills.

A few months after Porter and Fontayne captured these images, the specter of cholera revisited Cincinnati's streets, transforming them forever. Cholera had struck once before in 1832, but this second pandemic was terrifying in scale and intensity. Like all pandemics, cholera was more than a public health emergency. At a time of unprecedented economic and demographic change, disease was the medium through which rapid changes, already in motion, accelerated and converged. In addition to teeming, invisible pathogens, alcohol, violence, and crime festered behind the city's prosperous facade. Citizens linked demographic upheaval with fears of contagion, balking at "a plague of strangers" transforming everyday life.[1]

Figure 2.1 Cincinnati, from William S. Porter and Charles Fontayne's 1848 panorama. (Courtesy of the Public Library of Cincinnati and Hamilton County)

Porter and Fontayne's panorama now hangs in Cincinnati's Public Library, recording a cityscape obliterated by later development. It presents a field of vision broader than the human eye, heightened by the acuity of daguerreotype photography. The landscape looks beguiling enough beyond the squalid riverfront, but it is difficult to read despite its remarkable detail. While earlier illustrators of the Athens of the West beautified the urban landscape, the camera did not lie, instead recording the shambles of the public landing in the same frame as the still-pastoral vista of Mount Adams or the elegant twin spires of the Episcopal Christ Church. While the background details a landscape of prosperous stone villas and churches, the foreground points to the furious commerce driving the city's growth. But something else is missing. Apart from a few tantalizing silhouettes, the landscape is depopulated. The absence of human and animal life reflects the glacial exposure time of the daguerreotype process, adding to the panorama's surreal atmosphere.

Despite many glaring flaws, the Queen City beguiled visitors from across Europe and America with its eclectic energy. While later commentators imagined the city as a cultural melting pot, one breathless English tourist instead characterized it as "a salad, which to relish must be mixed from a variety of ingredients."[2] The noted French chronicler Alexis de Tocqueville recalled: "All that there is of good and bad in American society is to be found there in such strong relief, that one would be tempted to call it one of those books printed in large letters for children to read; everything there is in violent contrast, exaggerated; nothing has fallen into its final place: society is growing more rapidly than man."[3] Tocqueville's fellow countryman Michel Chevalier likewise hailed Cincinnati as "the rendezvous of all nations," marveling at the familiar accents of Alsace and the Rhineland.[4] No less bewildered than these foreign visitors, New England–born physician William Sherwood wrote home in 1848, describing Cincinnati as "one of *the* towns that you read of—a description of it cannot be given while rattling omnibuses and carts drown the senses. It is one great bee-hive—exhibiting more activity than New York and everything that ever was manufactured I suppose is made here."[5]

Nor was the city's bustle limited to its humanity. In the mid-nineteenth century, English travel writer Isabella Lucy Bird informed readers:

> The Queen City bears the less elegant name of Porkopolis . . . swine lean, gaunt, and vicious looking, riot through her streets . . . Cincinnati is the city of pigs. As there is a railway system and a hotel system, so there is also a *pig system*, by which this place is marked out from any other. Huge quantities of these useful animals are reared after harvest in the corn-fields of Ohio, and on the beech-mast and acorns of its gigantic forests. At a particular time of year they arrive by thousands—brought in droves and steamers to the number of 500,000—to meet their doom, when it is said that the Ohio runs red with blood![6]

In a similar vein, fellow visitor Charles Mackay noted: "All Cincinnati is redolent of swine. Swine prowl about the streets and act the part of scavengers until they are ready to become merchandise and visit Europe."[7] Though constituting a public nuisance, the semi-feral herds slaughtered each winter (when cold weather sufficed for refrigeration) were tolerated for economic and environmental reasons. Enclosure was prohibitively expensive, and their voracious consumption of refuse was deemed a public service. Though their teeming numbers, sound, and stench offended observers, they were noticeably absent from photographic and most other visual records of the city.

Unlike the swine-infested streets of Porkopolis, Porter and Fontayne's panorama was scrubbed and muted, but its details nevertheless revealed the city's underbelly to closer scrutiny. One detail stood out. As a small channel tapered down the public landing from the corner of Lawrence and Front Streets, it discharged itself into the ground toward the Ohio River. Perched

Figure 2.2 Banks of the Ohio. Detail from Porter and Fontayne's 1848 panorama. (Courtesy of the Public Library of Cincinnati and Hamilton County)

near some flotsam at the river's edge below, two men, perhaps fishermen, gazed out at the sluggish water—in any case, standing still enough to be captured for posterity. The river was low on the day the photograph was taken but prone to flood in heavy rains when the dry tracks running from the filthy streets to the water's edge became gullies of pollution, carrying outwash from privies and garbage heaps facing the riverbank.

"Drainage Is Destiny"

Early Cincinnatians identified strong connections among disease, ethnicity, and religion. Though rooted in visceral prejudice as much as rational objectivity, perceptions of squalor and moral decay influenced the city's development, shaping policies on everything from health care, sanitation, and temperance to public education. Moral alarm reflected growing concern at the declining urban environment. To borrow a phrase from historian Jack Kirby, Cincinnatians were discovering that "drainage is destiny."[8] Cincinnati ensured some of the nastiest sanitation in America, and while attempts to regulate civic hygiene were nothing new, legislation lagged behind growth. As early as 1802, municipal authorities enacted an ordinance aimed at *"preventing carrion from laying in any of the streets, lanes, allies* [sic] *or commons of the town."*[9] Such measures (if enforced) might have alleviated public health issues, but they did not address systemic challenges. In 1811, the editor of the *Western Spy* urged the creation of a municipal sewer system. "If the gutters of each street be conducted into the river," he warned, "the water along the shore of the western part of the town will soon be unfit for many domestic uses."[10] By 1819 nothing had changed, however, and the *Inquisitor and Cincinnati Advertiser* described the city's streets as a "cinque of pestilence and disease."[11]

Such conditions persisted over the coming decades, compounded by immigration, which pushed public health and urban infrastructure to the limits. Barely two weeks before Porter and Fontayne captured the filth of the public landing in their panorama, Louis Wright, editor of the *Cincinnati Daily Gazette*, complained that his city "is now looked upon, and with much truth, as the dirtiest city of its kind in the Union. Some of the gutters in the principal streets are so offensive to the eye and nose, as to make a walk along them disgusting."[12] Even by the eve of the Civil War, the question of sewerage remained unresolved, improvements in water supply focusing on quantity rather than quality. A joint stock–funded enterprise, the Cincinnati Water Company (1826) constructed a steam-driven pump house to the east of the city to funnel Ohio River water to a hilltop reservoir three hundred feet above the low water level, where a network of pipes irrigated the city.[13] The aqueducts of imperial Rome, however, these waterworks were not. Despite mechanical ingenuity, they recycled the riverine filth of Cincinnati, aiding and abetting the spread of waterborne disease.

Cholera, thriving in fetid Cincinnati, was among the worst pestilences of the nineteenth century. The earliest American outbreak in 1832 followed a devastating flood and measles epidemic in the city. Nearly six hundred Cincinnatians from a population of some thirty thousand perished, along-

Figure 2.3 Cincinnati's waterworks, from Porter and Fontayne's 1848 panorama.
(Courtesy of the Public Library of Cincinnati and Hamilton County)

side tens of thousands more Americans. Among the dead was Cincinnati's Catholic bishop, Edward Fenwick, stricken on a missionary tour of the Great Lakes. Despite calls for public health reform, new measures were slow to emerge. The only significant exception in 1832 was "An Ordinance to Establish a Board of Health in the City of Cincinnati," enacted in June of that year, creating a seven-member panel of physicians. This panel was charged with collecting information and complaints and overseeing the city marshal's enforcement efforts in declared public health emergencies.[14] But over the next twenty years, Cincinnati's population roughly tripled, immigration filling new neighborhoods and stretching the board's manpower ever more thinly.

Cincinnati physician J. P. Harrison, compiling a report for the American Medical Association's Committee on Public Hygiene on the eve of the 1849 cholera outbreak, described a city of 110,000 residents in "very good" health, with "but little bilious remittent fever seen within the limits of the town." In more crowded neighborhoods, he admitted, "especially among our German population, cholera infantum is very fatal during the hot months." While Harrison skirted over this disease, apparently unconcerned with epidemic threat, the signs were troubling. His report, while sanguine, gave plenty of evidence for the insanitary conditions of life in the Queen City. "The streets are cleansed by scavengers," he noted, "hired by the city authority; but . . . not kept in as clean a state as they should be." Swine still ran half wild downtown, devouring "what they will." Animal dung was routinely dumped from the public landing into the river, being "very rarely carried into the country, as the soil does not require any kind of manure." An irrepressible optimist, Harrison praised the city's health regulations as "pretty good; neither very stringent, nor altogether void of effectiveness," though admittedly "rather leaning to the side of laxity."[15]

Had Harrison been more skeptical, he might have foreseen the epidemic, but cholera's return surprised almost everyone. While cholera infantum (similar but separate from the pandemic Asiatic cholera) persisted as a killer of immigrant children in crowded tenements, complacency prevailed among municipal authorities and citizens alike as the 1832 cholera epidemic faded from memory, only to return by the spring of 1849. Worse, the city government and local press downplayed cholera's reemergence. "The general health of the city is now good," asserted the *Gazette* as late as April 12, 1849, "and all reports to the contrary are sheer fabrications." While isolated cases of cholera were inevitable, the article added that fears of an epidemic were "a perfect tempest in a teapot," puffed up by hearsay.[16] The editor of the *Daily Atlas* blamed "telegraphic rumors and the exaggerated statements of [steamboat] passengers" for stoking the epidemic scare.[17] Cincinnatians could hardly be blamed for their concern, however, given articles such as the one appearing in *Liberty Hall* on March 30, announcing that "cholera has been very prevalent on steam-boats arriving [at Louisville, Kentucky] from New Orleans since Saturday," when "the weather was hot and sultry and much sickness prevailed, principally among emigrants."[18] Through such reports, Queen City residents tracked the progress of cholera upriver while being sold the lie that their own neighborhoods were immune.

On May 16, 1849, a short notice by the city Board of Health in the *Gazette* acknowledged the severity of cholera. It stated: "There having been numerous exaggerated reports of the ravages of that dreaded disease, Cholera, in Cincinnati, the Board of Health was called upon by the daily papers to ascertain the actual state of affairs in this particular and make daily reports."[19] While the board honored its promise to report on the epidemic, their recognition of its severity came around four-and-a-half months *after* cholera first entered the city. Moreover, the board's admission that it was responding to local newspapers rather than city government or the medical profession underlined a weakness of institutional authority, while the press exerted its full influence in the absence of political leadership.

"Very Few Whom We Know Have Died"

From the outset, rumors of cholera stirred up a mixture of alarm, denial, and defiance. Many, including Stephen Foster (the famed songwriter then residing in the Queen City), dismissed the threat. "Tell Ma she need not trouble herself about the health of Cincinnati," he reassured a friend back home, "as our weather here is very healthy."[20] Others minimized the disease, provided it remained among immigrants. One man wrote his wife that 130 people had sickened and died the previous day. "But do not be alarmed," he added. "They are mostly German and Irish. Very few whom we knew have died."[21] Likewise exemplifying such complacency, one Protestant matriarch, Margaret Lytle, described how cholera was causing "quite a panic" in the streets, noting that "several cases have no doubt occur[e]d—generally among the labouring classes—no one that I know except Col Bruff." The colonel's death notwithstanding (he had overindulged at a wedding the week before), Lytle evidently saw little cause for alarm.[22] Cholera was something that happened to other people.

Most local newspapers promoted initial complacency, portraying cholera as almost exclusive to immigrants and the poor. According to the *Gazette*, it was "undeniable that Cholera is mainly confined to the poorer classes, and it is equally susceptible of proof, that the mortality is nearly exclusively restricted to that portion of the population." The typical "working man," it went on, "pays no attention to diet or regimen, is not particularly attentive to personal cleanliness, and eats anything that comes before him.—Hence he is naturally a fit subject for the disease."[23] Such generalizations in the city's leading commercial daily were revealing. No longer was Cincinnati the republican city on a hill of earlier years, synonymous with "industry, temperance, [and] morality."[24] Beleaguered by epidemic disease and class division, society was fraying.

Press coverage of the 1849 cholera outbreak was complex. Among numerous daily newspapers then available, the *Gazette* and its sister Whig journal, the *Daily Atlas*, led calls for civic and sanitary reform, though both hesitated to acknowledge the epidemic.[25] Following Drake's announcement, however, local editors rushed to deny rumors of misinformation, blaming such allegations on "some of the papers out of the city." One such denial in *Liberty Hall* addressed the allegation that Cincinnati merchants "move[d] in a body to induce the press not to publish the facts lest they should deter customers from visiting the city!"[26] Another article in the *Gazette* excerpted a January 4 editorial of the Indiana *Connersville Telegraph* to illustrate and refute "very exaggerated accounts" then circulating. According to the Hoosier press:

> The Cincinnati papers deny the existence of cholera in that city. We know not how to regard their statements—to keep the fact of the presence of this scourge of humanity in their midst, concealed from the people of the country—on whom they have to depend for their produce &c, and who in a great measure keep up the business of the city. Our private accounts from Cincinnati, however, differ very materially from the newspaper reports—they representing the cholera as raging with fearful fatality.[27]

For all his paranoia, the editor of the *Connersville Telegraph* understood the relationship between Cincinnati and its hinterland. The city stood exposed, as reports of pestilence radiated from its streets. Wherever cholera struck, panic ensued. Twenty-five miles downriver from Cincinnati, the city of Aurora, Indiana, was depopulated after 1,600 of its 2,000 residents fled in the summer of 1849.[28] In Eaton, Ohio, forty miles north of Cincinnati, some eighty houses were abandoned by August. Twenty-eight people died in a single week, while the remaining 544 residents numbered just 40 percent of the next year's census total. Even clergy despaired. One minister who remained denounced reports "that *all* of the pastors of the Churches of that town deserted their flocks."[29] Meanwhile, citizens of Lafayette, Indiana, agonized as cholera spread along the Ohio and Wabash Rivers. While the local paper republished articles from Cincinnati downplaying contagion, at least half of Lafayette's six thousand people fled the cholera epidemic, repeating a pattern found throughout the Ohio Valley. Despite relatively few foreign-born immigrants in Lafayette and other small towns, the press and clergy fixated upon their role in spreading the disease, just as in Cincinnati.[30]

Once cholera was acknowledged, Cincinnati's newspapers emphasized its impact on the urban margins—among the poor, immigrants, and racial and ethnic minorities. Concern for these groups dated to at least the 1830s, when Rev. Thomas Brainerd of the Presbyterian *Cincinnati Journal* described the "migratory nature of our citizens," rendering Cincinnatians "almost strangers to one another."[31] As Brainerd suggested, the fabric of church and family life seemed to be disintegrating. The cholera epidemic of 1849 only highlighted this decline. In an article entitled "Can Anything Be Done?," Louis Wright of the *Gazette* portrayed the disease as exclusive to "parts of the city . . . we know the least about, which are occupied by the poor and by strangers." An ardent Whig reformer, Wright, more than any other journalist, advocated for the city to be "cleansed" and for the establishment of citizen committees to visit the sick and report on cleanliness "in the streets, in the lots, [and] in the houses." Wright's muckraking showed how the other half lived. Many immigrants were "crowded, whole families, in a single room, used for cooking and for sleeping." Such households characterized Cincinnati's slums "from roof to cellar, accumulating filth and generating disease." The immigrants were "strangers among us—strangers to our language and to our habits," who knew "not what to do, nor where to seek relief."[32] Wright advocated that no citizen stand alone. Yet the challenges of forging trust and cooperation among native-born citizens, immigrant neighborhoods, and city government remained intractable.

Cincinnati's cholera epidemic of 1849 was worse than anyone anticipated, killing some 6,000 of the city's 115,000 inhabitants, or over 5 percent of the entire population.[33] Cincinnati's proportionate death rate was roughly triple that of Cleveland and Columbus, much smaller cities with populations of around 16,000 each.[34] And while urban size and density were key factors in the spread of disease, cholera mortality in Cincinnati outweighed the proportionate toll in large metropolises like New York City and London.[35] The Queen City's river location, poor sanitation, unfettered livestock, and centrality as a steamboat port magnified the pestilence.[36] Among Cincinnati's dead was the unfortunate J. P. Harrison, one of several physicians who succumbed. Across the spectrum, immigrants, the young, the elderly, and the poor suffered most. One German immigrant, for example, recalled 1849 as a summer of horrors. A girl of sixteen, newly arrived in the city, she witnessed twenty-eight deaths in the space of a week at the tenement where she lodged with her parents and nine siblings.[37] Among the dead was her brother Paul, two years old. Decades later she recounted "the frightful heat" from ubiquitous coal fires blazing at street corners as authorities sought to cleanse the air of miasma but succeeded only in worsening the torrid Ohio summer.[38]

"The Great Scourge of Cities"

Cincinnati's haplessness in 1832 and 1849 reflected political lassitude and the strangeness of a pestilence known by many names but understood by none.[39] This strange new disease came from the Old World. A disease of immigrants, it arrived in Europe from India through the nexus of colonialism, quickly spreading across the Atlantic. Victims experienced flu-like symptoms followed by "profuse discharges like rice-water from the stomach and bowels," often accompanied by a blue-gray discoloring of the skin, mental confusion, and seizures and death from fluid loss within forty-eight hours.[40]

Alarmed, Cincinnatians followed cholera's progress in their weekly newspapers as it struck from Quebec in Canada to the Great Lakes, along the Atlantic coast, and up the Mississippi to the Ohio Valley. It was "the great scourge of cities," terrorizing urban populations everywhere.[41] Even the largest city was not immune to panic: In 1832 one New Yorker scathingly described the sight of some "fifty thousand stout hearted" fellow citizens fleeing their homes "in steamboats, stages, carts, and wheelbarrows."[42] Such scenes replayed once again in 1849 through towns and cities across America.

Fear and discord ran rife in Cincinnati. Charles Cist, in 1851, estimated that around ten thousand "fugitives" from the 1849 cholera epidemic failed to return for the city's census the following year, fleeing in "every vehicle and conveyance" from the city and "its suburbs and immediate adjacencies."[43] Not until 1883 was the *Vibrio cholerae* bacterium identified, although preceding ignorance did not prevent wild speculation on the source of the disease. Cincinnati was an epicenter in this regard, with a medical profession as fractious as its clergy. Mainstream or "allopathic" practitioners (championing such dubious treatments as therapeutic bleeding and dosing with mercurous oxide, or calomel) vied for respectability with "sectarians" of alternative medicines such as homeopathy. Both sides proved similarly ineffective. "The *capriciousness of cholera*," noted one treatise, "has been frequently a subject of remark and astonishment:—attacking *this* part of a city and not *that*; *this isolated family*, and not the *one on the farm adjoining*!"[44] At the same time, certain patterns were evident. The urban prevalence of cholera was emphasized, with its tendency to afflict "first the lowest and dampest part of a city. . . . Crowded and destitute populations, damp and filthy locations seem to be its special hot-beds."[45]

Historians have identified two main interpretations of the era: the so-called contagion theory, positing that cholera spread from person to person, and the anticontagion, or miasma, theory, identifying airborne toxins as the culprit. The latter theory prevailed in Cincinnati, where Daniel Drake held sway over medical orthodoxy. A harsh critic of medical sectarians, Drake swore by "the tried and true therapeutics," declaring "those who disdain them from their velvet perches . . . traitors to the Hippocratic tradition."[46] His widely published advice to citizens was stolid, urging "*no one* [to] *leave the city* because the epidemic has come . . . it is not, like small pox, a catching disease, if it were, being out of the city would be a preservative."[47]

Downplaying of risk by Drake and others served social as well as medical ends, tamping down fears that the presence of disease was closing the city to business. Accusations of collusion between merchants and the press reflected the fact that Cincinnati was more than just a commercial center: Commerce defined its very being. As local editor James Hall observed, this identity supplied its own vocabulary and outlook: "The resources of this city are controlled chiefly by that class which, in our peculiar phraseology, we term 'the business community.'"[48] Arguments against contagion theory wove economic and cultural fear with medical anxiety. Drake himself identified fear as an "exciting cause" in sapping the morale of infected communities and the immune system of potential victims.[49] Drake's friend (and eventual biographer) Edward Mansfield went further, suggesting that "the *fear of cholera*" could prove deadly in itself, even among the otherwise healthy.[50]

Shifting attention from the city's sanitation and water problems, local physicians such as Drake's colleague Thomas Carroll blamed foreigners for cholera and other diseases. While legitimate concerns surrounded immigration and public health, fixation on the foreign born was a sign of desperation. Ambiguity concerning cholera and its spread led many physicians such as Carroll to be "non-contagionists in principle . . . [but] contagionists in practice," resulting in calls to isolate immigrant communities.[51] As Carroll argued, the typical immigrant was far removed from the vigorous, sanitary lifestyle of Anglo-Americans, exhibiting "not only filthy habits in his mode of living, but . . . a peculiar inclination to avoid ventilation in his building." Carroll was scathing toward the Germans, blaming "various kinds of unwholesome food, and, above all, the facilities for an indulgence in strong drink," for their allegedly weakened constitutions. While disparaging German appetites, however, Carroll struggled to explain some anomalies. He noted that "very few deaths" occurred along "the public landing from Vine Street to Deer Creek," despite its being occupied "by drinking shops of the lowest character," but he attributed this to "the greater facilities for ventilation that this quarter possesses."[52] The notion that beer protected against infection was inconceivable, as Cincinnati physicians stuck to received wisdom concerning diet, lifestyle, and disease risk. In contrast to the rich diet of sausage, alcohol, and pickled kraut enjoyed by German immigrants, Daniel Drake suggested a "plain and digestible" alternative including "codfish with potatoes . . . macaroni prepared with cheese . . . stale bread and crackers," as well as "mealy potatoes, well boiled hominy and rice." Salted meat was preferable to fresh, and while Drake deemed "sweet milk, tea, coffee and chocolate" acceptable, he frowned upon alcohol, especially "sour wines" and spirits.[53]

Although physicians and other authorities exaggerated links among ethnicity, religion, and cholera, Cincinnati's Catholics and immigrants suffered a grim toll, as the municipal Board of Health's records revealed. From May 1 to August 1849, 6,459 burials were recorded, as seen in Table 2.1.

Citing the board's report, Edward Mansfield claimed that "division of the cemeteries at Cincinnati, by nationalities and religions, is so complete, that it is easily determined how many of Americans, and how many Protestants died of cholera." Adding deaths from April, September, and October of 1849, Mansfield counted 7,000 dead over six months, including some 4,600 cholera cases. Based on 1850 census data estimating Cincinnatians born in Germany and Ireland at 40 percent of the total, Mansfield calculated deaths among them as "*four-fold* that of the [native-born] Americans, and *double* that of

TABLE 2.1 BURIALS REPORTED TO THE CINCINNATI BOARD OF HEALTH, MAY 1 TO AUGUST 30, 1849

	Cholera		Other diseases	
St. Joseph's, Irish (Catholic)	460	(62%)	284	(38%)
St. Joseph's, German (Catholic)	730	(66%)	369	(34%)
St. Peter's, Lick Run (Catholic)	913	(73%)	335	(27%)
Wesleyan Cemetery, Mill Creek	270	(53%)	235	(47%)
Methodist Protestant	115	(57%)	86	(43%)
German Protestant, Reading Pike	206	(72%)	79	(28%)
German Protestant, Walnut Hills	258	(67%)	126	(33%)
Spring Grove Cemetery	36	(25%)	144	(75%)
Episcopal, in the city	42	(70%)	18	(30%)
Presbyterian, in the city	50	(66%)	26	(34%)
Baptist, Catherine Street	77	(50%)	78	(50%)
Methodist, Catherine Street	59	(61%)	38	(39%)
Potter's Field	408	(61%)	258	(39%)
Friends	8	(67%)	4	(33%)
Hebrew	43	(77%)	13	(23%)
German Prot., St. Peter's, W. Row	286	(67%)	140	(33%)
American Association, Colored	72	(50%)	73	(50%)
Walnut Hills Cemetery	55	(63%)	33	(37%)
Warsaw	25	(83%)	5	(17%)
Total	**4,114**	**(64%)**	**2,345**	**(36%)***

*Adapted from table in: John Lea, "Reprints and Reflections: 'Cholera, With Reference to the Geological Theory: A Proximate Cause—a Law by Which It Is Governed—a Prophylactic,'" *International Journal of Epidemiology* 42 (2013), 40. Percentages rounded to nearest whole number.

the entire population, proportionately." Like Drake and Carroll, Mansfield linked cholera and lifestyle, arguing that immigrants "*huddle* together, many families in the same building," and that their susceptibility to disease reflected personal filthiness, "palpable to the eyes and nose of any who observe closely," alongside poor diet and "*inferior medical treatment.*" Such correlation, he asserted, was of interest "to the progress of social science," adding that the greatest cause of immigrant mortality was "the *inferior civilization* of the Germanic and Irish elements."[54]

Although Mansfield was a lawyer and journalist rather than a doctor, his association with Drake and other physicians lent his analysis credibility, even though his statistics were conflated. While Catholic and foreign-born Cincinnatians died at a greater rate than their Protestant and native-born neighbors, ethnic or sectarian division did not apply to all cemeteries, and the urgency of burial during the epidemic made such distinctions blurrier. Worse, the Board of Health's statistics bordered on guesswork. Responding to newspaper criticism, the board began compiling interment statistics in May, "by personal inquiry and from the sexton's reports." Many sextons struggled to keep count. One, unable to distinguish cholera from other causes, simply wrote "died very quick" beside names on his list. The sexton of St. Joseph's (Cincinnati's flagship Catholic cemetery) likewise struggled to identify how many died from cholera, noting that "a majority have been persons recently immigrated" and that burials were up one-third on the same period the previous year. Given the toll that summer, it is sobering that twenty-one of the fifty-nine burials at St. Joseph's from May 1 to May 16 of 1849 were children under twelve years of age.[55]

Cholera overwhelmed Cincinnati's cemeteries, closing many and bringing a surge in new burying grounds among neighborhoods still clinging to their rural character. The city's original Jewish cemetery on Chestnut Street was among the first to close its gates, leading the congregations of Bene Israel and Bene Yeshurun to pool their burials in a new United Jewish Cemetery (1850) some five miles northeast on Montgomery Road. Also that year, the German Evangelical Reform churches of St. Peter and St. Paul purchased a burial plot four miles north of the river on Vine Street.[56] Still, not all new cemetery development was due to cholera. As Methodist minister James Finley noted, "the crowding, pressing, teeming thousands of the city" already made "encroachments upon the resting-places of the dead," shutting down some of the city's original plots and creating new ones outside the city limits.[57] At the same time, the 1849 outbreak wrought havoc, piling new bodies upon older remains. Even the recently consecrated St. Joseph's in Price Hill (1842) struggled, and Delhi Township farmers were pressed into hauling victims' corpses on their return from market. Overcrowding led Catholic authorities to purchase sixty-one acres to the west of the original burying ground in 1853. Old St. Joseph's was designed with separate plots for the German and the Irish, but such ethnic distinctions were later cast aside. The New St. Joseph's grew to encompass 163 acres, including the tiny burial ground of the Delphi Universalist Church (1838–1872), an unlikely "cemetery within a cemetery," blurring sectarian lines among the dead.[58]

While Cincinnati's cholera victims might expect hasty interment in the city's sectarian cemeteries, most merited a grave marker and a burial record. Not all were so privileged, however. One 1841 city map, published by Doolittle and Munson, showed a cemetery where Music Hall now stands. Adjacent to the city orphan asylum founded in the wake of the first cholera epidemic, Potter's Field was the municipal burying ground for paupers and derelicts. An isolated plot named for the site of Judas Iscariot's death, its name reflected the Christian tradition of burying suicides and other undesirables in unconsecrated ground. The cemetery originated as a private burial site around 1818 and was taken over by the city in 1837.[59] Potter's Field welcomed more Cincinnatians in 1849 than any other non-Catholic cemetery—some 10 percent of cholera victims that year.

At the opposite end of the social spectrum was Spring Grove Cemetery, Cincinnati's prestigious necropolis. Encompassing some 170 acres to the north of the city, this "rural city of the dead," landscaped by German-born architect Adolphus Strauch, resembled a pastoral arcadia more than the familiar, overcrowded burying grounds downtown.[60] Modeled after Père Lachaise in Paris, as well as Boston's Mount Auburn, it embodied the now-familiar flight of affluence from the urban to the suburban, with interment exclusively by purchased lot. Unlike the city-owned Potter's Field or Cincinnati's denominational burying grounds, it was incorporated in 1845 and governed by the "Proprietors of the Cemetery of Spring Grove."[61] The height of the 1849 cholera outbreak saw only 144 burials at Spring Grove, fewer than one per acre, with only 36 of them—exactly one in four—ascribed to the epidemic. An official history published by Strauch in 1869 failed even to mention cholera, instead focusing on the "energy and taste" with which the cemetery was improved by trees, lakes, and monuments. Strauch did, however, emphasize the healthfulness of a "grass-covered" burial over "remain[s] unmixed with the earth, deposited on stone shelves above ground, and forming separate portions of preserved corruption, from which volumes of pernicious gases are continually exhaled."[62] While fears of miasma lingered beyond the grave, Spring Grove revealed correlations between health and wealth, regardless of religion, ethnicity, or other variables.

Religious Responses to Cholera

By 1849, religious adherence in the Queen City was it at its height.[63] Many Cincinnatians thus understood the cholera epidemic in terms of divine providence, ascribing profound significance to its spread. Among them was Margaret Lytle, who at first dismissed the pestilence as a minor outbreak. By July she had revised her tune, admonishing her son that "the Almighty has signally blest this city with many mercies for which I fear we have been unthankful." Describing cholera as an "evil [sent] to chastise us for our faults," she cautioned him to "reflect seriously on the uncertainty of life—and the importance of preparation for death."[64]

Despite the piety of Lytle and other citizens, Cincinnati's clergy seldom commanded automatic deference. As the democratization of American Christianity mirrored the democratization of American politics, evangelicalism did not empower the clergy so much as it elevated the congregation, placing the testimony of exhorters on a level with the preaching of ministers.[65] The panoply of Sunday schools; tract societies; relief funds for orphans, widows, and paupers; and other voluntary organizations suggested evangelicalism was alive and well in Cincinnati, but such evangelicalism depended on lay leadership as much as clerical authority, and the ecumenism of most benevolent societies removed denominations from monopolies of influence.[66] The main exception to this trend was the Catholic Church, whose strict hierarchy and perceived antidemocratic tendencies explained much of the hostility it faced. Yet even in the Diocese of Cincinnati, crises such as cholera challenged clerical authority as much as they bolstered clerical influence.

The cholera epidemic was hard on the clergy and their families. Many ministers suffered bereavements, including Lyman Beecher, who grieved for his infant grandson Charley. Beecher was revising his sermon manuscripts at the time but rushed them to the printers, remarking to a colleague: "There will be some defects, I can not doubt . . . but standing, as I feel myself to do, on the confines of eternity, and amid the shafts of death, I thought it better to do what I could immediately than risk doing nothing."[67] The loss of Charley, however, had its deepest effect on the boy's mother, Harriet Beecher Stowe. Stowe's grief inspired her antislavery novel, *Uncle Tom's Cabin* (1852), garnering international attention and encouraging middle-class sentiment toward abolition on the eve of the Civil War. "It was at his dying bed and at his grave," she recalled, "that I learned what a poor slave mother may feel when her child is torn away from her. In those depths of sorrow which seemed to me immeasurable, it was my only prayer to God that such anguish might not be suffered in vain."[68]

In contrast to many small-town minsters who saw their communities emptied in flight, most Cincinnati clergy stayed put. Some, including the majestically named John King Lord, paid with their lives "at the disposal of Providence."[69] As Cincinnatians sought meaning in disaster, the urge to moralize proved irresistible. During the first outbreak of 1832, for example, Rev. James Gallaher of Cincinnati's Third Presbyterian Church credited the decline of cholera in England to "the signal interposition of Divine Providence, in answer to prayer, . . . while France, which humbled not herself, and acknowledged not the God of heaven in this thing, had been swept of its thousands and tens of thousands."[70] Even children were not spared such pontification. The *Western Sunday School Messenger* warned young readers that "*Drunkards and filthy people of all descriptions*, are swept away in heaps, as if the Holy God could no longer bear their wickedness," but subtly mitigated this dismal picture, claiming that "cholera is not *caused* by intemperance and filth, in themselves, but it is a *scourge*, a *rod* in the hand of God."[71]

Cincinnati's Catholic priesthood differed little from the Protestant ministry in their response to the epidemic. The diocesan *Catholic Telegraph* admonished its readers that cholera signaled divine displeasure, at the same time cautioning them to avoid their traditional Friday meal of fish for fear of contamination.[72] At the epidemic's peak, Cincinnati bishop John Baptist Purcell calculated the toll among his parishioners at over seventy deaths per day or some five hundred per week.[73] In a pastoral letter, he acknowledged the grind of poverty behind this toll, reflecting on "the damp cellar, the ill-ventilated garret, [and] the loathsome alley" typical of immigrant ghettoization.[74] Such "filthy and disgusting hovels" should be razed, with "whole streets of comfortable cottages" built in their stead.[75] While subscribing to the dominant miasma theory, Purcell ascribed the epidemic to "crimes of intemperance, profane swearing, desecration of the Sabbath, contempt of religion, dishonesty, and oppression and insensibil[it]y to the wants of the poor."[76] At the same time, he proclaimed "every reason to hope in the justice and mercy of God that the cholera will cease" and called for "novenas and public prayers for the cessation of the pestilence."[77]

Amid terror and reflection, cholera drove religious and political leaders to vie for moral influence. At the height of the epidemic, "a number of ministers of different denominations" petitioned Cincinnati mayor Henry E. Spencer to declare July 3 "as a day of Fasting, Humiliation, and Prayer." Though seemingly ecumenical, the nine signatories represented a narrow demographic, numbering just three Episcopalians, three Presbyterians, two Methodists, and a token Baptist. The Catholic clergy was notable by its absence, as were Jewish and other minority religious groups. Even still, Spencer—a good Protestant Whig—gave the ministers' request his (and the city's) seal of approval. While this approval was expedient, the underlying impulse for self-preservation echoed the national mood. One month later, President Zachary Taylor assumed the role of minister-in-chief and declared the first Friday of August 1849 a national day of fasting, humiliation, and prayer—something Andrew Jackson had declined to do during the cholera of 1832. While echoing earlier, Puritan modes of communal piety, such penitence indicated a new chapter in the development of civil religion. Despite some misgivings against the blurring of church and state in Taylor's declaration, many Cincinnatians agreed with the Whig editor of the *Louisville Journal* that national salvation lay in "the progress of society, aided by the enlightening power of the Christian religion."[78]

Besides filling cemeteries and inspiring calls for greater piety, cholera strained social services provided by the churches, exemplified by the pressures on urban "asylums" for the orphans of disease and other misfortunes. Cincinnati's first such institution was St. Peter's Orphan Asylum (1829), one of the earliest instances of Catholic voluntarism in the city. Following the outbreak of 1832, however, German Catholics complained that their orphaned children were settled in the Irish-run St. Peter's Orphan Asylum and clamored for a German asylum of their own. In 1837, they formed the St. Aloysius Orphan Society, funding a home for boys orphaned by recent pestilence. While Swiss-born Father John Henni initiated the enterprise, the St. Aloysius Orphan Society relied on lay funding and support, mirroring other voluntary societies through the city. Within two months it boasted 155 subscribing members, and within two years the society purchased a nine-room house for orphaned boys on West Sixth Street.[79] While Catholics led the way in founding orphanages, they did not wield a monopoly. The Cincinnati Orphan Asylum (1833) was funded in the wake of the cholera by the "ladies of Cincinnati" and local Masonic lodges.[80] Though nondenominational, it offered an institutional refuge for Protestant orphans. A more explicitly sectarian (and ethnic) institution, the German Protestant Orphan Asylum was chartered in 1849. "An Asylum for Colored Orphans" also operated, but its population was small, "the children being put out to various employments, as soon as they become capable of usefulness."[81]

Cincinnati's Drinking Problem

Cholera was not the only epidemic of this era. Economic growth from the commercial revolution in the Ohio Valley brought its own concerns. The opening of the Miami Canal in the spring of 1828 connected Ohio River commerce to

Cincinnati's hinterlands as far north as the Great Lakes, extending via the Erie Canal to the markets of the Atlantic coast. From 1826 to 1840, Cincinnati's population swelled from sixteen thousand to forty-six thousand people, the fastest growing city in the West. A boom in commercial farming brought huge surpluses of corn, which ended up distilled into whiskey or consumed by pigs awaiting the slaughterhouses of Porkopolis. Overproduction and glut characterized the unholy trinity of corn, pork, and whiskey. The industrialization of agriculture thus fed into sumptuary concerns. One temperance campaigner denounced the practice of turning swine onto unharvested ripened corn as shockingly "unfarmerlike" in the 1840s. Still more of the surplus crop went on to distilleries, which typically kept a handful of pigs to consume the slops. These pigs were described as "a fine lot of topers—dirty, bloated, red-eyed, ears and noses bloody and slit to pieces in their drunken fights. They were once doubtless decent hogs, but whiskey had ruined their morals."[82]

Brawling pigs were one thing, brawling people another. The violence of Cincinnati's swine reflected a very human crisis, however, amid rising crime in the city. Murder threatened epidemic proportions. "Some fifteen years ago," lamented the *Cincinnati Enquirer* in 1853, "a murder in Cincinnati was but a yearly event, and when one occurred, our citizens held up their hands in sorrow . . . [now] scarcely a week floats off that the bowie knife or the pistol ball has not laid a human being low with the dead."[83] Crime statistics supported this concern. In 1845 only 873 arrests were made in Hamilton County; that number rose to 6,769 in Cincinnati alone by 1853. Reported murders increased sevenfold between 1846 and 1854. The professionalization of Cincinnati's police, with its accompanying focus on recording crimes, explained only some of this increase. Violent crime especially raised alarm. Even the esteemed Drake fell afoul of a local "footpad." His mugging left him decrying that Cincinnati seemed "greatly infested with bad men."[84] Immigrants were imprisoned disproportionately, making up 54 percent of Hamilton County Jail inmates by 1848. Certain ethnic enclaves became notorious, including the Irish "Gas Alley" neighborhood: "Filled with wretched hovels," it offered "more points of vice and depravity, in their most immoral forms, than any other point within the city limits."[85]

Like cholera, the scourges of crime and vice were intimately linked to the city's bibulous proclivities. Cincinnatians relied on water "drawn up in barrels from the river" for a host of uses, including drinking, but beer and whiskey were more attractive (and sanitary) alternatives.[86] By 1849 the Ohio River remained a key source of drinking water, directly or through wells, with catastrophic results. But even during cholera, the city's reformist papers found time to rebuke the scourge of alcohol. "Suppose this desolation of Life and happiness had been caused by any Disease, or Pestilence, with which the Earth has been visited," imagined the *Daily Atlas*, "with what horror, with what pale faces would men run from the Destroyer!"[87]

Nativist temperance, while evident in the 1830s, grew over the coming decade. Alcoholism, like cholera, was seen as a disease of poor and immigrant populations, although its etiology was similarly obscure. Dereliction reinforced stereotypes of the Irish as "vicious, ignorant, and ungovernable."[88] According to the *Cincinnati Commercial*, the Queen City was "more cursed and more imposed upon by the emigration of paupers into it, probably, than any city in the Union." Admittedly, some 40 percent of all municipal indoor relief cases on the eve of the 1849 cholera epidemic were Irish born, although such Irish natives were just 12 percent of the city population.[89] These Irish, along with other immigrants, placed a huge strain on city resources. One writer to the *Gazette* claimed "half of the applicants for labor or charity, clear out, as soon as work is offered to them. Their conduct often induces us to turn a deaf ear to those who need aid. Many arrive, who are not able to speak the language, or make their wants known."[90] While the Irish suffered much prejudice, the Germans were no more warmly received. Nativist Protestants acknowledged the industry of the Germans but regarded "their moral and religious condition" as "deplorable."[91]

Temperance evolved more rapidly than any other reform crusade in Cincinnati, except possibly antislavery. At first, advocates focused on the evils of hard liquor while not necessarily condemning imbibing out of hand. The antebellum period bridged the temperance movement of the early republic and the teetotalism of the nineteenth century, with many advocates still considering beer and hard cider wholesome alternatives to distilled liquor. Nevertheless, temperance radicalized so quickly that it left many advocates behind. Delegates at one Cincinnati meeting in 1849 were harangued for thinking that temperance "meant the moderate use of liquors. This was an error. Alcohol was a poison, and its temperate use was abstaining from it as a beverage."[92]

Reflecting moral preoccupation with immigrant lifestyles, newspapers like the *Gazette* complained "that intemperance appears to be greatly on the increase in our city. Almost every day we see . . . beastly intoxication on our thoroughfares."[93] Particularly abhorrent was drunkenness on the Sabbath and the German beer gardens in which whole families—men, women, and children—mingled in warm conviviality, or gemütlichkeit. "Our community are often shocked," wrote one Methodist to the Catholic press, "and their feelings outraged, when they see your people, especially the Germans . . . gathering on Sabbath, after the church hours have passed . . . in companies, and shooting guns."[94] Such frolics, wrote another, went hand in hand with an assault on "the entire sanctity of the Sabbath" by "the Roman Catholic idea of its being a day of recreation and mirth." Such irreverence was "heretofore but little known in our country," but it "threatened to change our national character."[95] Tensions rose in the holy season of Christmas, observed by Protestants as a time of sober reflection and "songs of thanksgiving." To many, the Catholic Yule seemed shockingly pagan, marked by "the sound of the canon [*sic*] and the oath of the drunkard; and . . . all kinds of revelry and frantic mirth."[96] Anti-Catholicism coexisted, moreover, with fears of creeping secularization. "We are glad to observe," noted the *Daily Atlas*, "this increasing disposition to recognize Christmas as a holiday . . . the universally joyous and charity-awakening festival of the year!"[97] But for many Protestants, such loosening of restraint was alarming.

Early temperance advocates called for regulation of the sale and consumption of alcohol, stopping short of absolute prohibition. Among evangelicals especially, the proliferation of saloons and alcoholic "coffeehouses" was worrying. "In Cincinnati, and probably in most other cities where coffee houses and grog-shops are licensed without limit," complained one Presbyterian, "the doors of scarcely one are closed on the Sabbath."[98] Attempts to control grogshops amounted to a primitive form of zoning within city wards, restricting businesses branded as morally corrosive. The struggle was uphill, though, given the value of liquor licensing to city coffers. By 1847, opponents could rally "an impressive" two thousand protestors on the streets, but such numbers paled in the face of the $15,000 raised by the city's licensing of taverns and saloons that year.[99] This stream became the city's largest revenue source by the 1830s: from a mere $145 per annum in 1818 to $1,562 in 1831 and $7,582 in 1831.[100]

Drinking dens were less architecturally prominent than churches but more numerous. In 1834, Cincinnati had some 223 saloons and taverns, or roughly 1 for every 38 drinking-age males fifteen and upward: a ratio sustained through the subsequent decades of the nineteenth century.[101] By contrast, a city directory for that year lists just 30 houses of worship, or roughly 1 for every 280 drinking-age males.[102] Despite relatively high levels of religiosity, saloon attendance dwarfed that of the churches.

Cincinnati's elected officials made concessions to the temperance movement, but activists clamored for more. In 1843, the city enacted a law requiring prospective licensees to submit "a recommendation signed by at least twelve respectable householders, residing in the immediate neighborhood of the house where such Tavern, Coffee House or Restaurat [*sic*] is intended to be kept . . . certifying that the petitioner is well qualified." The term "respectable householders" was vague, but the new law empowered citizens living near prospective drinking houses to determine the character of their community. No doubt such responsibility was open to abuse, including bribery and intimidation, but it represented a significant milestone. At the same time as this law empowered local citizens, however, it also empowered municipal authority, allowing city officials to levy fines and arbitrate who was, or was not, respectable. Further measures were passed outlawing gaming on premises, serving alcohol to minors, and—significantly—opening drinking houses on a Sunday. While such regulation superficially resembled Ohio's Blue Laws, it actually undermined organized religion, with government instead of ministers or congregations shaping the moral agenda. Another unintended consequence was the segregation of wet immigrant neighborhoods and drier, more "native" parts of the city. An additional law enacted in 1846 empowered Cincinnati officials to inspect newly licensed properties, reporting on cleanliness, number of rooms, "and whether such house is suitable and necessary for a tavern."[103]

Moderate legislation fell short of placating temperance radicals, many of whom wanted to revoke every single liquor license in Cincinnati.[104] The earliest attempt at an anti-coffeehouse ticket was roundly defeated in the 1841 city elections, however, and subsequent efforts came to little. The populist "log cabin and hard cider" spirit of antebellum politics proved tough to crack, even for the insurgent temperance wing of the Whig party.[105] Rather than accept defeat, coffeehouse reformers measured success less by the ballot box and more by social pressure.[106] Anti-grog sentiment proliferated, even in the normally proimmigrant *Cincinnati Enquirer*. In 1853, its editor admitted no problem with "properly conducted 'coffee houses,' where food and other refreshments are sold," but claimed "that nearly every murder that has been committed in Cincinnati of late years, has occurred in the low groggeries of the river wards, and by men whose residence in America has been too short for them to have . . . knowledge of the difference between freedom and outlawry."[107]

Though riddled with nativism, temperance gave early signs of grassroots reform, pitching local citizens against a powerful coalition that included urban political and business leaders, not to mention farmers whose surplus corn was processed into whiskey. One "committee of vigilance" in the fifth ward decried the contagion of immigrant drinking dens, hotbeds of degradation. Its report contrasted "the regular tavern, where the traveller alights and looks for accommodation," with "the groggery tavern [which] has its crowds—its eatables—all its stimulants to the indulgence of appetite, in full display."[108]

The power of citizen committees was vested in their numbers, participatory democracy, and the perception that they spoke for the majority. Like ancient Athenians, their ultimate sanction was social ostracism:

Resolved, That this meeting denounces any person, directly, or indirect-
ly, importing foreign distilled liquors of any kind, or engaged in the rec-
tification of ardent spirits . . . as an enemy of temperance, and a more
subtle enemy than the retailer of the poison in three cent glasses.[109]

Originally, temperance denoted moderation in all things, including social
relationships, civic discourse, and general patterns of consumption (not just
alcohol). By the mid-nineteenth century, however, abstinence became para-
mount, producing an emotional language of renunciation. One Cincinnati
Methodist declared himself "a degraded slave to tobacco" and its "poison-
ous fumes." Four years later, "with the help of God . . . vegetable food, and
abstinence from tea and coffee," he had vanquished addiction and restored
his health. While such absolutism was extreme, teetotalism was becoming
the norm by 1850: "the grand specific for reformation," in the words of one
contemporary critic.[110] Writing in the national temperance press, one "Dr.
Muzzey" of Cincinnati warned readers against too great a confidence in his
own profession. Medicinal alcohol, Muzzey wrote, "has made many a drunkard, and filled many a drunkard's grave. . . . Wine always has been, and we
fear it always will be, a mocker." He warned against being "hoodwinked by
medical men, who love their stimulants, both in health and sickness."[111]

The roots of temperance in Cincinnati traced back to 1832, when cholera
ravaged the streets and New England preacher Lyman Beecher arrived at
Lane Theological Seminary. Like many evangelicals, Beecher's fervent nativism shaped both his Americanism and his commitment to social reform. A
cofounder in 1826 of the American Temperance Society, his sermons anticipated the trajectory of the movement. He connected abstinence to broader
issues, foreseeing "the banishment of strong drinks from the list of lawful
articles of commerce, by a correct and efficient public sentiment, such as
has turned slavery out of half our land."[112] By linking alcohol abuse to un-
regulated commerce and appealing to legislative remedy, Beecher abstracted
temperance from the purely individual realm. But ironically, like many elite
temperance spokesmen, Beecher himself enjoyed moderate consumption of
fine wine while condemning its use among the poor and immigrants.

Reflecting growing national organization, the American Temperance Society merged with various state societies in 1833, rebranded as the American
Temperance Union (A.T.U.). The A.T.U.'s founding constitution resolved "by
the diffusion of information, and the exertion of kind moral influence, to
promote the cause of Temperance throughout the United States." While asserting that "*the use of ardent spirit as a drink is morally wrong*," no mention was
made of beer, wine, or hard cider. The document also called on "the females of

the United States, in view of the powerful and salutary influence which they may exert over all classes in the community, and especially over the young . . . to give to this cause their united and persevering efforts."[113] The A.T.U. was thoroughly Beecherite, reflecting refined middle-class values, Protestant clerical leadership, and the marshaling of wives and mothers into female "auxiliaries."

Washingtonianism

The American Temperance Society/American Temperance Union was the first national temperance society, established by Presbyterian clergy with a stated religious mission, but a more radical organization founded in April 1840 in Baltimore by six self-identified "reformed drunkards" eclipsed its influence in Cincinnati. Called the "Washington Temperance Society" in honor of America's first president, this movement spread nationally with the fervor of revival, proselytizing among alcoholics and encouraging pledges of total abstinence. In evangelical fashion, former drinkers underwent conversion, emerging as fully fledged abstainers after an often-harrowing public confession of past degradation. While nominally secular, self-styled itinerant "missionaries" spread the Washingtonian message. By July 1841, the first meeting of the Cincinnati Washington Temperance Society broke the ground for the Queen City to become "the western center of the temperance revival," with some eight thousand pledges by year's end.[114]

The Washingtonians published their own journal in Cincinnati. The *Western Washingtonian and Sons of Temperance Record* was funded largely by its publishing editor, Samuel Fenton Cary. Lofty, charismatic, and a fine orator, Cary was nevertheless an unlikely crusader. A wealthy trial attorney and Mexican-American War veteran, Cary spent an estimated $20,000 of his own money on temperance projects by 1853. Though never himself a hard drinker, his interest in temperance stemmed from witnessing the rising toll of criminality in the Queen City.[115] His idealism imitated the nation's founder, reimagined through his press as a temperate, archetypal American in tall tales celebrating virtuous deeds.[116] Like his hero, George Washington, Cary was also known by the title of "general," though his Washingtonian army was of a different cloth, made up of dried-out alcoholics and former drinkers.

Washingtonianism produced a plethora of offshoot and auxiliary organizations, notably the fraternal Sons of Temperance, the female equivalent Daughters of Temperance, and the youth organization Cadets of Temperance. The Sons of Temperance, in particular, spread quickly, boasting roughly 2,400 members and thirteen division in the Queen City by May 1846. This growth was not exclusively urban but included seventy-four Ohio divisions outside Hamilton County by January 1847, most near major road and canal routes. While alcoholism was imagined as a disease of the cities (reinforcing a dubious dichotomy between the vice of the slums and agrarian virtue), the reflex of reform was neither peculiarly urban nor peculiarly rural, with organized temperance flourishing among urban and rural communities bound together by commerce.[117]

Washingtonianism was not, strictly, religious, but its temperance went beyond political shades of meaning. *The Washingtonian Pocket Companion, Containing a Choice Collection of Temperance Hymns, Songs, etc.* (1842) underlined the movement's revivalist character. Published in Utica, New York (the burned-over ground of the Northeast), this widely circulated text advised Washingtonians how best to conduct their meetings:

> After the meeting has come to order, always open with a hymn or a song. Transact the business of the society with the utmost order and dispatch. . . . Then call for speakers. Let there be as many "experiences" as possible, interspersed with brief arguments, appeals, exhortations, news of the progress of the cause, temperance anecdotes, etc. Consult brevity, so as to have as many of the brethren speak as possible—the more the better. . . . And always be sure to call for persons to take the pledge, when the audience feel in the right spirit. When the pledges are being filled up for delivery, pour out the warmest appeals, or sing the most interesting hymns or songs.[118]

Unlike narrowly political temperance groups of the time, the Washingtonian movement offered a sanctuary for former drinkers as well as campaigning for legal restriction of alcohol. They also drew from tactics of mainstream evangelicals such as Charles Grandison Finney, whose bestselling *Lectures on Revivals of Religion* (1835) influenced *The Washingtonian Pocket Companion.*[119]

The Washingtonian movement blazed briefly in Cincinnati, but the "enthusiastic but ephemeral pledge signing" of the early 1840s began to wane.[120] For more genteel temperance advocates, including Lyman Beecher, its decline was no great tragedy. "Though the Washingtonians have endured, and worked well," Beecher wrote a friend, "their thunder is worn out."[121] Beecher shared common ground against the liquor trade but stood with his more conservative colleagues in opposing tearful expostulation, vulgar spontaneity, and secretive fraternalism. Washingtonianism's raw emotion echoed the camp meetings of the frontier, but its radical tone sounded increasingly out of kilter with bourgeois sentiment. Even the teetotal Methodists, the city's most populous Protestant denomination, began closing their doors. Their influential journal, the *Western Christian Advocate*, acknowledged "a peculiar fitness" to the Washingtonians' "species of instrumentality." Who better "to describe the horrors of intemperance than reformed drunkards"? Yet even the truest convert remained scarred by the bottle, risking "a necessarily crude and erroneous view of things . . . apt to jar the feelings of a part of the community."[122] Once a drunkard, always a drunkard! Following a rowdy temperance revival, trustees of the Sixth Street Methodist Church suspended such activities under their roof, prompting an angry riposte in the *Western Washingtonian*. "The progress of Religion is so intimately identified with Temperance," declared Samuel Cary, "that every church which regards its welfare, should not only throw open its church doors but labor most zealously in the cause."[123] Cary's words carried little weight among the city's Presbyterians, however, and in April 1846, the Cincinnati Presbytery resolved to condemn "*secret societies*." "Although the resolution was a general one," complained the *Western Washingtonian*, "it was understood to have special reference to the Sons of Temperance."[124]

The politics of temperance revealed class conflict in the Queen City as much as sectarian divide, as Washingtonians protested exclusion by fellow Protestants. "Why," declared the *Western Washingtonian*, "there are laboring men who work from early morn till late at night and yet will speak on temperance six times a week, and twice on Sundays." By contrast, it went on, professional clergymen eschewed their temperance duties for the flimsy of excuse of writing their weekly sermons.[125] Another article, satirically entitled "How to Promote Temperance," indignantly advised readers:

> Keep aloof from all temperance organizations, *profess* a great love for temperance, and by no means neglect to palliate, if you do not *defend*, the evils occasioned by Grog-shops. Whenever any lecturer is so "vulgar" as to denounce the traffic, although you know that it occasions three-fourths of all the pauperism, crime, disease and death, which afflict our land, cry out "moderation," and tell him that the rumseller is to be convinced and reclaimed by "*moral suasion*."[126]

As the Washingtonian societies grew less conspicuous, their revivalism ebbed, and temperance societies declined overall. Charles Cist's 1851 city survey revealed some twenty-eight Washingtonian-derived branches meeting weekly in the Queen City at midcentury, including ten Sons of Temperance, six Daughters of Temperance, and three Cadets of Temperance. These branches met in diverse venues. At least one met at a fire station. Others gathered at Foster Hall and Losantiville Hall, hired spaces attesting to the growth of the voluntary sphere in Cincinnati. Of special note was Temple Hall, purpose built for temperance meetings and the Washingtonians' greatest monument in the urban landscape. Some church doors remained open for Washingtonian meetings, but these were low key: the basement of a Methodist chapel and the Bethel Chapel on Front Street, an ecumenical mission for the Ohio's notoriously rowdy riverboat men.[127] But by 1853, the Sons of Temperance was down to just three divisions in Cincinnati, from a peak of sixteen in 1848. This decline reflected "structural and tactical deficiencies in the brotherhood itself," as well as "the rapidly changing social context of drinking and intemperance in the late 1840s." Cincinnati temperance agitators grew disheartened at their failure to reach immigrants. At the same time, Cary and others focused against "the traffic in intoxicating drinks [and] those who are engaged in it," lobbying for legal reform at the expense of grassroots organization.[128]

Evolution of Reform

Temperance divided Cincinnati along ethnic and sectarian lines, but it opened the public sphere to new voices. Calls to abolish Sunday liquor sales went hand in hand with broader Sabbatarian concerns, including campaigns to abolish Sunday mail delivery and efforts to preserve the Lord's day for pulpit and hearth. The domestic idealism of the movement had broader consequences, though, politicizing the moral suasion of mothers and wives over their sons and husbands. While some men saw it as "indelicate for females openly to advocate the temperance cause . . . imply[ing] a necessity on the part of women, themselves to be restricted in the use of alcohol," the rise of women's temperance reflected Protestant unease at promiscuous German drinking culture.[129]

Historians of temperance in America have focused on the anti-saloon movement, whose champions battled an immigrant milieu of male-only drinking establishments owned by large breweries. Such attention is understandable, given the leadership of the Anti-Saloon League and other nativist bodies in pushing the federal Eighteenth Amendment. Female leadership through organizations such as the Women's Christian Temperance Union (1874) is also well documented, reflecting calls for women's political representation in the aftermath of the Civil War. Both the anti-saloon and women's temperance movements shared common attitudes rooted in the antebellum period, however, seeing alcoholism as both a private scourge and a public health issue. Immigration transformed relationships among drink, gender, and ethnicity across the nation. Among native-born Americans in the antebellum era, particularly women, alcohol consumption was seen as a shameful, furtive vice. One male temperance activist noted that women "are *solitary* dram-drinkers, and so would men be, had not the arbitrary opinions of the world invested the practice in them with much less moral turpitude than in the opposite sex."[130]

Maintaining separate spheres of gender was a fraught enterprise for temperance men like Samuel Cary and Daniel Drake. While Cary identified alcoholism as a masculine disease, its ravages threatened emasculation. Throughout history, empires such as Rome and Babylon exemplified the pitfalls of drinking, their populations being "reduced to effeminacy and poverty through excessive indulgence."[131] By contrast, Cary asserted, the Sons of Temperance promised an American empire of manly self-discipline. In an unpublished temperance address of 1841, meanwhile, Drake condemned the erosion of gender boundaries, singling out, among the "motley multitude" of the drunk, "the elegant and fashionable lady, who at the hour of midnight assembles her young friends—of both sexes—round her ostentatious and luxurious table, to reanimate their drooping spirits, with *ardent* spirits," as well as "young ladies with tastes which enable them to enjoy the company of young gentlemen, whose breath send up the mingled stench of Tom & Jerry, whiskey punch and squealing pig!"[132]

Mirroring nativist temperance, the Diocese of Cincinnati mounted its own drive against alcohol, despite the lackluster enthusiasm of many Catholics. While some Irish clergy shared their bishop's temperate leanings (though Purcell, like Beecher, served wine at his table), their German counterparts worried that temperance was a front for "fanaticism, intolerance, and ultra-views on politics and religion," promoting what one priest described as "spiritualism, Mormonism, free-lovism, infidelity, and materialism."[133] With German-speaking clergy thin on the ground and unlikely in any case to be swayed by Purcell's temperance leanings, converting the German laity was an uphill task. The main diocesan newspaper, the *Catholic Telegraph*, was published in English only. Secular and at times radically anticlerical voices dominated Cincinnati's German press. The one German Catholic weekly, *Der Wahrheitsfreund* (1837), played no discernible role in promoting the cause, displaying animus against such national temperance voices as Horace Greeley.[134]

Anxious to assuage lager-loving German Catholics, Bishop Purcell trod carefully. As far as personal conviction went, temperance implied moderation, as opposed to the total abstinence coming into fashion. Purcell criticized the A.T.U. for promoting the latter and, when asked to preach on temperance by two Methodist churches in the city, pointedly declined. He instead focused on his fellow Irish, among whom temperance enjoyed a toehold.[135] Nevertheless, this strategy risked further division. One priest in Sandusky, writing to Purcell in 1842, captured the divisive mood: "On St. Patrick's Day . . . I took first the temperance pledge and was followed by twenty-five Irishmen. . . . Among the Irish Catholics I do not know a single man who might be called a drunkard. It is not so with the Germans, [a] few of them are often giving a very bad example and only one of them took the temp. pledge."[136] With Irish notoriety for drink and disorder, however, temperance cut across the grain of ethnic stereotype, laying the groundwork for new forms of social organization.

Catholic temperance, and Protestant notice of it, coalesced around the aging but cherubic Father Theobald Mathew, a Capuchin friar from County Cork in Ireland (whence Purcell also originated), noted on both sides of the Atlantic as an ardent teetotaler. Mathew led a charismatic campaign in 1838, converting thousands to total abstinence and winning over Ireland's Catholic hierarchy while securing his name within the ethnic diaspora. No less a figure than Daniel O'Connell, the great emancipator of Irish Catholicism, sang his praises after converting to teetotalism.[137] Mathew's influence was remarkable. Charles Dickens, visiting Cincinnati in 1842, witnessed "a great Temperance convention" the day after his arrival. Proceeding below his hotel room marched "several thousand men," including "members of various 'Washington Auxiliary Temperance Societies,'" marching bands, and "the Irishmen, who formed a distinct society among themselves, and mustered very strong with their green scarves; carrying their national Harp and their portrait of Father Mathew, high above the people's heads." Dickens applauded this show of ethnic pride, noting that the Irish "looked as jolly and good-humoured as ever; and . . . were the most independent fellows there."[138] What escaped Dickens's pen, however, was the class solidarity on display. The ranks of Protestant Washingtonians marching with their Irish neighbors marked a high point of ecumenism in the temperance movement, one sadly destined to fade.

Father Mathew visited Cincinnati in 1850, among the final legs of a grand tour of the United States begun the previous year. Skepticism and mistrust greeted the Irishman's progress. The *Cincinnati Enquirer*, for example, claimed Mathew's conversion rates were grossly exaggerated, while the *Western Christian Advocate* had long insinuated that Mathew was part of a Vatican scheme for colonization of "agrarian free states in the northwestern valley."[139] In general, however, Mathew's arrival met with enthusiasm. Though recovering from a recent stroke, his presence was galvanizing. By the time he departed the United States in November 1851, he claimed an astonishing six hundred thousand American pledges.[140] Whether or not such figures were accurate, they were impressive. In the end, the Queen City was Mathew's platform for "a long, and thank Heaven, a successful campaign." Though "enfeebled in health,

[and] shattered in constitution," he declared, "yet with the Apostle, I glory in my infirmity, contracted as it has been in the noblest of causes . . . no sacrifice, whether of health, or property, or life, is too great to save from ruin or perdition the humblest of those for whom our divine Saviour has willingly shed His most precious blood."[141]

As Father Mathew proved, temperance was not an exclusively Protestant concern, although ethnicity and sectarian identity mattered. Cincinnati's German population remained resolutely wet, while the prominence of local nativists such as Samuel Cary and politician Thomas Spooner gave temperance an anti-immigrant edge. Despite confluences, however, temperance and anti-immigration politics were never identical. During the mid-1850s, nativism effervesced into a potent political force in Cincinnati and other American cities as the old Whig party imploded. Where nativists came to local power under the Know-Nothing banner, they were consistent in promoting temperance reform, even enacting prohibition statutes in states such as Indiana and New Hampshire. Nevertheless, Know-Nothing leanings can be attributed as much to expediency as to any principled stand. Father Mathew notwithstanding, critics consistently tarnished the Catholic-Democratic alliance with the immigrant love of alcohol.[142]

While cholera and alcohol plagued Cincinnati, to the reform minded, such epidemics were symptoms of deeper malaise. By midcentury, the Queen City's population reached its high point, relative to the national total, amid concerns about the nature of urbanization. In 1847, for example, the *Cincinnati Commercial* reported on the rise of able-bodied relief cases. It blamed the influx of foreign immigrants for the breakdown of society: "The increase of our cities,—the increase of our Foreign Commerce,—the increase of manufactures; in fine all that sort of civilization, which drives men from the cultivation of the soil, more or less tends to enlarge the class of the Poor." In addition, it claimed "one *half* of the whole number" entering the city's hospitals were "strangers" and only "*one fourth* are the real poor of the township." As the article suggested, hospitalization and poverty were as synonymous as transience and disease. Of the 2,038 hospital cases listed for 1846, 998 were "strangers," 444 were "boatmen," and only 494 were "residents" (the remaining 102 were listed as "lunatics and idiots," a class unto themselves). Such sad statistics revealed the nature of "Commercial Civilization . . . render[ing] men more dependent on the fluctuations of Trade and Government; and less connected with the steady and almost sure returns of the Harvest Field."[143]

Civic leadership in this era was limited, and concerns over disease and alcohol did not automatically produce municipal reform. Elected city leaders relied on medical authorities and the newspapers to encourage confidence.

While some efforts were made in street cleaning and other services, no sooner did the cholera decline in 1849 than critics decried "a manifest abatement in attention to the cleanliness of the city."[144] During the agitation over licensing of saloons and coffeehouses, legislators conceded to the temperance lobby, but they proved equally beholden to commercial interests in shaping policy. No matter the circumstances, Cincinnati's immigrants became the scapegoat. While not directly contagious, cholera was seen as the consequence of private squalor and public degradation. Protestant ministers joined the chorus against Catholic immigrants, but their missionary impulse outweighed the simple hostility of secular nativism. Foreign-born Catholics, especially Germans, were ripe for conversion, but they resisted reforms by those seeking to drag them from the beer garden and the saloon.

The ravages of cholera and the agitations of temperance offered glimpses into Cincinnati's future. In 1849, cholera paved the way for heightened ethnic and sectarian tensions. Nativist politics and civil disorder fed upon the anxieties, fears, and frustrations of the pandemic, as shown in Chapter 4. The national implosion of the Whig Party—divided over the Mexican-American War and expansion of slavery—accelerated this upheaval, channeling former energies. If Washingtonianism was the cultural phenomenon of the 1840s, Know-Nothingism became the political phenomenon of the 1850s.

Fears of intemperance and disease encouraged suburban population flight in the later nineteenth century. Emblematic was the Mount Pleasant neighborhood, a holdout against the 1849 cholera pandemic. An enduring urban legend holds that Mount Pleasant renamed itself Mount Healthy in 1850 to commemorate its miraculous deliverance. In fact, while the neighborhood suffered fewer deaths than neighboring communities, Mount Healthy had been used as a postal address for several decades owing to the existence of a separate Mount Pleasant, Ohio, and postal regulations preventing duplication of place names.[145] This mundane etymology, however, did not prevent the Mount Healthy legend from taking root, encouraged by local boosters promoting the sanitary appeal of their suburb. Mount Healthy stood in relative isolation, but as public transport enabled greater physical mobility, leafy suburbs like Clifton (incorporated 1850) and Wyoming (1861) arose as exclaves for prosperous Cincinnatians. As wealthier, native-born citizens migrated out, the city center declined economically, and its religious landscape became increasingly dominated by German and Irish Catholic communities.

3

"The Destiny of Our Nation"

Missionary Competition in the Ohio Valley

> American history has been in a large degree the history of the
> colonization of the Great West. The existence of an area of free
> land, its continuous recession, and the advance of American
> settlement westward explain American development.
>
> —TURNER, "The Significance of the Frontier"

Long before the Civil War, America's West loomed as an object of fascination on both sides of the Atlantic. Almost thirty years before the rebel barrage at Fort Sumter and nearly six decades before the 1890 United States census declared the nation's frontier closed, Rev. Calvin Colton, overseas agent for Cincinnati's Lane Theological Seminary, toured Great Britain, speaking at crowded fundraisers in London and other cities. "The Alleghany ridge," he declared, "makes not only a natural division, but constitutes a sort of moral boundary, in the United States. From that line West, all sympathies, and all passions, and all energies, unite with the rivers, and send forth their products upon the wide world, from the mouth of the Mississippi." Colton evoked the moral geography of the Great Valley of the West, where unprecedented economic growth stoked unprecedented anxiety. He warned "a mighty flood of population is seen abandoning schools, and churches, and all the multiplied advantages of a long established and improved state of society." He insisted "the means of intellectual and moral culture must be *forced* into the Mississippi Valley by the efforts of the benevolent, [or else] one generation to come will find the government of that mighty Republic in the hands of an ignorant and depraved people." Stressing the gospel maxim "*the field is the world*," he declared that "the Atlantic States . . . must stand or fall with the great Western Valley" while arguing "it is by the East, that the redeeming power attempted to be organized and applied to the West, is principally sustained."[1]

Colton's implications could not be clearer: if the West was not won for Protestantism, it might be won for infidelity or worse. America faced the greatest immigration in its history, an influx transforming the nation over the next two decades. Its upheaval resonated from New York City down to the smallest canal town, but the question of immigration especially vexed those preoccupied with the character of the young republic beyond the Alleghenies. Two years before Colton's overseas mission, Lyman Beecher—soon to assume the presidency at Lane—told his daughter Catharine his plans to move from the comfort of Boston to the relative frontier of Cincinnati. "The moral destiny of our nation," he wrote, "and all our institutions and hopes, and the world's hopes, turns on the character of the West, and the competition now is for that of preoccupancy in the education of the rising generation, in which Catholics and infidels have got the start of us."[2] While identifying education as the cornerstone, Beecher asserted the leadership of mainline Protestant clergymen like himself as the foundation of America's cultural, economic, and spiritual development. In pointing to Catholic and "infidel" inroads, Beecher acknowledged the challenge to Protestant hegemony—a challenge to the complacency of many in his generation.

Like Beecher, Colton stood at the vanguard of evangelical Protestant expansion, but unlike his more famous colleague, his convictions proved surprisingly fragile. In 1832, he represented the Benevolent Empire, or Evangelical United Front, of Protestant laity and clergy marshaled into a loose-knit legion of voluntary societies. Like-minded evangelicals hoped the "grand moral machinery which the spirit of Jehovah has put into operation, and [which] his Providence is carrying throughout the land," would straddle the globe, redeeming humanity for Christ.[3] The model of Protestant benevolent societies originated in Great Britain a generation earlier, with such organizations as the British and Foreign Bible Society (1804), but their growth caught on in the United States. Up to 1828, for example, the federal government spent some $3.6 million on domestic infrastructure, whereas the cumulative receipts of the nation's benevolent societies totaled more than $2.8 million.[4] In private economic terms, this was indeed an empire, and Colton told his London audiences what they needed to hear. He had been sent to raise money and sounded the right notes. Just four years later, however, his tune had changed, and he denounced the Benevolent Empire as "Protestant Jesuitism," a "combined attempt to establish a spiritual supremacy over the mind of this country." Almost overnight, he observed, "the economy of society in this country, in all that pertains to moral reform and religious enterprise, has been formed on a model entirely new to ourselves, but not without type in history."[5] The model in Colton's mind was Rome, the epitome of spiritual despotism. What had arisen on the religious landscape to so alarm him?

Origins of the American Home Missionary Society

This chapter aims neither to debunk nor to rehabilitate mythical notions of the American frontier but instead follows other trails into less familiar territory. Such territory radiated from the urban to the rural, from Cincinnati and other large cities to extensive hinterlands. Catholic as well as Protestant proselytizers itinerated these domestic circuits, at times competing among the same communities for the same converts. Before considering such competition, however, this chapter explores the Benevolent Empire, the national network of evangelical voluntary societies that became the "functional equivalent of an established church" in the wake of church-state disestablishment.[6]

The largest cities of the eastern United States enveloped Cincinnati in their outreach, just as Cincinnati enveloped the Ohio Valley and territory beyond. By 1830, Protestant benevolent societies had grown into a national network, incorporated in such sprawling concerns as the American Board of Commissioners for Foreign Missions (founded 1810, in Boston); the American Education Society (1815, Boston); the American Bible Society (1816, New York); the American Sunday School Union (1824, Philadelphia); the American Tract Society (1825, Boston); and the American Temperance Society (1826, Boston). Most extensive in both its national reach and scope, however, was the A.H.M.S., founded 1826 in New York City.[7]

Missionaries of many stripes sowed the gospel through the antebellum United States, but few did so as methodically and with an eye to the settlement of religion as the A.H.M.S. The society's "great object," according to its founding constitution, was "to assist congregations that are unable to support the Gospel Ministry, and to send the Gospel to the destitute, within the United States."[8] Still, the A.H.M.S. was anything but parochial. Its emphasis on education and societal reform went deeper than any comparable scheme among Protestant evangelicals. This thoroughly modern organization was nonetheless rooted in a Puritan heritage, romanticized by cultural elitists such as Lyman Beecher.

The A.H.M.S.'s cultivation of an educated, settled ministry contrasted with the less formal methods of rival Protestants who relied on sporadic revivalism and the itinerancy of the sort of preachers who allegedly insisted "larnin isn't religion, and eddication don't give a man the power of the Spirit."[9] Admittedly, the A.H.M.S. often struggled against these more aggressive rivals, particularly Methodists, Baptists, and Disciples of Christ (commonly but erroneously referred to as "Campbellites"). For their part, battle-scarred itinerants such as Methodist Peter Cartwright scorned A.H.M.S. interlopers from "the eastern states, where they manufacture young preachers like they do cabbages in hot houses."[10]

Demographic shifts revealed changes in the landscape in Ohio by 1850. The Methodists emerged as the largest faith: some 37.3 percent of the population, against just 21.6 percent for Presbyterians and Congregationalists combined. By contrast, Catholicism accounted for just 5.2 percent of Ohio's population, fifth overall.[11] While Methodists, Presbyterians, and Congregationalists spread throughout the state, however, Catholics concentrated in and around Cincinnati, forming 35 percent of city's population by midcentury.[12] Their urban influence particularly alarmed the A.H.M.S. and other national Protestant societies.

Attempts to establish a national (as opposed to merely local or statewide) domestic missionary society gained traction after the War of 1812 against a backdrop of assertive nationalism and consolidated regional infrastructure. The United Domestic Missionary Society founded in New York in 1822 was the precursor to the A.H.M.S. Though drawn exclusively from the Reformed and Presbyterian clergy and centered in the northeastern United States, the United Domestic Missionary Society boasted an annual receipt of some $10,000 in 1825 and 125 missionaries scattered as far afield as Michigan in the North, Florida in the South, and Missouri in the West. Missionaries such as Connecticut-born Timothy Flint, who came to Cincinnati in 1815, typified the experiences of Yankee evangelicals in the Ohio Valley. Writing a relative in Hartford, Connecticut, Flint described how his newly founded churches at nearby North Bend and Newport, Kentucky, promised "some stability and permanence, after I shall have left them," but he was less sanguine concerning outlying communities on his three-hundred-mile circuit, which enjoyed "none, but casual preaching." Traveling down the Ohio River with a box of Bibles, Flint described Indiana as especially "destitute" while noting, "destitution in the Illinois & Missouri territories is said to be almost entire."[13] It was precisely such destitution and the dispiriting itinerancy it entailed that the A.H.M.S. sought to remedy, weaving the hinterlands into the urban American fabric.

The idea of a national home missionary society arose from the ashes of state religious establishments, which fell one by one in the wake of the American Revolution. Rather than weakening religion, the removal of tax support from specific denominations galvanized evangelical activism. "They say ministers have lost their influence," noted Lyman Beecher (who opposed the disestablishment of his native Connecticut in 1818), "the fact is, they have gained. By voluntary efforts, societies, missions, and revivals, they exert a deeper influence than they ever could by queues, and shoe-buckles, and cocked hats, and gold-headed canes."[14] In 1825, delegates at a domestic missionary convention at Andover Seminary clamored for even greater reforms:

> We want a system which shall be one;—one in purpose, one in action;—which shall be pervaded by one spirit, and palpitate with one heart . . . a National Domestic Missionary Society. . . . Let no sect raise its banner—no section stand alone—no party wake to strife—but blow the trumpet in Zion, and ALL SHALL COME.[15]

The A.H.M.S. was established the following year at a national convention in New York City that included members of the Congregationalist clergy in addition to Reformed and Presbyterian ministers. While still reflecting the eastern leadership and denominational narrowness of its predecessor, the notion of a national domestic missionary society struck observers such as Alexis de Tocqueville as one more shining example of American democracy. "I met with wealthy New Englanders," he marveled, "who abandoned the country in which they were born, in order to lay the foundations of Christianity and of freedom on the banks of the Missouri or in the prairies of Illinois."[16] Like other observers, however, Tocqueville foresaw challenges for evangelical reformers, foisting their ideals on recalcitrant settlers. Tocqueville was especially skeptical of efforts to reshape the culture of the Ohio Valley, where the "amalgamated" population "creates a moral being whose portrait it would be very hard to draw."[17]

National Scope of the A.H.M.S.

From its earliest years, the A.H.M.S. focused on two geographical regions: the northeastern United States and the trans-Appalachian West. The society was founded to supply educated ministers to frontier communities at the written request of local lay leaders. This arrangement lasted until such congregations became self-sufficient, indicating both economic health and religious stability. Beyond New England, the Atlantic Seaboard, and the broadly identified "West," however, the society's presence was negligible.[18] Its tenth annual report (1836) recorded a total of 755 missionaries, including 15 in Canada. The society supported only 10 missionaries in its southern field and none whatsoever in South Carolina, Louisiana, and the District of Columbia. New England (319) and the remaining northeastern states (220, including 183 in New York) accounted for well over two-thirds of all A.H.M.S. preachers, while only 191 of the society's preachers (25.3 percent) were stationed in the West, including 80 in Ohio. The income of the A.H.M.S. revealed even greater regional disparity. Of the $100,786.88 receipts in 1836, 71.6 percent came from New England alone, with an additional 23.9 percent from the remaining Northeast. Just 3.6 percent of receipts came from the western United States, mostly from Ohio ($3,315.77 of $3,664.89).[19] Fifteen years later, the A.H.M.S. grew to support 1,065 missionaries, including 311 in New England and 224 in the remaining Northeast. The geographic center had shifted, however, and there were now 515 missionaries in the West, including territorial additions such as California. Yet, economically, at least, the A.H.M.S. radiated from the eastern United States. In 1850, the six New England states funded receipts of $60,814.92: more than quadruple Ohio, Indiana, Illinois, Missouri, and Michigan combined ($14,054.35).[20]

From its beginning, the A.H.M.S. faced challenges of distance, expansion, and democracy, felt nowhere more keenly than in the Queen City. By the summer of 1830, the many hundreds of miles dividing the society's headquarters in New York from the trans-Appalachian Ohio Valley prompted the creation in Cincinnati of the Central Committee of Agency for Home Missions in the Western States. This cumbersome entity oversaw "those portions of the West which have a natural relation to Cincinnati as a commercial center," an area including the entire state of Indiana and parts of Kentucky, as well as most of Ohio.[21] Though this new creation was "entered on with much deliberation," the A.H.M.S. conceded "that the missionary business of the states west of the Allegany [*sic*] mountains could not long be transacted with the best effect by a committee located in New York or Philadelphia, and that the western churches would call for another center of action within their own bounds." Sure enough, the Presbyterian Church, under the local leadership of the Cincinnati Presbytery, resolved in April 1830 "to use their best endeavors to unite in the west, the operations of the A.H.M.S. and the General Assembly's Board, in the appointment of one Board of Agency."[22]

The A.H.M.S.'s Central Committee was a who's who of Cincinnati's Protestant establishment, initially including all four of the city's Presbyterian pastors. One prominent member, Elijah Slack, was both president of the Lancastrian Seminary and, later, common school principal in the city. Lyman Beecher's eventual membership from 1832 cemented linkage between the board's remit under the A.H.M.S. and its commitment to educational uplift in the Ohio Valley. New England clergymen including Henry Little, Thornton Mills, and Samuel Cushman dominated the committee's board, but it also included local religious leaders such as Joshua Lacy Wilson, the white-haired patriarch of Cincinnati's First Presbyterian Church. Given such a distinguished roster, the committee's success should have been practically assured, but the weakness of the A.H.M.S. lay in its foundations.

America's sectional boundaries have always been elastic, but A.H.M.S. demographics nevertheless pointed to some troubling conclusions. While the society avoided a strong position on the question of slavery, for example, its Yankee character readily explains why so few preachers were requested in the South. Throughout the antebellum period, the A.H.M.S. trod a fine line. Until 1850 the society warned its ministers not to alienate congregations by preaching against the "peculiar institution" while at the same time it avoided assigning fundraising agents to slaveholding states (though it continued sending handfuls of preachers).[23] Relations between the A.H.M.S. and the South were mutually suspicious at worst and mutually ignorant at best. Even when southern evangelicals petitioned for assistance, the result was generally underwhelming. In one telling exchange, for example, the A.H.M.S.'s Central Committee asked a lay evangelical to clarify where he was writing from, as the small town of Thibodauxville, Louisiana, was "not on our maps."[24]

The Problem of Slavery

Although relatively few Cincinnatians were born below the Mason-Dixon Line (some 26 percent of American-born male heads of household in 1841), the city's proximity to slaveholding Kentucky, together with its commercial relations and racial fault lines, made A.H.M.S. ambiguity toward slavery corrosive.[25] The society's Central Committee was founded one year after Cincinnati's worst rioting drove over a thousand black residents to permanently flee in 1829, leaving the city's remaining black residents vulnerable to further depredations. While the Queen City's strategic location attracted abolitionists such as newspaperman James Gillespie Birney and charismatic preacher Theodore Dwight Weld, antislavery activists routinely faced harassment, intimidation, and even violence.

The treatment of Weld offers a particularly revealing instance of anti-abolitionism in Cincinnati. Weld was best remembered for leading an 1834 abolitionist insurrection at Lane during his time there as a seminarian. Previously, Lyman Beecher had censured Weld for ministering to the city's black residents, or "carrying the doctrine of intercourse into practical effect," as he euphemistically described it.[26] Summoned by the Board of Trustees to explain his students' wayward behavior, Beecher stated:

> When they founded colored schools, I conversed with Weld repeatedly, and pointed out these things. Said I, you are taking just the course to defeat your own object, and prevent yourself from doing

good. If you want to teach colored schools, I can fill your pockets with money, but if you will visit colored families, and walk with them in the streets, you will be overwhelmed.[27]

Like the A.H.M.S. he represented, Beecher was not against humanitarian or even educational outreach to black Cincinnatians, but he opposed fraternization between seminarians and black citizens that might jeopardize the reputation, funding, and safety of his seminary. Meanwhile, Weld and other students at Lane who embraced the principles of racial equality pursued an immediate abolitionism closer to that of Beecher's former parishioner William Lloyd Garrison than to the laissez-faire of Beecher, who described himself as both a colonizationist and an abolitionist "without perceiving in myself any inconsistency."[28] Unfortunately for Beecher, the radicalism of Garrison, Weld, and others made fudging such distinctions increasingly problematic. His dismay, therefore, was palpable when Weld staged a series of unsanctioned student debates over the question of immediate abolitionism versus gradual emancipation. These debates, in turn, caught the attention of the local press and, once again, the Lane Board of Trustees, who embodied the converging interests of commerce and evangelicalism in the Queen City. The trustees resolved immediately to outlaw all student associations "except such as have for their immediate object improvement in the prescribed course of studies." The result was disastrous. Led by Weld, some forty seminarians—the majority of those enrolled at the time—went north to Oberlin College at the invitation of its radical president, Charles Grandison Finney, leaving Lane struggling to survive.[29]

The A.H.M.S. Gospel

The A.H.M.S.'s reluctance to address questions of slavery and racial justice contrasted with its eagerness to shape the Ohio Valley in its own image. In 1832, for example, national corresponding secretary Absalom Peters informed the *Cincinnati Journal* that his society had "granted aid to more than 400 congregations and missionary districts, in the support of 260 ministers . . . more than one-third of the whole number of Presbyterian ministers now laboring in the 'Valley of the Mississippi.'" While vindicating the society's efforts, Peters warned that "this labor of love has been hitherto prosecuted under many embarrassments in the western states.—Among these have been the difficulty of obtaining suitable agents, and the repeated interruption of the labors of such as have been employed in this field."[30] Worse, Cincinnati was just recovering from its first cholera epidemic, and its prospects were looking decidedly shaky.

Led by northeastern ministers such as Absalom Peters, the antebellum A.H.M.S. was bourgeois, orderly, urban, and nationalistic. It embodied the postmillennial theology that had dominated evangelical America since the Great Awakening. Advocates hoped that a thousand years of civil and religious progress would precede Christ's imminent, triumphant return. In their view, the City of God was no metaphor but a template for social reform. According to Cincinnati minister Henry Little, A.H.M.S. preachers were performing "a work, which though silent, will be seen, in the light of another day, to have been truly great and glorious."[31]

Emphasis on the "silent" progress of the gospel suggested the taming of the evangelical spirit, governed by human reason and technology, in contrast to the supernaturalism of Cane Ridge and similar revivals. Redemption was thus a question of "homogeneity and nationalization," according to David H. Riddle, one of the A.H.M.S.'s leading ministers. "Men every where, and in all ages," he preached in an 1851 sermon, *Our Country for the Sake of the World*, "love darkness rather than light." Only the guidance of an educated ministry, he argued, offered Americans spiritual relief: "Such is the character of the population crowding the West. Scorched by revivals, and restive under the restraints of other States, they go like Cain of old to found or find a city of repose." Riddle envisioned "the great American church of all denominations" redeeming not only the United States but spreading across the entire globe.[32]

If the A.H.M.S. was global in its mission, its globalization was thoroughly domesticated, a template imposed on the religious landscape. Throughout the nation, refined places of worship became the hallmark of polite society, replacing worn and crumbling meetinghouses. In 1839 the society commended "a plan of a neat church, of moderate dimensions, accompanied by an estimate of the expense." Described as "*neat* in appearance, *commodious*, and *cheap*," its estimated cost of $1,500 to $2,000 nevertheless reflected the cost of lumber and other building materials in New York City, from whence prefabricated supplies were shipped. The society's promotion of standardized architectural plans underwrote its arguments for physical and cultural homogenization, contrasted against a regional hodgepodge of churches "constructed and furnished with so little regard to comfort and taste, that the endurance of them is to many persons a present misery."[33] At the same time, the New York–centric vision of the A.H.M.S. competed with regional cities such as Cincinnati, a noted center of construction and manufacturing in such fields as church organs and furnishings. Therefore, the A.H.M.S. struggle should be understood in terms of economic as well as religious influence. Such national influence, for example, prompted one leading Queen City artisanal association, the Ohio Mechanics Institute, to complain that "the

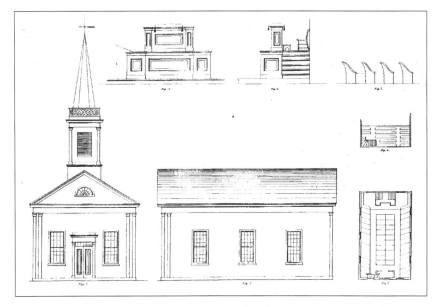

Figure 3.1 Standardized church plan promoted in the *Home Missionary and American Pastor's Journal* (December, 1839).

ingenuity of western artists" was "neglected and unknown . . . languish[ing] for want of patronage, while thousands of dollars are annually sent across the mountains."[34]

As A.H.M.S. evangelicals strove in millennial hopes of God's kingdom, to many easterners the Ohio Valley remained a moral lowland. "The free use of ardent spirits . . . profanity & sabbath desecration" characterized many small communities under the society's Cincinnati jurisdiction.[35] Questions of moral reform weighed heavily, none more than slavery, the very question the A.H.M.S. skirted most consistently. The peculiar institution divided communities on both sides of the Ohio, but rather than preaching emancipation, A.H.M.S. ministers reframed the problem around white morality. One minister a few miles north of Kentucky, for example, lamented the influence of slavery on his congregation, many of whom came from slaveholding Virginia. "Like Lot in Sodom," he lamented, "my soul is continually harassed & vexed by low conversation & filthy morals of the wicked." Raised among slaves, they picked up "the habit of lying to such a degree that they have no control of the tongue. Tattling, slander & low intrigue is common." Sundays were marked by "party visiting, swimming, Hunting, political electioneering," and similar worldly pursuits.[36]

The Puritan tradition of the Errand into the Wilderness remained alive and well within the A.H.M.S., with the Midwest regarded as ripe territory for cultural as well as spiritual conversion. Beecher's description of Cincinnati as "the London of the West," populated by "intelligent, New England sort of folks," reflected this missionary mentality. Another senior official of the A.H.M.S. prayed "that the 'Spirit of the Pilgrims' . . . arouse itself to the work of Home Missions—and N[ew] England be as distinguished for her preeminence in this department of benevolent effort, as she has been in Foreign Missions."[37] Such parochialism reduced the Midwest to a domestic Sandwich Islands, the Pacific archipelago then preoccupying Protestant missionaries on the far side of the globe.

The educational background of A.H.M.S. preachers confirmed the society's eastern bias. Most missionaries to the Ohio Valley were graduates of one of three colleges: Princeton, the nation's leading Presbyterian stronghold, or the Congregationalist bastions of Andover and Yale.[38] Soon enough, graduates from Lane supplemented their ranks, but even these early Lane graduates tended at first to be New England natives rather than locally recruited.[39] Lane's trustees reinforced the template of eastern evangelicalism by boosting their institution as "the great Andover or Princeton of the west," destined "to give character to hundreds and thousands of ministers."[40] While not technically affiliated to the A.H.M.S., Lane's connections were implicit in the association between Beecher and other officials, not to mention the shared commitment to the 1801 Plan of Union, combining the national resources of the Congregationalist and Presbyterian Churches for the evangelization of the frontier.

Cloistered as it was, the A.H.M.S. boasted remarkable assets. Above all, it was a vast intelligence-gathering network. The society's records, amassed over its years of labor in the field (1826–1893), provided a panoramic overview of the spiritual landscape. A.H.M.S. missionaries, commissioned from the ranks of newly ordained Congregationalist and Presbyterian clergy, submitted a quarterly report to the society's corresponding secretary in New York City. Such intelligence, in turn, determined distribution of resources, with ministers being instructed "to make a *perfect statistical return . . . that we may make out a complete return, at our Anniversary Meeting, of the hopeful conversions, additions, &c.* which have occurred in the churches where missionaries of the A.H.M.S. labour."[41] The society's first corresponding secretary, Princeton alumnus Absalom Peters, coped with an avalanche of correspondence. This influx was essential to reckon the needs of different communities, he asserted, "and thus to seize upon the most important points to be occupied."[42]

The A.H.M.S. mission to the Ohio Valley depended on lay participation in terms of finance and guided migration, as much as on the exertions of missionaries and other agents. In theory, the relationship between laity and clergy was symbiotic. "A half dozen families of the right stamp," wrote one official, "in company with the missionary, in many places would render his labours doubly efficient." Every missionary was therefore advised to "have his little colony selected to accompany him."[43] Recognition of domestic mission work as *colonization* underscored the A.H.M.S.'s New England character, whether such colonization was undertaken by missionaries responding to a call or lay settlers under their own volition. "It is not uncommon," boasted Andover-educated Henry Little, secretary of the society's Central Committee, "to meet men whose principle [*sic*] design in emigration was to assist as laymen in doing good in the west." Little claimed to have known two such settlers who "took up their residence in one of our towns where there was very little religious influence exerted. Shortly a good Sabbath school was in operation. Each of them subscribed $100 for the support of a minister."[44] While the A.H.M.S. was designed to supply ministers in response to congregational demand, where no such demand existed, it was deemed necessary to provide it. Otherwise, "in the sparse communities of the West, where there is not, and probably cannot be, very soon, a regular ministry, with its settled plans," the A.H.M.S. depended on "do[ing] good in such ways as Providence puts out."[45]

The ideal of the pious midwestern pioneer mixed a grain of truth with a peck of humbug. In any event, domestic missionary growth went together with other forms of civic boosterism, depending on economic fortune as much as any other line of business. In its first year, for example, the A.H.M.S. already attracted over $23,000 in receipts.[46] By 1836, this figure rose to over $100,000, but national financial panic the following year significantly shrank A.H.M.S. growth across the United States.[47] While this economic crisis was a national calamity, Cincinnati, as a commercial hub, was particularly vulnerable to "pecuniary embarrassments, and the prostration of mercantile credit," as the Central Committee's reports underlined.[48] Its then secretary, Thornton Mills, wrote his opposite number in New York, admitting "that we are under obligation for about $500, or $600, more than our treasury can meet . . . owing to the fact that the commercial affairs of the West are embarrassed." Mills asked if "the situation of your Treasury [is] such that for the present we can draw upon you?" Equating moral economy with financial health, he requested a new visiting agent, "a man from the East . . . who will not only raise funds, for us, but who will exert a good spiritual influence in the churches he visits." Such influence was apparently wanting, and Mills complained of the transience of A.H.M.S. missionaries, moving from place to place. Too many funds were being "squandered, or at any rate they do not answer the great end the society has in view, the establishment of a permanent ministry in our land."[49]

Things were bad in Cincinnati but no better in Ohio Valley's rural hinterlands, bound to the city by chains of debt and dependence. In Johnstown,
Ohio, local lay leaders addressed New York society headquarters in 1840, noting that "the times are hard." The cash-strapped Cincinnati committee declined them one hundred dollars in matching subscription toward a qualified
Presbyterian minister despite fierce competition from Baptist and Methodist
preachers.[50] Elsewhere across the region, missionaries struggled with poor
harvests, dwindling subscriptions, the lure of "gold fever" in California, and
other disruptions. Their appeals for help directly to New York underlined the
marginal influence Cincinnati exerted through its Central Committee.[51] "It
is almost literally true," observed Henry Little, "that away from the centers of
business, there is no money." Congregations in the Ohio Valley were reduced
to paying their dues "in such articles of produce as the people could give."[52]

Even as the A.H.M.S. struggled financially, it strove to expand its influence through the medium of the printed word. As a major publishing and
printing center, Cincinnati was ideally placed to promote the cause of religion. Presbyterian journals such as the *Western Luminary* and the *Cincinnati
Journal* cultivated readers through the Ohio Valley, but the A.H.M.S. wanted
a broader, national base. Within two years of its founding, it first published
the *Home Missionary*, a hugely influential monthly periodical printed in New
York and circulated throughout the United States. Under the scriptural byline
of Mark 16:15 ("Go . . . preach the gospel"), the first issue outlined its purpose with reference to the A.H.M.S.'s mission as a whole:

> The design of the American Home Missionary Society is to promote,
> not the interests of any one section or denomination of the church,
> but the religious benefit of a great and growing nation. The business
> of such an institution cannot be conducted properly, nor can its ap-
> peal be effectually presented to the public, without a vigorous and
> active correspondence with the citizens of every State. Facts must be
> gathered from every portion of the field of the Society's operations,
> and these must be communicated to every other portion, before a
> common and national sympathy can be expected to be awakened.

The *Home Missionary* was a counterpart to the *Missionary Herald* (published
by the American Board of Commissioners for Foreign Ministers) and was
meant to "bear none of the local characters, which belong to most publications devoted to the interests of particular sections of the church, but, like
the Society, in whose name it is issued, is intended to be truly *national*."[53]
The A.H.M.S.'s emphasis on a national platform, and the *Home Missionary*'s

reinforcement of homogenous national character, underlined a view of the Ohio Valley first and foremost as mission territory, rather than as a coequal partner in the work of reform. Viewed in this light, Cincinnati's logistical resources, particularly its printing and distribution networks, were valued more than its cultural identity, which was seen as both malleable and unfinished.

"The Jesuits Are Making Rapid Strides Here"

The *Home Missionary* became one of America's leading anti-Catholic periodicals, but early issues showed little evidence of its eventual obsession. Drawing heavily on edited reports of A.H.M.S. field missionaries, it rarely addressed Catholicism by name through the early 1830s, instead focusing more generally on struggles with irreligion and conversions among the unchurched. Furthermore, the *Home Missionary*'s national focus kept it aloof from local controversies between Protestant journals such as the *Cincinnati Journal* and the Catholic diocesan press, though the A.H.M.S. missionaries were often passionately embroiled. For example, the journal's editor, Rev. Amos Blanchard, was a member of the A.H.M.S.'s Central Committee and took up against the "new *papal* paper in this city," avowing his "duty to hold up its manifest corruptions in their true light, to the public gaze."[54] For its part the *Catholic Telegraph* (established 1831), under editor James Mullon, served as a lightning rod against "those who are in the habit of inveighing against the Catholic Faith," adding that "we expect their opposition, and are prepared to meet it."[55]

Anti-Catholicism in the *Home Missionary* reflected overseas immigration. At first, editorial discussion of the faith was largely limited to historical enclaves like St. Charles, Missouri.[56] There, warned one correspondent, "the Jesuits are making rapid strides here in their usual way, building chapels, school-houses, and establishing nunneries. Large contributions, by protestant people, are made to erect those buildings, and many send their children to these schools."[57] Such reports betrayed various anxieties but, coming from the old French interior of the Midwest, would have caused only limited consternation to readers in Cincinnati. More to the point, the willingness of local Protestants to fund and support Catholic education suggested that assimilation, not conflict, was the reality on the ground. Early volumes of the *Home Missionary* also highlighted Catholicism in Canada, anticipating later conspiracies surrounding transnational Catholic colonization of the Great Lakes. "Catholics," wrote one Canadian correspondent, "are treading more boldly and closely upon us. . . . The vast sums of money, and the great number of emigrants which arrive in this land from Europe, enable them to establish their schools wherever they please."[58]

Catholic consolidation in historic centers like Canada and French pockets of the Midwest elicited Protestant shudders in the 1830s, but German and Irish immigration to the Ohio Valley was another thing entirely. In Cincinnati alone such immigration contributed to a near doubling of population from 24,831 in 1830 to 46,338 in 1840. Germans were only 5 percent of this total in 1830, compared to 23 percent in 1840 and 27 percent by midcentury.[59] At that juncture, observed Bavarian-born editor Max Oertel, "part of Cincinnati is almost entirely German . . . there it swarms with German faces and one hears the dialects of Baden, Austria, Frankfurt, Berlin, Low German, and even some Yiddish."[60]

Oertel emphasized the kaleidoscopic diversity of German settlers, although increasing numbers of Cincinnatians viewed immigration through the lens of nativism. Nativism prevailed especially among both evangelical Protestant and anticlerical German immigrants, whose suspicion of their Catholic brethren was most violently tinged with recent conflict and ancient history. In an article entitled "Progress of German Immigration," Rev. B. C. Wolff, a Reformed pastor from Easton, Pennsylvania, decried the recent influx of his fellow Germans from Catholic strongholds such as the Rhineland and Bavaria: "The Catholics are now far ahead of us. They have already possession of the field."[61] Wolff's detection of the Vatican's hand in the Ohio Valley echoed in the *Home Missionary* over the coming years, with one 1839 editorial reporting "The Catholic boast—'We have got the West.'"[62] An advocate of German-language missions, Wolff maintained that conversion of immigrants was key to redeeming America. He directed the settlement of German-speaking A.H.M.S. missionaries, including F. M. Raschig, a native of Saxony who came to Cincinnati in 1834, serving seven years at St. John's Evangelical Church and thirty more at St. Mattheus in Over-the-Rhine, among the city's leading German Protestant congregations by the Civil War.[63]

Anti-Catholicism may have been "the deepest bias in the history of the American people," but it took European immigration to rouse it from slumber.[64] The mid-1830s witnessed hardening anti-Catholicism, both nationally and in Cincinnati, and the A.H.M.S.'s mission must be understood in this context. Besides Lyman Beecher's nativist tract *A Plea for the West* (1835), two nationally bestselling publications stoked the flames in that decade. The first was Samuel F. B. Morse's *The Foreign Conspiracy against the Liberties of the United States* (1835), which popularized the idea of a Vatican conspiracy to colonize America with Catholic paupers and erode the United States Constitution. Second was *The Awful Disclosures of Maria Monk, or, The Hidden*

Secrets of a Nun's Life in a Convent Exposed (1836), a lurid tale of abuse from a Montreal convent. Though Maria Monk was fictional, her exposé—ironically memorialized as the "Uncle Tom's Cabin of Know-Nothingism"—was presented and widely read as fact.[65] Strikingly similar allegations of abuse had led mobs to torch the Ursuline Convent in Boston the year before, though some arsonists were allegedly inspired by hearing a series of anti-Catholic sermons delivered by Lyman Beecher, who was visiting from Cincinnati at the time.

Were the A.H.M.S. and its allies to blame for sectarian violence? Even accounting for Beecher's utterances, evidence directly connecting evangelical fervor with urban unrest is cloudy to say the least. Admittedly, the discourse of the A.H.M.S. grew increasingly militant and anti-Catholic over the antebellum period, reflecting patterns of immigration and the westward shift of missionary frontiers. In 1843, for example, the *Home Missionary* envisioned phalanxes of Catholics "rushing in to occupy the still vacant lands of our country."[66] An 1839 editorial identified the Ohio Valley in similarly Beecherite terms: "The great battle is to be fought [there] between truth and error, between law and anarchy—between Christianity, with her Sabbaths, her ministry and her schools, on the one hand, and the combined forces of infidelity and Popery on the other."[67] Practically, this "great battle" translated into debates over education, temperance, and similar issues. To evangelicals, however, such moral suasion was a far cry from the sporadic rioting, ethnic gang fights, and other hooliganism they saw erupting on the streets of Cincinnati and other cities. Few denounced the burning of Boston's Ursuline Convent more forcefully than Beecher himself, and sectarian violence in Cincinnati was low compared to similar cities, including nearby Louisville, Kentucky.[68]

The A.H.M.S. had anxieties aplenty within its own congregations without worrying about Catholic competition. Despite their best efforts to establish Zion in the West, its missionaries labored in a fractious landscape where nothingarianism and anythingarianism prevailed. In a typical field report to the A.H.M.S., one Ohio minister despaired that there were "almost as many denominations as there are individuals."[69] Another missionary described his "little flock" as "much scattered, and thickly interspersed with almost every description of character and sentiment Baptists, Methodists, Camelites [*sic*], Chrystians, Episcopalians & Universalists of two kinds no-hell-ers & hell redemptionists."[70] Illustrating the prevalence of "infidelity and universalism," a third missionary described a female parishioner "either so ignorant, stupid, or hardened in sin, that . . . she would not wish to go to heaven if her relations and friends were to be sent to hell."[71] Such encounters indicated a broader struggle between traditional ministerial authority and the democratization of religion.

In 1847 New England preacher Horace Bushnell published a sermon for the A.H.M.S. entitled *Barbarism the First Danger*. Bushnell, among the leading Congregationalist thinkers of his era, identified aesthetic refinement, or taste, with moral purity, and his florid prose style influenced a generation of sermonizers. He wrote that taste (as opposed to mere fashion) was "God's legacy to him in life, which legacy he cannot surrender, without losing the creative freedom and dignity of his soul."[72] Unlike *A Plea for the West* (1835) by his friend Lyman Beecher, Bushnell put in context—even if he failed to contradict—Catholicism's putative threat to Protestant America. Acknowledging readers who were "half frighted by the cry of Romanism, and half scorn it as a bugbear," Bushnell asserted: "We are in danger, first, of something far worse than Romanism, and through that of Romanism itself. OUR FIRST DANGER IS BARBARISM." Where others, including Beecher, viewed Catholic immigration as an invasion, Bushnell was more circumspect, regarding Catholicism as just one more symptom of upheaval in a nation uprooted by westward expansion. A believer in Christian civilization, Bushnell even acknowledged the relative appeal of Catholic institutions:

> If we must have a wild race of nomads roaming over the vast western territories of our land—a race without education, law, manners or religion—we need not trouble ourselves further on account of Romanism; for such a people, Romanism, bad as it is, will come as a blessing.

If the West was in a parlous state, according to Bushnell, it should nevertheless count its blessings. The South was worse, laboring under the barbarism of slavery. Making "a waste where God had made a garden," he wrote, "slavery gathers up the relics of bankruptcy, and the baser relics still of virtue and all-manly enterprise, and goes forth to renew, on virgin soil, its dismal and forlorn history." The solution to America's ills was clear. "Religion," Bushnell concluded, "is the only prop on which we can lean with any confidence; and Home Missions are the vehicle of religion."[73]

In the mind of the A.H.M.S., then, religion was a panacea for the nation's troubles, whether mitigating the ills of slavery or, increasingly, immigration. In Cincinnati, German immigrants were a particular concern, although cultural ignorance and a dearth of German-speaking ministers made reaching them problematic. While two-thirds of Cincinnati's German population was Catholic, Protestant reformers viewed Catholicism as an affliction of national identity rather than an essential feature. An 1832 *Cincinnati Journal* article on "Sunday School Efforts," for example, described German Catholics as "universally opposed to sending their children to any of our schools." Those children who attended once "have almost invariably been kept away the second Sabbath." The next paragraph, however, described German immigrants in general as a "very considerable and interesting portion of our population. . . . Most of them are poor, but generally industrious and frugal; many moral, and some of them religious."[74]

While German Catholics were an obvious challenge to the evangelical gospel, many A.H.M.S. ministers regarded German Protestants as equally problematic. They were widely suspected of lax religiosity and their ministers accused of dubious leadership and unorthodox preaching. One minister in Columbus described "the deplorable and destitute condition" of German Protestants in Ohio's cities, lamenting that many "are led off into the coarse forms of rationalism and infidelity by those who impose themselves on them as ministers of the gospel."[75] In Cincinnati, the A.H.M.S. Central Committee observed "a decided disposition on the part of many of the German churches, to make a convenience of, & impose on us, and we are compelled to watch them narrowly." Committee chairman Thornton Mills described one German minister, Rev. Schiedt, as "an evangelical man" who received "his members on the same principles which our churches do," although Mills questioned "how faithful he is in applying those principles to individual cases." In fact, Schiedt neglected public confession of faith and spiritual conversion, considered sine qua non by Anglo-American evangelicals, in favor of open-door membership of his church. Although he continued receiving his stipend from the A.H.M.S., Mills advised "not to increase his appropriation."[76] In the absence of interethnic communication, such sanctions were typical of the society's efforts to coerce and cajole the immigrant clergy.

Some twenty miles north of Cincinnati, Hamilton, Ohio, was as a microcosm of its larger neighbor. Connected to the Ohio River via its tributary of the Great Miami and by canal and turnpike to the Queen City itself, Hamilton was situated to receive many immigrants then arriving in the region. Like Cincinnati, Hamilton soon boasted a large Catholic population, including many Germans concentrated in the west of the city. In 1830, however, when the city's first Catholic church, St. Stephen's, was established, the city's Catholic population was barely existent. Hamilton's leading Protestant citizens cannily invested the initial $400 to found the parish and attract the immigrant labor that came with it, laying foundations for industrial growth.[77]

In Hamilton, as in Cincinnati, German Protestants posed problems for the A.H.M.S. The society retained a German pastor at Saint John's Lutheran Church, whose fortunes highlighted challenges among immigrants in the region. Unlike the wayward Rev. Schiedt, Louis Richter was orthodox by A.H.M.S. standards, but his congregation was varied, consisting "principally of Lutherans, a small number of Presbyterians, and one family of Baptists." Ethnicity rather than denomination characterized his flock, and infighting between recent immigrants and established lay members ensued. Two of Richter's elders complained to the A.H.M.S. "of many unconverted and infidel members in the congregation." They noted that "since the revolution in Germany of 1848, a large number of rationalists and infidels have come from there to this country," and that Richter "thought it a sacred duty to preach repentance and conversion in the most urgent manner; he had the pleasure of seeing some converted, but others in consequence became his most bitter enemies." By 1850, matters came to a head, and the congregation split. Richter was forced from his pulpit by the more numerous moderates. Three years later he was without a roof over his head, still supported by the A.H.M.S. but reduced to leading services in a room at the courthouse. Maintaining his convictions and admitting to communion "only good and true Christians" while eschewing "those who are only Christians by name," Richter struggled to maintain his family and his social standing.[78]

The Wilson-Beecher Controversy

Ultimately, all was not well within the A.H.M.S., and local opposition increasingly arose from disaffected Old School Presbyterians. In Cincinnati, this fell to Joshua Lacy Wilson, Lyman Beecher's redoubtable antagonist. A native of Virginia, Wilson was licensed as a Presbyterian minister in Kentucky in 180, before moving to Cincinnati six years later. A Scotch Irish theocrat, he initially supported Lane's mission as a Presbyterian seminary, but his support was short lived. Wilson caused trouble for the A.H.M.S. as early as 1830, convinced that it was "aiming to overthrow the Presbyterian Church" in the Ohio Valley.[79] Whatever the A.H.M.S.'s goals, he took umbrage at its influence, which he denounced in an 1831 pamphlet entitled *Four Propositions Sustained against the Claims of the American Home Missionary Society*. His four arguments were that Christ had ordained missions to the care of the church; the Presbyterian Church was, "by her form of government, organized into a Christian Missionary Society"; the A.H.M.S. was "not an ecclesiastical, but a civil Institution"; and, finally, the society "disturbs the peace and injures the prosperity of the Presbyterian Church." He complained, "This Association has no visible connection with any branch of the Church of Jesus Christ, being amenable to no ecclesiastical body. . . . To whom did Christ say, 'Go ye to disciple all nations'? He said this to the church, not to the world."[80]

Wilson's antagonism to the A.H.M.S. was partly temperamental, but it had a broader context. Wilson did not oppose voluntary societies as such, provided they remained under constituted denominational authority (ideally Presbyterian). He had long championed benevolent enterprises, including the Lane Seminary at its founding. Nor was Wilson's opposition the mere cussedness of a western minister in the face of eastern cultural imperialism. Old School his Presbyterian may have been, but he had broad national connections. In 1817, for example, Wilson toured New England, meeting with numerous religious leaders, including Beecher. At the time, Wilson seemed satisfied with the state of Yankeedom, reflected in such institutions as "the Connecticut Asylum for the education of deaf and dumb persons," where he later referred an orphan boy under his care, assisted by "the First female society of Cincinnati for religious purposes," an all-female charity attached to his congregation.[81]

Between Wilson's tour of New England in 1817 and Beecher's arrival in Cincinnati in 1832, the religious landscape changed. Voluntary benevolent societies eroded the monopoly of mainline denominations as the guiding hand of Presbyterian influence loosened its grip. While Wilson did not oppose cooperation between congregations and religious charities, he condemned the national structure of societies such as the A.H.M.S. Despite the society's efforts at devolution, Wilson pointed to its origins and headquarters in New York, a city of "twenty thousand Infidels" who might well, he suggested, "purchase membership" in order to make "a Board of their own stamp . . . taking control of the Society into their own hands."[82] Wilson's anti–New York prejudices were far from unique, echoing those of many clergy, including one New Englander of the A.H.M.S. who deplored "the most fatal errors—many of the vices—and the Infidelity & Atheism which are spreading through this country . . . brought from the same State & City of New York."[83]

In 1832 the A.H.M.S. stood at a crossroads in Cincinnati. Early that year Corresponding Secretary Absalom Peters declined an invitation to "remove west" to the Queen City, an offer extended by leading local ministers, including Lyman Beecher. Had Peters accepted, he would have signaled a bold commitment in the society's operations, reflecting the demographic center of the nation. Instead, he cited the objections of his New York colleagues against the move. If he had thought them "probably right" in their veto that spring, subsequent developments confirmed his suspicion.[84] Ralph Cushman, chair of the A.H.M.S.'s Central Committee in Cincinnati, had died suddenly the previous summer, and his replacement, Virginia-born Presbyterian James W. Douglass, found business in Cincinnati untenable. "What is the use of this Central Committee?" he asked, in a remarkably frank letter to Peters. Amid "frequent and sudden" cholera deaths and the makeshift transformation of Presbyterian churches into hospitals, the city resembled a charnel house. On top of everything else, Douglass described how the A.H.M.S.'s Cincinnati committee was fraying at the seams. Its purpose was "'no sense, no how,'" complained one of its "Rev'd members" (probably Wilson). Cholera adjourned the Central Committee's scheduled meetings as it adjourned much else, but however morbid the occasion, it afforded some truce between pro-A.H.M.S. "brethren" and Old School "partizans," whose factions were already apparent. Douglass warned the A.H.M.S.'s New York executive that putting too many eggs into Cincinnati's basket was "do[ing] you more harm than good." To his mind, traditional denominations, not voluntary mission societies, best fitted the work of the gospel. "The churches of the valley are the organizations I should wish. Of these I would ask good wishes, prayers, money, young men." Douglass concluded his letter by resigning his A.H.M.S. commission, complaining that he had come to see his position "in the light of a diocesan Bishop"—a sentiment echoing Calvin Colton's charge of "Protestant Jesuitism."[85]

Lyman Beecher's 1832 arrival in Cincinnati triggered Wilson's troublemaking, spiraling toward denouement three years later. In November 1834 Wilson brought charges of heresy against Beecher before the Cincinnati Presbytery, accusing his colleague of "propagating doctrines contrary to the word of God and the standards of the Presbyterian Church on the subject of the *depraved nature of man*."[86] While there was some theological distance between Wilson and Beecher, the former's grievances were political in their origin. Wilson's concerns stemmed from his first meeting with Beecher in 1817 and an 1827 sermon entitled "The Native Character of Man." Wilson found the latter to be riddled with errors, asserting human free agency as a means to individual salvation instead of Calvinist dependence on divine sovereign grace. The red flag was raised, however, when the Congregationalist Beecher was received into the Presbyterian ministry without adopting its standard confession of faith, an oversight attributable to the exigencies of the 1801 Plan of Union but one leaving Wilson "surprised, grieved and alarmed."[87] In March 1835 Wilson wrote the Lane Board of Trustees, declining to pay $105 balance on a $150 pledge to the seminary "on the ground that a professor has been appointed, who accepted and whose salary has been paid, who was not at the time of his appointment, nor has he ever been since 'a member . . . in good standing.'"[88] In June of that year, Beecher was tried before the Cincinnati Presbytery under the roof of his own church, some two blocks north of Wilson's pulpit.

Beecher and his allies survived their trial, but their experience left him unsettled, deploring that "there is so much of popery in the Presbyterian system of settling doctrines."[89] Wilson appealed Beecher's acquittal to the regional synod, followed by the General Assembly of the Presbyterian Church. Though unsuccessful in both cases, Wilson succeeded in causing an irreparable schism between Old School and New School Presbyterians in Ohio.

Waning Fortunes of the A.H.M.S. in Cincinnati

In addition to intradenominational rivalry and local jealousies, the A.H.M.S. ultimately suffered the same strains and stresses that tore apart the antebellum United States. Since the A.H.M.S. presence in the South was negligible to begin with, it avoided sectional schism, but the question of slavery still drove a wedge in its ranks. In 1846 abolitionist missionaries, disillusioned with the A.H.M.S.'s weak position on slavery, broke away to form their own society, the American Missionary Association, aimed at ministering to African Americans and American Indians. The chief architect and financial backer of the American Missionary Association was Lewis Tappan, a teetotal New York City dry-goods merchant who amassed a fortune with fixed prices on articles in his stores (customers at that time were accustomed to haggling). Alongside his brother Arthur, he gave more money to evangelical causes than anyone in the antebellum era, including prominent donations to the A.H.M.S. and Lane. Increasingly, however, Tappan's benevolence (and that of others like him) switched to more radical institutions, including Oberlin and the American Antislavery Society. "As the American Missionary Association belongs to no sect," he stated, "it has a claim upon all. Its simple object is to send out a pure gospel, free from every compromise."[90]

The A.H.M.S. transferred its long-suffering Cincinnati Agency to Columbus in 1854, eliminating its missionary territories in Indiana and northern and eastern parts of Ohio. From the perspective of domestic missions in the Ohio Valley, this was a closing of the frontier, though one largely doomed to obscurity. Even within the agency itself, there was resignation at the declining significance of the Queen City. In 1853 its chair, Thornton Mills, wrote to New York suggesting a change of location might appease those "brethren in the interior who perhaps have been (unjustly) a little jealous of Cincinnati influence." The city was no longer the natural hub of influence, he argued: "We were central at first to the West when it was all in our field, and afterwards central to Ohio & Indiana united. Indiana is now cut off from us & is, as it ought to be, a field by itself." Mills ventured his opinion that the A.H.M.S.'s mission would "be more satisfactorily & efficiently done hereafter by Presbyterial, Associational, or Synodical Committees, in direct connexion with the office at New York."[91] Ironically, the leading voice of dissent against the Cincinnati agency's relocation was Marcus Hicks, an A.H.M.S.

preacher in Columbus. Hicks highlighted Cincinnati's "facilities of getting intelligence from all parts of the field & keeping thoroughly posted . . . to all the churches & ministers." Merchants and farmers traveling to the city were regularly relied upon by congregations to ferry "S. S. [Sunday School] Books, Bibles, & tracts," he noted, and where "25 ministers visit Cincinnati . . . one visits Columbus."[92] Though Cincinnati never became—like Chicago— "Nature's Metropolis," it remained a major midwestern city.[93]

Roots of Catholicism in Cincinnati

The Catholic Church in many ways resembled the A.H.M.S. but ultimately proved more resilient, having weathered more than one thousand years of change. Though seen as alien by many Americans, Catholicism in the United States was no less national in its character than the Benevolent Empire and no less urban in its structure, embodying the pre-Christian idea of the "Eternal City." The doctrine of apostolic succession applied to the church's bishops, but it might equally have applied to its cities, church hierarchy evolving through various iterations from Rome to Cincinnati. Before the War of Independence, all Catholics in British North America were subject to the Apostolic Vicariate of London, itself a post-Reformation entity created in 1623 from the titular See of Chalcedon. Following the revolution, Catholics in the United States looked to the Diocese of Baltimore (established 1789; elevated to archdiocese in 1808) as the new seat of hierarchical authority. For Catholics as well as Protestants, nationhood heralded religious independence. The American religious landscape became more "democratic" in its contours. Lay Catholics assumed a greater leadership role than their counterparts in Europe, most notably through the "trustee system," a uniquely American innovation placing church property under the administration of elected parishioners. As the nation grew—and its Catholic population with it—diocesan territories were added. In 1808, Bardstown, Kentucky, became the first new diocese in the United States, extending to Michigan in the north and Missouri in the west. The Diocese of Cincinnati was established from its bounds in 1821 and obtained metropolitan status as the Archdiocese of Cincinnati in 1850, confirming the influence of the Queen City.

Catholicism's early years in Cincinnati were quiet but not quiescent. Catholics kept a low profile, and as late as 1833 they were "so obscure as to be quite unknown to the citizens generally," according to one traveler.[94] On the ground, however, Catholics showed an unassuming willingness to self-organize. An 1811 notice in the *Western Spy* first indicated that lay worshipers were building their own communities and congregations while seeking the supply

of a pastor. Although alluding patronizingly to the virtues of civic republicanism, mere acknowledgment of Catholicism underscored a widening of the
public sphere in Cincinnati.[95] "As the constitution of the United States allows
liberty of conscience to all men, and the propagation of religious worship,"
began the notice,

> it is earnestly requested by a number of the Roman Catholics of Cin-
> cinnati and its vicinity, that a meeting be held on the 25th of Decem-
> ber next, at the house of Jacob Fowble, at 12 o'clock A.M. when it is
> hoped all those in favor of establishing a congregation and giving it
> encouragement will attend and give their names and . . . appoint a
> committee of arrangements.[96]

Efforts to establish the first Catholic congregation in Cincinnati continued for the best part of a decade. In 1818 a lay committee of citizens appealed to wealthy Catholics across the United States for funding to establish
their congregation. In a letter to one Baltimore merchant, they identified as
"the lost sheep of Israel, forlorn and forsaken, destitute of the means of exercising our Holy Religion, without Guide, Church, or Pastor, while we behold
all other members of the community enjoying these benefits."[97] As this letter
suggested, Cincinnati's Catholics considered faith part of their identity as
citizens as they laid the groundwork for their church.

Catholicism was never the invasive phenomenon its critics alleged, its
assimilation instead reflecting religious hospitality among the broader population. Thus, successful fundraising enabled the construction and incorporation of Christ Church, the original Catholic house of worship in Cincinnati,
where mass was first observed on Easter Sunday, 1819. The church's site on
Liberty Street was inauspicious, lying beyond the corporation line at that
time. Nevertheless, the parish trustees were able to purchase the land at a
fair discount from its Protestant owner, as well as an adjacent lot for $400,
which became the city's first Catholic cemetery. Though the Catholic Church
remained strapped for cash, three years later it purchased a second lot further downtown for $700 credit. The old log church on Liberty was then
physically mounted on rollers and relocated to Sycamore Street—collapsing
en route only to be reassembled at the new site. Subsequently renamed St.
Peter in Chains, this new cathedral became a thriving center of missionary
enterprise.[98]

As the emergence of Catholicism suggested, sectarian relations in early
Cincinnati were generally pragmatic. As citizens of a commercial city, Cincinnatians welcomed Catholics as economic migrants and appreciated their

cultural influence. Following the 1821 foundation of the Diocese of Cincinnati, for example, an editorial in the *Liberty Hall and Cincinnati Gazette* congratulated "the Roman Catholicks [*sic*] of this city and environs" on the arrival of Edward Fenwick as their first bishop. Fenwick's presence, "not only interests Catholicks, but all the friends of literature and useful knowledge, as we understand that his intention is ultimately to open a school, aided by members of his Order, long distinguished for their piety and learning."[99] Excepting the ugly years of antebellum nativism, Protestants generally cultivated good relations with their Catholic neighbors, whether through financial dealings, attending worship services as spectators, or even contributing to parish collection plates.[100] Such was the boosterism of many citizens: welcoming newcomers who might elevate society in any way, regardless of sectarian differences.

Though some harmony endured in the Queen City and its hinterlands, sectarian tensions increased as Catholicism grew on the religious landscape. Under Bishops Fenwick and Purcell—who succeeded Fenwick in 1832—the Catholic Church embarked on a wave of expansion, including ambitious church construction and fundraising. Such projects continued to draw support across sectarian lines. In 1825, for example, Fenwick noted that while a subscription for one new church was failing to meet the requisite sum, "many non-Catholics contributed."[101] Competition shaped Catholic-Protestant relations, however, overshadowing earlier ecumenism. While the A.H.M.S. and the Catholic Church fought to corner their respective, overlapping markets, measures adopted by the Catholic clergy, such as itinerant preaching circuits and religious revivals, suggested that the Great Revival had rubbed off on them. This turn toward revivalism was most remarkable given the scathing critique by Badin and others of such methods and coming at a time when the A.H.M.S. and other Protestant evangelicals were abandoning the enthusiasm of Cane Ridge for a bourgeois "gospel of respectability."[102]

The Parish Mission System

Catholic revivalism in the Ohio Valley did not evolve in isolation but as part of broader renewal efforts directed by the Vatican. Rome classified the United States as "missionary territory" until 1908: a special region demanding proselytization.[103] Toward the close of 1825, Pope Leo XII announced a global jubilee year, uniting Catholics in a concert of prayer, penance, and missionary outreach. On Christmas Day, 1826, Bishop Fenwick promulgated this jubilee in the Diocese of Cincinnati, the Holy Year having been delayed locally for the construction of the city's cathedral of St. Peter in Chains. In addition, the pope granted Fenwick two years to promulgate the jubilee through his sprawling diocese, which at the time included Illinois, Indiana, most of Michigan, and Wisconsin. An eight-day service was held at the new cathedral, with sermons in English and German and some two hundred communicants. The length of this religious gathering curiously echoed that of the Cane Ridge revival twenty-five years before, likewise the epicenter of a much larger, regional revival. Fenwick's efforts reaped considerable rewards through the following year and beyond as he and colleagues toured diocesan bounds, preaching sermons and offering the Eucharist. As a result, perhaps four hundred converts came over to the church in 1827 alone.[104] Missionary successes extended beyond the jubilee, with some 150 Cincinnati Protestants converting to Catholicism in 1829 and more than 50 receiving First Communion in the city cathedral on April 28 alone.[105]

Catholic apologists were sensitive to parallels between Protestant evangelical revivals and what they dubbed "parish missions" or "folk-missions" within their own church.[106] As imitation is the sincerest form of flattery, Catholic priests took pains not to appear too Protestant in their modes of religion. One itinerant priest, for example, reported to Fenwick having addressed an audience including some one hundred Presbyterians, Baptists, and Methodists in Newton, Ohio, for some two hours until his voice gave out. He invoked "the example of many missionaries, in the early days of the church," as his warrant for such fervor.[107] Meanwhile, among leading national Catholics, earlier, more primitive modes of Catholicism were likewise resurrected. In his widely read essay "Protestant Revivals and Catholic Retreats," Orestes Brownson distanced Catholic revivals from "the vulgar fanaticism, the shouting, and anxious benches, prayer meetings, and other clap-trap" of Protestant evangelicalism. The son of evangelical farmers from Vermont, Brownson might easily have entered the Presbyterian ministry. Instead, he carved out a literary career and converted to Rome following dalliances with Unitarianism and transcendentalism. Brownson traced Catholic revivalism to the earliest Dominicans and Franciscans, especially St. Anthony of Padua, who drew "immense crowds, both of the nobles and the common people." Acknowledging resemblances between Protestant and Catholic camp meetings, Brownson nevertheless insisted that the former "have, to some extent, followed in the wake of Catholic missions . . . and have sprung out of efforts inspired by a spirit of rivalry."[108]

Brownson's medievalism betrayed his romantic bent, but his observation of Protestant-Catholic rivalry was astute. In private correspondence, for instance, the usually mild-mannered Bishop Fenwick made no bones about competing with Protestants. "We often see," he boasted in 1824, "the communion rails crowded, which is a source of great edification to spectators; the church is constantly filled by persons of every denomination."[109] Throughout the diocese by the early 1830s, "great numbers have been added by conversions, which are very frequent, especially in Cincinnati."[110] Protestant conversion, while rare in the early republic, grew in the antebellum period, with an estimated 57,400 American Protestant converts between 1831 and 1860.[111] This statistic included distinguished figures such as Brownson, who lectured in Cincinnati on several occasions. Another convert was Brownson's friend and ally Isaac Hecker, a son of German immigrants who itinerated in the Midwest and became a leading light of the "Americanist" movement, asserting the dual values of patriotism and Catholicism. In Cincinnati, converts were notable for social prominence as well as numbers. They included local politician Donn Piatt and Sarah Peter—daughter of Ohio's sixth governor, Thomas Worthington. In at least one case, moreover, public endowments from a wealthy Catholic convert ensured both financial gain and propaganda appeal for the church. Rueben Springer, a prominent Cincinnati river merchant married into a wealthy Catholic trading family, financed the 1854 construction of an elegant spire for the cathedral, the city's most visible religious monument at the height of nativist agitation.[112]

Conversion fueled alarm in the age of Beecher and the A.H.M.S., but Catholicism succeeded in reaching constituencies other denominations left behind. In addition to competing head to head with Protestant evangelicals, the Catholic Church offered layers of stability, tradition, order, and beauty that gave comfort in an often turbulent and impersonal world. Such experience held true for Brownson, who deplored the "barren, dry, tasteless, and wearisome" banality of most Protestant worship services.[113] Fenwick similarly explained Catholic success in terms of two factors: aesthetic appeal and the spiritual outreach of the clergy. "Music and singing at services . . . prove a strong attraction" to many converts, he noted in a letter to an Italian colleague. But in other cases, Catholic ministry simply reached people otherwise neglected on the margins of society. Fenwick related the case of "a sick negress" dying in poverty. When a Methodist minister ignored pleas from her deathbed, "she sent for a priest . . . [and] was baptized and died a Catholic."[114]

Missionary successes aside, the Diocese of Cincinnati endured early hardships, struggling to supply clergymen to its growing population. When Fenwick first visited Cincinnati in 1816 as a humble Dominican preacher, there were perhaps 150 Catholics in Cincinnati. Fifteen years later, the now bishop Fenwick supervised "twenty-four priests, missionaries, twenty-two churches and several more congregations without churches, whereas fourteen years ago there was not a church, and I the only missionary in the State of Ohio."[115] Such growth was promising but still trailed demand. By the early 1840s, his successor, Bishop John Baptist Purcell, estimated fifty thousand Catholics in Ohio. Their numbers strained basic infrastructure, with many Catholic families forced to provide temporary housing for immigrants of their faith.[116] In these circumstances, the rate of ministerial supply took time for the church to resolve. "There is no subject connected with our faith in America," declared one diocesan letter, "which so often engages our attention, as the small number of our clergy, and the means by which the increasing want may be supplied. . . . Fifty additional clergymen would find ample employment in Ohio." Catholic parents were urged to consider the priesthood as a "sublime career" for their sons while being warned that "God is under no obligation to perform miracles for us, if we show no disposition to correspond with his designs."[117] Four years later, the number of Catholic priests in the state had grown to fifty (though not yet the hoped-for "additional" fifty). This was roughly double the total under Fenwick but still trailed population growth. Nevertheless, it promised enough for his successor to predict "a brighter era . . . when we shall have a Catholic house to stop at every ten miles and a Catholic Church every twenty miles, even in Ohio."[118]

The Catholic Church became the largest denomination in Cincinnati by the 1840s and the largest in the United States by 1860, its local and national growth reflecting its global reach.[119] European donors and organizations supported and enabled Catholic growth. Even so, the Diocese of Cincinnati did not always receive the assistance for which it hoped. Protestant nativists led by Beecher and Morse railed against Catholic benevolent societies such as the Society for the Propagation of the Faith in Lyon, France; the Ludwig Missionverein of Bavaria; and the Leopoldine Foundation of Vienna.[120] While claims of Jesuit cabals and Vatican-inspired colonization in the Ohio Valley were rooted in paranoia, overseas assistance to Cincinnati and other urban dioceses piqued the jealousy of Protestant sects and voluntary associations, who lacked the cultural networks and resources of their Catholic counterparts.

The Diocese of Cincinnati in Transatlantic Perspective

Drawn from Europe and the United States, the Diocese of Cincinnati's early missionaries were diverse, dynamic, and cosmopolitan.[121] Priests such as Stephen Badin—a refugee from revolutionary France—were equally familiar with the cornfields of Ohio and the streets of Paris and Rome. By contrast, few among even the worldliest of the Ohio Valley's Protestant missionaries were at ease beyond the Anglophone Atlantic, bound up as they were in their missionary jurisdictions. Admittedly, clergymen with A.H.M.S. connections such as Calvin Colton occasionally ventured across the Atlantic, but they were the exception rather than the rule. Other Protestants, such as the Baptists and Methodists, traveled huge distances for the gospel but were even more domestic in their focus. Even the English-born Methodist Francis Asbury, the most saddle-worn itinerant of his era and a man who traveled an estimated 270,000 miles by horse or carriage, preaching "not less than sixteen thousand four hundred and twenty-five sermons," was fundamentally provincial in his worldview and narrowly circumscribed by national boundaries. Following his October 1771 debarkation in America, for example, Asbury never once strayed beyond circuits in the United States.[122]

Fenwick himself traveled to Europe, raising some $10,000 dollars for his diocese in 1823, but overseas fundraising was mostly delegated to his subordinates. Chief among these was his vicar-general, Stephen Badin, an indefatigable toiler whose reputation for piety belied Fenwick's private opinion of him as "bustling, noisy, & fractious."[123] Badin spent the best part of the 1820s in Europe fundraising on behalf of the church in Ohio and Kentucky. His letters to Fenwick, written in tiny, meticulous script, revealed his frustrations. England was "a prodigal, proud, and vicious country" where he garnered a pittance and his expense account barely covered board and lodging. Shunned even among his fellow religionists, he discovered "that there are continual calls made on the Catholics for churches, schools, and all sorts of charities . . . [and] a great many questors and also imposters from foreign countries." Badin was also dismayed by the callousness of the English church hierarchy, notably when the Bishop of London rebuked him for administering last rites to a dying man "absente parocho." All told, it is hard not to sympathize with Badin: "How rude and inhospitable is John Bull compared to the Americans!" His reception was "much more favorable" in the provinces, but even there it was tough. "I have walked many miles and climbed the Lancashire hills many times with my bag on my shoulders streaming almost with sweat in winter," he confessed. "All this to save the mission-funds; from which I have scarcely drawn a penny."[124]

Badin was more warmly welcomed in his native France, although obstacles remained. Under the reigns of Louis XVIII and Charles X, the French state promoted Catholicism at home and abroad. Of note was the Society for the Propagation of the Faith, founded in Lyon in 1822, providing overseas support through finance, prayer, and recruitment of clergy for America. While such assistance was welcome, noted Badin, the association suffered an archaic understanding of the missionary field in the United States. Writing to Fenwick, he warned that his support from the association

> will be great or little, in proportion to the interest which you will excite . . . by yr. letters or the details of yr. priests respecting the Ohio mission, especially among the Savages. You must bear in mind that the object of the Association is <u>precisely</u> the conversion of the Indians.

Badin added that the association had pledged 11,000 francs for Cincinnati's diocese that year, with the king himself adding 2,000.[125] The purpose of such donations was clear, however: The French Catholic hierarchy was more interested in converting tribal peoples than in the welfare of fellow religionists across the ocean.

Back in Cincinnati, widespread Catholic immigration from Germany belied naive European images of the Ohio Valley as frontier, populated by American Indians and backwoods folk. While the diocese struggled to supply German-speaking clergy from its ranks (dominated in the early years by ethnic Irish), shifting demographics provided opportunities to deepen existing European connections. Cincinnati's first German-speaking priest, Hanover-born Frederick Rese, was one of a handful of leaders in this regard. Handpicked by Fenwick from the Urban College in Rome, Rese arrived in Cincinnati in 1824 and set about cultivating the city's German Catholics. Like Badin, Rese also returned to Europe to raise funds and recruits—a mission in which he excelled. In 1828 (the year of Badin's final return to America) Rese persuaded Austrian emperor Francis I to establish a fundraising organization, the Leopoldine Society, designed to promote Catholicism in the Ohio Valley. Unlike previous bodies such as the Society for the Propagation of the Faith, this new body focused efforts on just one region of the United States. Propaganda circulated by Rese and others in Europe depicted Protestant inroads in the Ohio Valley at the expense of Catholic expansion.[126] While mirroring and inadvertently fueling the flames of the more familiar Protestant nativist narrative, such strategy worked. By 1835, the Leopoldine Society had given some $32,000 to the Diocese of Cincinnati, yet such beneficence sparked Protestant fears of conspiracy between the Vatican and Vienna's powerful Habsburg dynasty.[127]

Despite richly propagandized conversions among Cincinnati's Anglo-American elite, the city's most heavily proselytized group was German Protestants. Uprooted and often distrustful of their own religious leaders, this demographic proved as amenable to the gospel of Rome as to the A.H.M.S. Rese was especially successful in this regard, converting no fewer than thirty-three German families between 1825 and 1826 alone. This exodus exasperated the city's Lutheran minister, who spat "fire and flame" against Rese in his sermons, as Bishop Fenwick wryly noted.[128] Rese's successes were no fluke but reflected his valuable ability to communicate directly with the German laity in their own language. Such was Rese's reputation in Cincinnati that Francis P. Kenrick, bishop of Philadelphia, requested his temporary services for a German congregation in Pennsylvania, "much dissatisfied" with their Anglophone priest.[129] Until Fenwick's death in 1832, however, Rese was pledged to remain put. The Vatican thereafter acknowledged his usefulness in 1833 by naming him bishop of Detroit, though he had hoped for the vacant See of Cincinnati. Detroit was an unhappy fit. Rese was permanently recalled to Rome in 1838, his mind and body unraveling under private strains and heavy drinking. In 1859 he was placed in a Catholic asylum in his native Germany, where he died twelve years later decrepit and insane: a sorry footnote to his heyday in Ohio.[130]

Besides Rese, the Swiss-born priest John Martin Henni did most to build the Diocese of Cincinnati's mission to German immigrants. Recruited as a young theology student in Rome, Henni came with Rese to Cincinnati in 1829 and was ordained by Fenwick. His first posting was to Canton, Ohio, replacing the deceased parish priest, but his main energies were spent itinerating among scattered communities around Canton, Zanesville, and Somerset. With completion of the Ohio and Erie Canal in 1832, immigrants in this part of the state rose tenfold from around two hundred in 1829 to more than two thousand in 1834. Henni ministered to them with the zeal of an Asbury or a Badin, baptizing over a hundred people; presiding over fourteen weddings, twenty-two funerals, and twenty-four communions; and winning seven new converts in his first year alone.[131]

Henni established his reputation in outlying provinces but returned to Cincinnati in 1834 as pastor of Holy Trinity (Heilige Dreieinigkeit). The first German-language Catholic church west of the Alleghenies, Holy Trinity struggled to house its growing congregation. By 1840, parish meetings overflowed into the basement.[132] The following decade saw unprecedented Catholic expansion, with eleven new Catholic churches in Cincinnati by 1850, including five additional German churches.[133] Henni was a key player, founding many of the city's German institutions. Shortly after arriving at Holy Trinity, for example, he opened up the first bilingual parochial school with classes in German and English, some six years before German was introduced into the public school curriculum of the city. In consequence, the Holy Trinity school catered to huge demand. Most of its students were, in fact, Protestant. Henni was also instrumental in missionary and philanthropic enterprises, both through his fundraising and recruitment trips to Europe but especially in helping establish the city's St. Aloysius orphanage (1837). Another service in high demand, the city's first German orphanage took on upward of fifty boys per year, many from foster homes. Realizing the need to support these ventures financially, and the importance of carving a space for Catholic Germans in the public sphere, Henni also established *Der Wahrheitsfreund* (The friend of truth), a newspaper modeled on the *Catholic Telegraph*, whose profits were earmarked to the St. Aloysius Orphan Society. Though many articles were translated from the *Telegraph*, *Der Wahrheitsfreund* endured for eighty years as a voice for the Diocese of Ohio's German Catholics. By 1838, over 3,300 people had already subscribed their annual $2.50 for the paper, the vast majority—some 3,000—outside the city.[134]

German-speaking priests remained in high demand through the antebellum period, making up at most a quarter of diocesan clergy for a population that was mostly first-generation German.[135] At the start of Bishop Purcell's tenure in 1833, with Rese gone to Detroit, there was still only one German-speaking priest in Ohio for some five thousand German parishioners.[136] This population was set to explode. Between 1834 and 1859, twelve new German parishes were founded in Cincinnati alone, although the shortage of ministers meant they were often without a German-speaking priest.[137] In addition to demand in Cincinnati, Bishop Purcell faced calls from outlying towns such as Dayton, where one local priest was "much pleased with the zeal and piety" of the local Germans while noting that "few of them speak English . . . it will be a difficult task for any but a German to attend them."[138] "Five hundred miles of heavily populated Erie Canal Zone . . . need [German] priests," complained the polyglot preacher John Neumann to Bishop Purcell, "we shall need not only good priests, but a Francis Xavier."[139] Despite the shortage of German-speaking priests in Cincinnati, Purcell was forced to field requests from other dioceses, including New Orleans, where recent German immigration left German speakers, especially those fluent in English and French, in high demand.[140]

While German Catholic immigrants outnumbered their Irish fellow Catholics three to one in southern Ohio (a mirror image to national immigration trends), the Irish played a key role in sectarian identity. The first-generation Irish, including the mercurial Bishop Purcell, continued to dominate the clergy. The Irish as a whole, however, were disdained as "hewers of wood and drawers of water," the poorest white ethnic cohort at the time. Brutalized by famine and persecution, Irish refugees were a dubious advertisement for their native soil. One Ohio priest reflected this poor estimation to Bishop

Purcell, noting that only one-tenth "of our Irish on the railroad" regularly attended mass while "one half are grown up to 20–25 years & never made their first communion [and] know nothing of their catechism even some of those that come from the old country."[141]

Conclusion

Though Catholics endured hostility in Cincinnati, they had come to stay. Bolstered by overseas funding and centuries of experience, the missionary model of the Catholic Church surpassed the A.H.M.S. in adapting to conditions in Cincinnati, the Ohio Valley, and beyond. Although the A.H.M.S. enjoyed success in its early years, bitter division eroded its vision of reform locally and nationally. The society amassed over $4 million in receipts by the eve of the Civil War, but the demand of administering to the distant West was proving ever more costly.[142] Opposition and dissent from conservative Old School and evangelical New School Presbyterians revealed the persistence of denominational fault lines, and divisions over slavery replicated themselves in the home mission movement. In 1860 there were only three A.H.M.S. missionaries in the entire South. The Civil War further eroded the society's base of operations, shrinking its coffers and narrowing its activities. While it limped on until 1893, changes in the religious landscape left the A.H.M.S. a Congregationalist concern in all but name.[143]

By the mid-nineteenth century, A.H.M.S. nativism failed to reverse the society's sliding fortunes, instead alienating potential allies. Beecher's former colleague Calvin Colton, for example, welcomed immigrants to the United States "with the true missionary spirit, desiring the conversion of papists to pure Christianity, and confiding in Protestant principles, their immigration here is the very thing to be desired."[144] Among Protestant German observers, criticism of A.H.M.S. anti-immigrant tendencies was especially trenchant. One Lutheran missionary, a veteran of the Ohio Valley, criticized "the often silly views that they have, of the doctrine and inner essence of the Roman Church, [which] will make victory all the easier for the latter once it begins, with its flexibility, to adapt to the [American] temperament."[145] Instead of embracing foreigners, the A.H.M.S. blamed immigration on Catholic designs against the United States, sowing fear among many Protestants but failing to alter demographic trends.

Ironically, given nativist perceptions of Catholic hierarchy, a culture of individualism in the United States bolstered grassroots Catholic identity. At the same time, evangelicals, including Calvin Colton and Harriet Beecher

Stowe, sought a middle path between American Protestantism and Catholic aestheticism. During his sojourn in England, Colton was moved to tears by the solemnity of Handel's *Messiah* at Westminster Abbey. On his return to the United States, he was appalled to witness the moral hysteria stirred up by maverick Presbyterian Charles Grandison Finney, leading a national crusade against prostitution. Colton's response was to embrace Episcopalianism, with its liturgy and Catholic roots. Revivalism, by contrast, dwindled at the hands of Finney and his ilk. No longer understood as "*dependent on Divine influence,*" it was instead "boldly and publicly declared to be *dependent on man.*" Undue emphasis on human agency was "a leaven diffused through the religious community," eroding church authority. Above all, revivals, like forest fires, burned all they touched. "Protracted meetings from day-to-day," complained Colton, "are making demands upon ministers which no human power can sustain."[146]

Alexis de Tocqueville summed up the melding of Protestant Christianity and republican politics in the United States, originating with "men who, after having shaken off the authority of the Pope, acknowledged no other religious supremacy: they bought with them . . . a democratic and republican religion." Tocqueville went on to acknowledge that the Roman Catholic population (numbering some one million Americans in 1830 but set to grow radically) repudiated those who sought to "*harmonize* earth with heaven." Scorning notions of Protestant republicanism, Tocqueville celebrated Catholic immigrants instead, calling them "the most republican and the most democratic class in the United States." Among their ranks, he noted, "the religious community is composed of only two elements: the priest and the people. . . . If Catholicism predisposes the faithful to obedience, it certainly does not prepare them for inequality; but the contrary may be said of Protestantism, which generally tends to make men more independent than to render them equal."[147]

A lapsed Catholic who eventually reconciled with his childhood faith, Tocqueville's assessment of American Catholicism was generous, underlining his impressions of the religious landscape. Extolling the "spiritually satisfying" faith and civic-mindedness of North American Catholics, he foresaw their rise to demographic plurality as a blessing, noting that "the *curé* is indeed the shepherd of his flock; there is nothing here of the industrial religion of most American ministers."[148] Writing in the early 1830s, his observations were sanguine but warranted by the toleration he witnessed firsthand in Cincinnati and throughout the United States. His characterization of American Protestantism as "industrial" was intuitive, moreover, foreshadowing the westward expansion of the gospel along steel rails and telegraph cables. In the thirty years or so before the Civil War, American Protestants discovered "the cloven foot" of Vatican conspiracy at the root of overseas immigration.[149] Evangelical voluntary societies such as the A.H.M.S. expanded alongside the commercial infrastructure of the nation, competing with the growth of the Catholic Church in the Ohio Valley and beyond. At the same time, nativist xenophobia and sectarianism of the Know-Nothing variety fostered the paranoia, bigotry, and violence that form the subject of the next chapter.

4

"The Cause of America"

Nativism, Toleration, and Freedom

> The cause of America, and of liberty, is the cause of every virtuous
> American citizen; whatever may be his religion or his descent,
> the United Colonies know no distinction, but such as slavery,
> corruption and arbitrary domination may create.
>
> —WASHINGTON, "To the Inhabitants of Canada"

The limits of toleration in Cincinnati were not always inscribed in law but unfolded in the relations between different classes, races, ethnicities, and sectarian communities. On any given day, itinerant preachers, religious processions, and political protests fomented in the streets, but not all modes of expression, or all voices, were equally welcomed. Black people and women were especially marginalized.[1] Political and religious antagonism might escalate, and Cincinnati was no stranger to violence. But the Queen City remained a prodigious social laboratory whose culture shaped ideals of religious and political freedom beyond its immediate hinterlands.

On May 1, 1853, "a vast multitude" thronged into the marketplace at the corner of Fifth and Vine Streets, where Cincinnati's Fountain Square now stands. Though described as "sober and orderly," the crowd cut a spectacle, massing in their thousands, leaning out of balconies and windows, and transforming the square into a sea of black hats. They had come to hear an evangelical preacher deliver his sermon, and a hubbub of anticipation drowned the silence of the Sabbath morning. But this was no ordinary revival. The audience exuberated in the atmosphere of a political rally, quite unlike the mixed gatherings of camp meetings. Women were noticeable by their absence. While immigrants made up virtually half the city's population, they overwhelmingly gave this gathering a wide berth. Though the crowd was peaceful, there was a menacing undercurrent, heightened by the uncanny location. This was, after all, a butchers' market built over the leveled remains of an American Indian mound.

Around nine o'clock, a makeshift aisle formed through the crowd. A hogshead barrel of sugar was carried into the center of the square, followed by an unassumingly dark-suited preacher with a disheveled beard who mounted the rostrum with the assistance of a wooden plank. The audience greeted him with enthusiasm, but Hugh Kirkland, the "American Christian Catholic Apostle," cut a weird figure even in an age of religious eccentrics. His wild gestures and "deranged" delivery evoked the image of a frontier revivalist while his elongated vowels and foreign diction marked him as a stranger. Born in Ulster around the turn of the nineteenth century, Kirkland migrated to Canada in his youth and later moved to Pennsylvania. There he served as a preacher in the ultra-Calvinist Associate Reformed Presbyterian Church but in 1834 "was excommunicated for some improper conduct." Despite his alleged impropriety, he established himself as a popular itinerant. Unattached to any denomination, he developed his own primitive theology and preached hellfire sermons against the Roman Catholic Church that won him a loyal following.[2] He printed his own nativist journal, the *Street Preacher and Pittsburgh True Catholic*, of which no known copy remains extant. All told, Kirkland is a figure of maddening obscurity. Even his death was strange. Some ten years after his dramatic revival meeting on Fifth and Vine Streets, he drowned in the Ohio River after falling (or jumping?) from a steamboat between Pittsburgh and Cincinnati.[3]

This was not Kirkland's first sermon in the Queen City, as the thronging audience indicated. Had the self-styled apostle not fallen afoul of local authorities, he might have remained yet another voice amid the cacophony of the urban religious landscape. But the previous month, when Kirkland had preached at Fifth Street Market, a force of police led by Mayor David Snelbaker broke up the meeting. Snelbaker, a brusque Democrat from the proslavery, proimmigrant "Miami tribe" wing of his party, worried the sermon on April 17 would bring violence on a day when local Catholics were holding a procession for the cornerstone of a nearby church. The mayor denied reports he had manhandled Kirkland, protesting that he had "not arrest[ed] him, or put my finger on him, or so much as touch[ed] the hem of his garment." Nevertheless, on April 23 he issued Kirkland a cease-and-desist letter. "The right of the people," he wrote, "to assemble together in a peaceable manner to consult for the common good is undoubted; but the right of any to perch himself upon an elevation, and use inflammatory language, as to cause a riot . . . and that too on a Sabbath Day, and in a Christian country, is another and different thing, and cannot be tolerated."[4]

Snelbaker's letter lit a fuse. Kirkland and his followers rallied, condemning the mayor for trammeling free speech and religious worship and clamoring for his impeachment. Four days after Snelbaker's letter, a mass meeting of some of the city's leading anti-Catholics, including future Know-Nothing leader Thomas Spooner, assembled at the Ohio Mechanics Institute to debate its implications. A pamphlet entitled *Narratives of Scenes and Events Which Occurred Lately in Cincinnati*, self-published by Kirkland, recorded excerpts from the debate, including one Presbyterian minister, Rev. James Prestley, who denounced "the general principles of the Catholics." Prestley especially distrusted "their position on the school question" versus the supposedly nonsectarian ethos of the city's public schools. "The Catholics," he complained, "thought that because they could 'come it' in Austria, France, Spain, and Italy, they could 'come it' here; but that in free and enlightened America, they would find they had 'waked up the wrong passenger.'" Another protestor spoke for many when he exclaimed: "Are we in Austria, that our right to express our sentiments in public spaces freely is thus suppressed?"[5] Beneath the hyperbole was genuine fear. Kirkland and others spoke against timeserving politicians like Snelbaker, the selling of religious liberties to the highest bidder, and the malign influence of European Catholic autocracy.

If he was not the worst of Mayor Snelbaker's problems, Kirkland was certainly a headache. His May 1 sermon was a rallying point for anti-immigrant, anti-Catholic, antiestablishment voices. Kirkland warned that his fellow citizens were "not practically intelligent regarding the devices of Satan, or the God of this world, who has the science and art of blinding the understandings of men . . . through the instrumentality of bands of magnetizing cripples and jackasses called clergy, lawyers, and even editors of newspapers." He railed against "Romish heresy" as "a fraud on mankind." He alleged that Catholic mobs had assaulted Cincinnatians for refusing to uncover their heads before processional icons (suggestively, Samuel Morse likewise claimed to have had his hat knocked off on a visit to Rome). The history of Cincinnati, Kirkland insisted, showed the Roman Inquisition alive and well. Why had the mayor arrested him but not challenged several other revivalists preaching in the streets that day? Among those left to their own devices were two drunkards "preaching in favor of the old harlot. Having drank freely of her sorceried cup so as to be in dalliance with her, in her commission of fornications and abominations . . . they wished to keep her red petticoats from being furled up, lest the shame of her nakedness and deformity should appear to all men." By contrast to these intemperate papists, Kirkland vaunted his credentials as an apostolic patriarch of Christianity. He was "neither a heretical Roman Catholic nor a Protesting Catholic," scorning "the business of protesting against so vile an imposture, so dirty, trashy an excrescence as Romanism."[6] His American Catholic Church was the apostolic body of believers in Christ, tailored to the nationalistic anxieties of his day.

Kirkland's spleen reflected a deeper crisis of authority. His self-published *Narratives* was a mishmash of excerpts from public meetings, press cuttings about himself (both flattering and denunciatory), and text from his sermons, yet it was more than the sum of its parts. The silhouette of a popular movement can be traced between lines denouncing the Catholic Church for threatening to "have our American cities wrapped in flames" and a resolution dated May 3, 1853, to establish "a committee of two in each Ward" petitioning for Snelbaker's impeachment. Unsuccessful though its efforts were to oust the mayor (although Snelbaker refused to run for a second term), this was a political campaign disguised as a religious revival, echoing broader currents of reform—most notably temperance—in its militancy. As one Columbus newspaper, cited in Kirkland's *Narratives*, wryly observed: "Mr. Kirkland has made a decided hit in Cincinnati and if he will but only take advantage of the opportunity, we would not be *very much* surprised to hear of his being elected as Mr. Snelbaker's successor to the mayoralty of that city. Stranger things *have* happened."[7] As it turned out, Kirkland eschewed the campaign trail in 1855. Nevertheless, Cincinnati's mayoral elections that year proved troublesome enough, pitching immigrants against nativists at the polls and in the streets, where brickbats served for arguments.

Freedom versus Toleration

Kirkland preached to a regional audience, but his fiery gospel reflected tensions between political order and freedom of conscience older than Christianity itself. The question of religious freedom dated back to the Old Testament, via the upheavals of the Protestant Reformation and the American Revolution. Most Americans understood its historical outline, albeit imperfectly. Cincinnatians divided by faith and politics read the same Bible, which told how the sixth-century B.C.E. Persian founder Cyrus decreed: "The Lord God of heaven hath given me all the kingdoms of the earth; and he hath charged me to build him an house at Jerusalem, which is in Judah."[8] This city builder established the model of cosmopolitan empire, couching his edicts to reflect the diverse religions of his subjects. Nearly one thousand years later, Rome's adoption of Christianity confirmed a different relationship between power and faith, as state support for monotheism replaced a pantheon of pagan cults. In a crucial development, Augustine of Hippo laid the theological foundations for modern ecclesiology in late antiquity. Augustine wrote: "Mankind [*hominum*] is divided into two sorts: such as live according to man, and such as live according to God. These we mystically call the two 'cities' or societies, the one predestined to reign eternally with God, the other condemned to perpetual torment with Satan."[9] For Augustine and Catholics generally, God's grace determined human salvation. At the same time, salvation lay only within the communion of the Catholic Church. The highest order of freedom was thus freedom to obey church teachings and institutions.

Augustine's theology survived the upheavals of the Protestant Reformation. Luther retained Augustinian views even as he rejected Rome's influence. Augustine's insistence on the role of the magistrate in a Christian society was the foundation of Calvinist theocracy in sixteenth-century Geneva. In early America, the Augustinian tradition underpinned legally established Protestant churches in eight of the thirteen colonies, and state support for religion enjoyed broad support in other parts of the Atlantic world. Colonial dissent, moreover, was strictly circumscribed. Even John Locke, the ideological grandfather of the American Revolution, drew the line at Catholics and atheists. "Promises, covenants, and oaths," he insisted, were "the bonds of human society," underwritten by the sovereign authority of "the Supreme Magistrate in the State." Locke questioned Catholics who "*ipso facto* deliver themselves up to the protection and service of another prince."[10] In England, he insisted, political liberty compelled obedience to a Protestant monarch.

The fruits of American independence were not immediate, but they were far reaching. Secular liberals such as Thomas Jefferson and James Madison forged an unlikely coalition with Protestant evangelicals, ushering in disestablishment of religion by federal and state governments and a wall of separation between church and state. At the same time, many mainline Protestants advocated that government should police religious toleration, a position far short of the Jeffersonian ideal. Among them was lexicographer Noah Webster, whom Absalom Peters, corresponding secretary of the A.H.M.S., quoted approvingly in a letter to the Presbyterian *Cincinnati Journal*: "*Toleration* implies a right in the sovereign to control men in their opinions and worship."[11]

Protestant conservatives viewed the First Amendment as dangerously democratic, creating a free-for-all in religious authority. Likewise, in the political sphere, many nativists equivocated. Samuel Morse, for example, praised freedom of religion as "a beautiful feature of our constitution" but warned that in "tolerating all sects, we have admitted to equal protection not only those sects whose religious faith and practice support the principle on which free toleration of all is founded, but also that unique, that solitary sect, the Catholic, which builds and supports its system on the destruction of all toleration."[12] To those who doubted his convictions, Morse pointed to Catholic suppression of republican nationalists in Continental Europe.

Even as America's religious landscape shifted, an Augustinian appetite for theocracy persisted, transplanted from New England and the Northeast to the Midwest. Over time, however, the position of Lyman Beecher and other theocrats softened from championing religious establishment to more subtly defending Protestant values in public life. Tellingly, Beecher remembered the 1818 disestablishment of the Congregationalist Church by the Connecticut legislature as "a time of great depression and suffering" but later acknowledged its cathartic effects: "It cut the churches loose from dependence on state support," he wrote, and "threw them wholly on their own resources and on God."[13]

"The Very Seat of Western Warfare"

In 1832, Lyman Beecher came to Ohio as an apostle of self-sufficiency, its ideal embodied in the manual labor model of Lane Theological Seminary. His Boston ministry established numerous voluntary societies, including the Mechanic Apprentices Library Association and the Laboring Young Men's Temperance Society, foreshadowing future preoccupations. "The great aim of the Christian Church in its relation to the present life," he wrote, "is not only to renew the individual man, but also to reform human society."[14] For Beecher, the reform of society went beyond the planting of new churches, embracing endeavors including temperance reform, stricter Sabbath laws, publication and distribution of tracts and scripture, and, crucially, free public education.

Beecher's recruitment to Cincinnati—painstakingly negotiated by Lane's Board of Trustees—was hailed as a coup, a geographic shift in the evangelical map of America. "Boston and the East generally would sustain an irreparable loss in giving up Dr. Beecher," conceded one board member in 1830, "and yet . . . the good of the Church, the awakening of the East in behalf of the West, loudly demanded that one of their best generals should occupy the very seat of Western warfare while the enemy is coming in like a flood."[15]

When it came to saving the Ohio Valley for Protestantism, images of warfare and inundation proliferated. Such proliferation only mounted in 1835 with the publication of Beecher's nativist tract *A Plea for the West* and Samuel Morse's equally vituperative *Foreign Conspiracy against the Liberties of the United States*. Nativist evangelicals, Beecher and Morse held that the work of salvation began in the life of the soul. They preached the habits and culture of Protestant republicanism, but for all their devotion to Puritan ideals, they were not simply reactionaries wallowing in nostalgia. Nevertheless, their prejudices revealed ambivalence toward forces of modernity they themselves had nurtured. When Morse sent the first transatlantic telegraph on the morning of May 24, 1844, it read simply: "What hath God Wrought!" These words, wrote Daniel Walker Howe, "baptized the American telegraph with the name of its author."[16] But if Morse saw technology as the instru-

Figure 4.1 Rev. Lyman
Beecher (1775–1863): Lane
Theological Seminary's
influential president.
(Wikimedia Commons)

ment of providence, he also feared its Promethean nature. Heeding Morse's
alarm, Beecher regarded the salvation of the Ohio Valley—and, by extension, of America and the world—as a race between the gospel and economic
development: "What is to be done must be done quickly; for population will
not wait, and commerce will not cast anchor, and manufactures will not shut
off the steam nor shut down the gate, and agriculture, pushed by millions of
freemen on their fertile soil, will not withhold her corrupting abundance."[17]

The nondenominational structure of the Benevolent Empire was itself an
innovation. New printing techniques and distribution systems enabled evangelicals to reach beyond traditional church networks. By 1836, for example,
colporteurs of the American Tract Society (A.T.S.) distributed almost one
hundred million pages of religious literature per year—an astonishing figure,
placing the A.T.S. at the forefront of American print culture alongside collab-
orative agencies such as the American Sunday School Union and the American Bible Society.[18] New York businessman Arthur Tappan (brother of Lane
beneficiary Lewis) donated $5,000 to the A.T.S. for new printing presses. As
early as 1829, he announced: "I want to give two tracts to every family in the
valley of the Mississippi, so none shall be passed by. I will give $1,000 for this

project." Recognizing the twin virtues of godliness and sobriety, Tappan also endowed a separate fund of $2,000 for the benefit of A.H.M.S. congregations that expelled habitual drunkards.[19]

While dry goods merchants exerted the moral suasion once reserved to synods and congregations, inventive clergymen still found new ways to influence society. The quintessential civic text of American evangelicalism (not counting the King James Bible), *McGuffey's Eclectic Reader* sold over 122 million copies in multiple editions from the 1830s through the middle decades of the twentieth century. While nominally unsectarian—at least in the sense of eschewing any particular denominational affiliation—McGuffey's textbooks promoted a vigorously Protestant republicanism. Penning an introduction on behalf of his friend and fellow local minister McGuffey, Lyman Beecher thus proclaimed himself "not a little gratified to know that our youth have access to so perfect a series of Reading Books. They are excellent for educational purposes—their religion is *unsectarian*, true religion—their morality the morality of the gospel."[20]

For all his evangelical morality, Beecher was politically conservative to a fault, especially when it came to the question of slavery. Though he despised the practice of slavery, he feared to antagonize public opinion on the matter. No issue was more combustible in Cincinnati than abolition and no group more broadly disliked than abolitionists. Already, abolitionism had brought Lane Seminary to the brink in 1834, when Theodore Weld led students in support of the American Anti-Slavery Society. Fear of violence had then led the school's Executive Committee to outlaw "all associations or societies among the students . . . except such as have for their immediate object improvement in the prescribed course of studies." Committee members argued: "The location of this School, in the vicinity of a large city, & on the borders of a slave state, calls for some peculiar cautionary measurements in its government, which under other circumstances, might be entirely unnecessary."[21]

Cincinnati's location only fostered its peculiar conservatism. Though the city was a hub of the Underground Railroad, its fortunes were intimately tied to the plantation economy, with its pork industry feeding millions of slaves.[22] While many Cincinnatians helped fugitive slaves find freedom in the North, the city was dominated by powerful vested interests looking to the South.

The Philanthropist

In January 1836, a public meeting gathered at Cincinnati's courthouse, attended by influential citizens including Daniel Drake and the plutocratic Nicholas Longworth. The focus of their debate was *The Philanthropist*, a radical antislavery weekly inspired by William Lloyd Garrison's *The Liberator*, which was quickly garnering notoriety for its "pestiferous" politics.[23] *The Philanthropist* was published by James Gillespie Birney, a hard-living southern lawyer-cum-planter born again as an evangelical Presbyterian. Though never an ordained minister, Birney was a missionary of sorts. A close friend of Theodore Weld, whom he had first met in Huntsville, Alabama, Birney was a midlife convert to the abolitionist cause. Emancipating his slaves, Birney arrived in Cincinnati in 1835, just one year after the Lane rebellion, and soon caused a stir with his abolitionist newspaper. Reflecting its controversial nature, *The Philanthropist* contained no commercial advertisement. Even sympathetic merchants feared the attention their association might bring, so funding came instead by private subscription and sponsorship of the American Anti-Slavery Society. In the face of public condemnation and anonymous death threats, Birney defiantly reprinted fellow abolitionist William Ellery Channing's maxim: "A NEWSPAPER,—which openly, or by innuendoes excites a mob, should be regarded as sounding the tocsin of insurrection."[24]

In their resolutions, the courthouse delegates denounced "the nature and tendency of Abolition Societies," which, "if not treasonable," were "highly revolutionary." While asserting "toleration" of free speech, the meeting resolved "every lawful effort to suppress the publication of any abolition paper in this city or *neighborhood*." Witnessed by Birney himself, the anti-abolitionists directed attention to the Ohio Anti-Slavery Society (an auxiliary of its New York–based national society) and read its Declaration of Sentiments, signed by founding members. Drake objected to the inclusion of signatories' names in the reading, which threatened "respectable citizens, with whom they daily associated, a measure of obloquy, to which they ought not to be exposed." Drake's objection was overturned by Colonel Charles Hale, whom Birney described as giving "no quarter" to such "hide-bound notions of delicacy."[25] Abolitionists, Hale insisted, deserved the ostracism of their peers.

Despite its ostracizing tone, the courthouse gathering was about more than abolitionism. What troubled delegates most was Birney's unfettered liberty of speech. Ironically, if they had only focused on editorial content, these critics might have discovered much in common with the red-haired Alabamian. For one thing, Birney, like most Protestant abolitionists, was a nativist who denounced slavocracy and popery alike. He filled his paper with correspondence from fellow abolitionists, including New York's William Jay, who believed immediate abolitionism had "been merged into the vastly more interesting enquiry, how far we ourselves are to enjoy the freedom purchased for us by the toils and blood of our fathers." Jay wondered out loud whether "the vast body of foreigners among us" would corrupt the body politic, inducing politicians "to scatter as 'disturbers of the peace,' the various 'native American associations,' who are contending that Americans only should govern Americans."[26] In a similar vein, Birney insisted, those seeking to regulate freedom of the press under the pretense of limited toleration (including those seeking to muzzle *The Philanthropist*) opened the door to all manner of abuses.

For Birney, in the liberal tradition, mere toleration had outlived its usefulness. Instead, he called for a free market of ideas, unimpeded by the hand of magistrates. In an open letter, he rebuked the secretary of the anti-abolition meeting held at the courthouse: "Our constitution, our laws, (if we yet have them,) know no such word as '*toleration*'—it is not to be found in the language of republican freemen." In contrast to the United States, where religion enjoyed free range, Birney noted, Protestantism was only "*tolerated* in many of the Catholic countries of Europe. . . . The rights of conscience are taken into the hands of the governments—and the use of them doled out, as may best suit their convenience." Toleration was not enough to secure a public sphere, though it might do for crowned heads of Europe. "But how lame and spiritless such language—we 'approve and advocate toleration,' &c., when compared with that of our constitution," Birney complained. "There is no toleration here sir, nor, before the anti-abolition meeting of Cincinnati, was there any one, who claimed power to *tolerate* or to grant *permission* to the citizens of Ohio to use, as should be prescribed to them the freedom of speech or of discussion."[27]

Birney promoted abolitionism from libertarian as well as humanitarian motives, whatever the cost. One January 1836 letter in the *Philanthropist*, coinciding with the courthouse meeting, warned of a plot by locals "in conjunction with some Kentuckians" to attack his press and to scatter his "'tell-tale' types."[28] With characteristic defiance, Birney continued to publish, moving his printing operation to downtown Cincinnati. In response, that July, an anti-abolitionist mob ran riot. They seized Birney's printing press, tipping it into the Ohio River, and killed or injured an untold number of black Cincinnatians. The violence was an ugly expression of the majoritarian impulse denounced by Tocqueville and others.[29] The custom of "Regulators" breaking loose to reclaim, or "regulate," social boundaries originated in colonial society.[30] Such action furnished the riotous "social exclamation points" of Cincinnati history, both through informal mobs and, more formally, committees of vigilance, all of which flourished in this period.[31] At the height of the violence, abolitionist sympathizers, including Henry Ward Beecher (son of Lyman Beecher), formed armed patrols to protect antislavery and black businesses and property. But as his sister Harriet Beecher Stowe observed, almost all the local papers "were either silent or openly mobocratic" during the unrest.[32]

Although Birney was personally humane (in 1837, he stood trial for harboring a fugitive slave), he remained skeptical of those professing humanitarian ends for their own sake.[33] His born-again faith drew him toward the enslaved, but his politics distinguished him from mainstream benevolence. *The Philanthropist*'s byline quoted Genesis 42:21—"We are verily guilty concerning our brother, therefore, is this distress come upon us"—reflected his own unexpiated guilt in the sin of slavery. In an open letter, Birney rebuked the pharisaical "Clergymen of Cincinnati," who were "zealously engaged in many of the benevolent enterprises of the day—in foreign and domestic missions—in bible and tract societies—in educating the poor children of our white population, and the German and Irish emigrants." Such enterprises were worthy, conceded Birney, but "where are your prayers, your alms, your sympathies, for the poor, despised, and persecuted among you, who differ in nothing from other men, but in the color of their skin?"[34]

Birney's religion was as radical as his politics, reflecting a rift between moderate antislavery and abolitionist evangelicals. As a layman, Birney clashed with Presbyterian authority. The Synod of Kentucky's noncommittal stance on slavery influenced Birney's relocation from Kentucky to Ohio.[35] His association with Theodore Weld—the Lane rebel who had converted him to abolitionism—and the fact that Lane students were using their seminary as a forwarding addressing for *The Philanthropist* reflected this radicalism. While those who ransacked the downtown offices of Birney's paper spared Beecher's seminary (isolated by its semirural location), concern at student activism prompted Lane professor Thomas Biggs to worry that "it has surmounted all rule and all authority," threatening to turn the college into "the great laboratory [of Abolitionism]."[36]

The reaction to Birney played out against a broader sectarian landscape, inflamed by press sensationalism. "*Society seems everywhere unhinged*," lamented the editor of *Nile's Weekly Register*, reviewing some five hundred press cuttings relating to urban violence. "The demon of 'blood and slaughter' has been let loose upon us!"[37] Intolerance pervaded the public sphere. All within its bounds were contaminated, including Lyman Beecher, his reputation sullied by one of the period's ugliest incidents of sectarian violence.

The Anti-Catholic Gothic Imagination

In August 1834 Beecher revisited New England "to speak of the character, wants, and dangers of the great valley . . . [and] to kindle the interest of the churches and draw forth their liberality."[38] While he preached the salvation of the West from his old pulpit in Boston, a working-class mob besieged and set fire to the Ursuline Convent in the nearby suburb of Charlestown, chanting "Down with the Pope! Down with the Bishop! Down with the convent!" Police held back as the nunnery burned to ashes. Although the convent was evacuated, the fire could have proven fatal.[39]

Local Catholics blamed Beecher for inciting the mob, but deeper causes provoked the burning of the Ursuline Convent. Throughout the northeastern United States, nativist sentiment was rising. In New York City, the American Protestant Association (founded 1831) propagated anti-Catholic literature. The Massachusetts General Association of Congregational Churches railed against "the degrading influence of popery."[40] In New England, especially, sectarian conflict focused on matters of education. Since their arrival in 1820, Boston's Ursuline sisters ran a day school for local Catholic girls. In 1824, they relocated from cramped downtown quarters to the spacious hilltop estate in Charlestown. Coinciding with their new prospects, the nuns opened a second academy catering to daughters of local merchants and professionals. They taught up to sixty girls at any one time, most from Protestant families.[41] The contrast between the refinement of the Ursuline mission and the incendiary "truckmen and brickmakers" who burned it down was striking.[42]

Class conflict alone did not explain the violence at Charlestown. Beecher's return to Boston fit a growing pattern from Cincinnati to New England, as Protestant congregations in major cities hosted a circuit of anti-Catholic preachers and lecturers.[43] Boston mayor Theodore Lyman (Beecher's distant kinsman) assembled a public committee at Faneuil Hall to investigate the motive for the arson. While resolving that "the late attack . . . was a base and cowardly act, for which the perpetrators deserve the contempt and detestation of the community," the report failed to identify the ringleaders and reflected the prejudices of prominent Protestants on the committee. Beecher's visit to Boston was nowhere mentioned, the culpability of the press only hinted at.[44]

Despite absolving Beecher, the report on the Ursuline Convent acknowledged anti-Catholic conspiracy. Its authors insisted "the destruction of the convent might be attributed primarily to a widely extended popular aversion, founded in the belief, that the establishment was obnoxious to those imputations of cruelty, vice, and corruption, so generally credited of similar establishments in other countries." Notably, the case of one young novice, "Mrs. Mary John, formerly Miss Elizabeth Harrison," incited the mob, with allegations that she "had been put to death, or secretly imprisoned," after leaving holy orders. Such "assertions and reports were not only prevalent in this city and its vicinity," reported the committee, but "pervaded many parts of the commonwealth, and have extended into other states; affording a monitory lesson of the extent and excitability of public credulity."[45]

While Boston's authorities blamed anti-Catholicism in general, Cincinnati's Catholic clergy blamed events at Charlestown on "fanatical preachers in Boston and the adjacent towns . . . glad of so favorable an opportunity to excite the public." The *Catholic Telegraph* accused Beecher, stating that he had assailed the Catholic faith "last Sunday in three sermons, which he delivered in three different churches." Beecher's itinerancy placed him in company with "violent fanatics . . . evidently the most dangerous of the enemies to good order, and to the peace and harmony of society."[46] Responding to the *Telegraph*'s accusations, Beecher countered that the actions of the mob were "regarded with abhorrence and regret by Protestants and patriots," but he took pains to defend his own reputation. "The sermon of mine to which the mob was ascribed," he wrote, "was preached before my presence in the city of Boston was generally known, and on the very evening in which the riot took place . . . not an individual of the mob, probably, heard the sermon or knew of its delivery."[47] Other American nativists were less apologetic—with Samuel Morse, for one, reiterating charges against the Ursuline nuns.[48]

Mary John was not the only Ursuline novice whose alleged abuse roused anti-Catholic sentiment. Rebecca Reed's harrowing memoir, *Six Months in a Convent*, was published in 1835, shortly after the Charlestown fire. Reed detailed her arrival in Boston as an impoverished single woman, her conversion to Catholicism, her initiation into the Ursuline order, and torments at the hands of her mother superior—which included floor kissing, drinking water used to clean dirty feet, and even chewing shards of glass—before her escape and refuge with a local Protestant family. However brutal these accusations, the agenda of the Catholic Church was allegedly equally concerning, focused on converting Protestant children to the malign cause of Papacy. Reed also reported that Bishop Benedict Fenwick of Boston (brother of the late bishop of Cincinnati) anticipated welcoming the pope on American soil—an alarming prospect to many.[49]

The abuses, real or imaginary, at the Ursuline Convent in Boston confirmed the fears of many Cincinnatians—perhaps unsurprisingly, for, as historian Richard Hofstadter observed, "Anti-Catholicism has always been the pornography of the Puritan."[50] An antebellum genre thus exposed the veil on alleged abuses of women and girls, colored by gothic literature. The most lurid example was *Maria Monk's Awful Disclosures of the Hotel Dieu Nunnery of Montreal* (1836), which outsold every other American book until *Uncle Tom's Cabin*.[51] Like Reed, Maria Monk was a documented figure. Her narrative was presented as factual, although its horrors, including rape, infanticide, and murder, surpassed even Reed's in their sensationalism. *Awful Disclosures* sold some three hundred thousand copies, but not before the book's true author was exposed as Rev. J. J. Slocum, a New York Presbyterian and stalwart of the American Board of Commissioners for Foreign Missions.[52]

The success of *Six Months in a Convent* and *Awful Disclosures* corresponded with the volume of anti-Catholic publication in the Queen City. Through the antebellum era, hundreds of convent-themed books describing rape and abuses sold hundreds of thousands of copies. Cincinnati authors jumping on this bandwagon included Isaac Kelso, whose *Danger in the Dark: A Tale of Intrigue and Priestcraft* (1854) racked thirty-one editions in its first year alone.[53] Though acknowledging "the guise of fiction," Kelso hoped his novel "may prove no less acceptable to the sober-minded and truth-loving than to the mere novel reader, who seeks in books nothing beyond amusement." Kelso denounced "the spirit, principles, and tendency of anti-republican Romanism in this country" crudely but effectively. "All good Catholics," stated one character, "pray that the time may speedily come when the church will have power to establish the Holy Inquisition in America."[54] Novels like Kelso's enjoyed a wider readership than more sober anti-Catholic tomes produced by Cincinnatians, including Rev. Charles Elliott's one-thousand-page *Delineation of Roman Catholicism, Drawn from the Authentic and Acknowledged Standards of the Church of Rome* (1841), which explained how "Romanists" threatened to "retard or destroy true religion, and overturn the civil and religious liberties of the United States."[55]

Scholars of American anti-Catholicism have focused on Anglophone culture, but in Cincinnati, the fiercest opponents of Rome were German immigrants. Among the anti-Catholic novels of this time was a remarkable German melodrama, *Cincinnati, oder, Geheimnisse des Westens* (Cincinnati, or the mysteries of the West, 1854). Its author, Emil Klauprecht, edited one of antebellum Cincinnati's flagship German newspapers, *Der Republikaner*. A leader of the *Dreissiger* Germans (émigrés from the failed revolutions of the 1830s), Klauprecht denounced the papal state for oppressing European revolution in 1848. His novel was in the style of the urban mystery thrillers popular in Europe, though, as Klauprecht acknowledged, "the drawings which are offered in this little work are coarse cartoon sketches, quickly drawn . . . for the ravenous German American daily press."[56] Nevertheless, one scholar called *Cincinnati* "the most important piece of creative literature produced by a German-American during the nineteenth century."[57]

Like *Uncle Tom's Cabin*, published by Harriet Beecher Stowe two years before, Klauprecht's *Cincinnati* was serialized for mass-market consumption. Both Stowe and Klauprecht imagined the Queen City as a crossroads of

America: Stowe focusing on the city as a hub of the Underground Railroad, Klauprecht on urban immigration. While Klauprecht's *Cincinnati* numbered multiple subplots, including nods to *Uncle Tom's Cabin* (a southern slave auction, pursuit of fugitive slaves by bloodhounds, and even a scene featuring an iced-over river), its central theme was a conspiracy to steal the inheritance of the young Washington Filson, grandson of Ohio pioneer John Filson.

Klauprecht's plot bears summarizing. A cabal of Jesuits frames the naive protagonist for murder, throws him in jail, and attempts blackmail. Through a tangle of intrigues (including unlikely intervention by Missouri senator Thomas Hart Benton), Filson is exonerated, his persecutors thwarted. After Benton reveals his identity, Filson renounces his inheritance, which turns out to be the land on which Cincinnati was built. Tearing up the deed on a hill overlooking the city, he exclaims, "The people ha[ve] made this ground their own," as his fortune wafts away on the wind. The novel ends with Filson marrying his German sweetheart, redeeming her from engagement to a crooked local pork merchant. The happy couple head off for a new life in Iowa, enjoying "the free country of the West"—allowing the author to eulogize "the real Americans . . . our heroic pioneers."[58]

His novel ended happily, but Klauprecht was at pains to reveal the Jesuit order as the foremost threat to liberty in America. For Klauprecht, Jesuitism was the Catholic Church at its worst, its mere presence proof enough of Vatican conspiracy. While the Society of Jesus was, in fact, a latecomer to the Queen City, predated by the Dominican and Redemptorist orders, Klauprecht portrayed the order as commanding the Catholic Church in Cincinnati.[59] Notably, Klauprecht identified the Jesuits with the interests of southern slaveowners and foretold the eradication of both in a coming civil war:

> Jesuitism had always seen in European absolutism its truest friend and ally, as the manifesto of its disciples to the King of Naples most recently demonstrated. In America, cotton is king, the absolute ruler in politics. United with it, as it is, the Black Band can ignore all storms which might break against it in the political field. Only the collapse of the slaveowners' party, only the victory of freedom and enlightenment with the spiritual weapon of the vote can tear from Jesuitism the triumph of which it now boasts so openly. But this demands the cooperation of the united patriotism and intelligence of the Republic. The primeval enemy of human welfare has used its time well to gather the means to make the soil of Washington and Jefferson into a place for a baleful conflict for which it has prepared through so many hundred years of Europe's civil peace.[60]

Klauprecht's fiction raised pressing questions. Like many German radicals, Klauprecht viewed sectarian conflict as all but inevitable. Why, then, if hostility to American Catholicism was so intense, was sectarian violence not correspondingly more widespread? Why, when civil war came to America, were the dividing lines geographic and racial instead? These questions cut to the heart of sectarian and ethnic encounters in Cincinnati.

Transatlantic Currents

Klauprecht's fears of Jesuit tyranny resonated beyond German readers in Cincinnati. Catholics numbered over one-third of the city's population by 1850 and had become the largest denomination in the Ohio Valley.[61] Alexis de Tocqueville, anticipating this demographic shift twenty years earlier, painstakingly addressed nativist concerns. He conceded that the British colonies were "peopled by men who, after having shaken off the authority of the Pope, acknowledged no other religious supremacy: they bought with them . . . a democratic and republican religion." Tocqueville acknowledged that the Roman Catholic population (some one million inhabitants in 1830) challenged those who sought to "*harmonize* earth with heaven," yet he defended American Catholics as "the most republican and the most democratic class in the United States." The Catholic community, he noted, "is composed of only two elements: the priest and the people. . . . If Catholicism predisposes the faithful to obedience, it certainly does not prepare them for inequality; but the contrary may be said of Protestantism, which generally tends to make men more independent than to render them equal."[62]

Despite Tocquevillian assurances that Protestantism and Catholicism were complementary sides of the American coin, anti-Catholicism proliferated. In *A Plea for the West*, Lyman Beecher inquired: "What is to be done to educate the millions which in twenty years Europe will pour out upon us?" If Catholicism was "now rolling its broad tide at the bidding of the powers of Europe," the danger embodied by immigrants was ignorance and tractability. "Is this a vain fear?" he asked. "Are not the continental powers alarmed at the march of liberal opinions, and associated to put them down? and are they not, with the sickness of hope deferred, waiting for our downfall?"[63]

Was Beecher justified in his suspicion of European monarchy and autocracy? To some extent, his fears were reasonable, albeit exaggerated. During the revolutionary era, Americans witnessed convulsions of the Old World, as democratic upheavals in France led to political terror, total war, and oppression in Europe. At first eschewing foreign entanglements, the United States was drawn into conflict as Great Britain harassed neutral shipping on the

Atlantic and reasserted dominion through the United States backcountry. Britain's defeat in the War of 1812 confirmed American independence but underlined frailties of national sovereignty. Following Napoleon's defeat at Waterloo, meanwhile, Austria, Russia, and France (under Bourbon restoration) united in a self-styled Holy Alliance. Vowing to extinguish the forces of the French Revolution, these Christian autocracies combined against nationalist, liberal, and socialist uprisings. Looking across the Atlantic, the Holy Alliance had reason to fear America as a bastion of republicanism while, as Beecher complained, papal autocracy was "sustained by Austrian bayonets."[64]

Mirroring the European fundraising voyages of the American Catholic clergy, a steady stream of European exiles came to America in search of solidarity, refuge, and finance. Following the thwarted liberal-nationalist uprisings that riled Germany, Italy, and the Austrian Empire in 1848, many Americans, native and foreign born, embraced charismatic revolutionaries, such as Italian patriot Giuseppe Garibaldi and his Hungarian contemporary, Louis Kossuth, with the same enthusiasm that welcomed the return of Lafayette to the United States in 1826. Kossuth received an especially rousing welcome in the Queen City in 1852, when fifty thousand people thronged a procession led by the mayor and local militia companies. His itinerary was relentless. One member of his entourage complained of endless festivities, "the want of homogeneity in the population of Cincinnati" reflecting the city's dynamic but bewildering landscape. Though wearied by his American tour, Kossuth addressed eight different venues in Cincinnati, including a banquet of dignitaries, a gathering of local women, an assembly of workingmen, and separate audiences of both northern and southern German immigrants.[65] For native-born Americans, the struggles of patriots such as Kossuth resonated with the birth pangs of their republic. For émigrés from Germany and elsewhere, torn between Old World heritage and ethnic Americanism, the struggles were even more emotionally raw.

Amid transatlantic upheaval, the Catholic Church's global organization was at once a strength and liability. Classifying the entire United States as missionary territory, the church encouraged new congregations and transatlantic immigration, sounding nativist alarm bells. In November 1842, for example, the *Home Missionary* published an editorial exposing a "Grand Scheme for planting Irish Catholic Colonists in the Western States." Accompanying this headline was an even bolder map, illustrating "the contemplated field of the SOCIETY FOR COLONIZING THE IRISH CATHOLIC POOR." Composed of the former Northwest Territory states of Ohio, Indiana, Illinois, Michigan, and Wisconsin, together with a chunk of eastern Iowa, the projected colony also included Upper Canada (present-day southern Ontario).

The source of "the Grand Scheme for planting Irish Catholic Colonists" and its accompanying map was a pamphlet printed in London and Dublin in 1841 entitled, "Proposed New Plan of a General Emigration Society; By A Catholic Gentleman." As the *Home Missionary* noted, the anonymous author was inspired by the "Centralization system" developed by British colonialists in Australia. The scheme commended itself on five merits: "to dispose of the *excess of population* . . . to create a larger demand *for British manufactures* . . . to render *the Catholic religion* predominant in the United States . . . [to secure] *pecuniary profit* on the capital invested," and, finally, to prepare "an agreeable asylum for a large class of persons, whose present situation is uncomfortable, such as the younger sons of the nobility and gentry." In light of such concerns, the *Home Missionary* insisted that the only safeguard was "unceasing vigilance, and the most strenuous efforts to make the Gospel light so intense in our land, that error shall find no corner so dark that it may securely abide there."[66]

Echoing the concerns of Morse and Beecher, the *Home Missionary* depicted North America as a blank canvas for Catholic Europe. Even though the existence of any central design to colonize the Midwest remained unproven, the editor pointed to "the stimulus applied in all Catholic countries, to induce immigration to America, and the rapid increase of that emigration," not to mention "the immense expenditure of Papal Societies, for the purpose of planting Romanism in the Western states."[67] Catholic networks such as the Habsburg-endowed Leopoldine Foundation fueled nativist fears. Although Catholic fundraising for the Midwest reflected transatlantic migration and patterns of diocesan development, critics beheld sinister designs behind groups such as the Leopoldine Foundation and the French-based Society for the Propagation of the Faith.[68] More schematic attempts to settle Catholics in the United States struggled, however, and should be seen in light of the utopianism of the period. Catholic immigration to America was at best modestly funded by church sources, and most immigrants, Catholic and non-Catholic, came to the Queen City for economic rather than religious reasons.

Cincinnati's demography gave anti-Catholicism a complex dynamic, strongly articulated by two immigrant groups. The first was Protestant Germans. The other was freethinking, anticlerical nationalists, including refugees from the revolutions of the 1830s and 1848. Both groups had grievances with the Catholic Church, stretching from the European Reformation and Wars of Religion to recent struggles between German nationalists and autocracies allied with Rome. German Protestants included Presbyterians, Lutherans, Methodists, and Reformed (Calvinist) congregations, all sharing common attitudes.[69] Many questioned the laissez-faire secularism of their adopted homeland. One

Lutheran minister warned that "America is the country in which the Catholics can develop their power unhindered." Most risky was "the unfamiliarity with church history that generally prevails among Americans, and particularly the often silly views that they have of the doctrine and inner essence of the Roman Church." Complacency, he added, "will make victory all the easier for the latter once it begins, with its flexibility, to adapt to the American temperament."[70]

Though sharing a dislike of Rome, German Protestants and freethinkers were at odds in other ways, torn between assimilation and maintaining their heritage in the New World. Secular Germans especially promoted voluntary associations, festivals, and mutual self-help. By midcentury a distinctly German subculture emerged in Cincinnati, characterized by beer halls, Sunday picnics, *sängerfesten* (singing contests), *shützenvereinen* (gun clubs), ethnic militia, and Turnervereinen (or Turner societies). This latter movement was a uniquely German blend of gymnasium, sports club, and fraternity introduced to the Queen City in 1848. While the Turners were primarily a social organization, Cincinnati was also home to the Freimanner, or Society of Freemen, radical republicans who paraded the black, red, and gold tricolor of Germany. Such display looked a lot like ethnic separatism, although the Freemen's abhorrence of Catholics and Catholicism resonated with the prejudices of American nativists.

Although critical of American foibles, many German Protestants strove to assimilate. William Nast, a German-born Cincinnati Methodist, was scathing of "the Germans in America [who] have conceived the idea of maintaining their nationality in this new world, with its peculiar life and customs." Describing immigrant life in Over-the-Rhine—the ethnic enclave bordered to the west and south by the Miami and Erie Canal—Nast added: "If a native of Germany could fall asleep in his own country, and wake up in this part of Cincinnati, he would still believe himself in the fatherland."[71] Nast's fellow countryman Franz von Löhner corroborated this observation of German insularity, irritating "an American woman" by claiming to have spotted her in the German district. "'No sir,' she said sharply, 'I never cross the canal.'" Though separated by the width of a waterway, lamented Löhner, the city's German population was isolated from their neighbors. Worse, they were isolated from each other: "split into strong factions, religious and political."[72]

Catholic Americanization and the Mexican-American War

The diverse character of Cincinnati's German diaspora was equally evident within the Catholic community. The city's Irish-born bishop, John Baptist

Purcell, only inherited one German-speaking priest for the city's five thousand German Catholics in 1833, but he strove to close the gap as European immigration increased.[73] Cincinnati Germans hailed from various territories, with local customs, dialect, and traditions. Before the Bismarckian Kulturkampf of the later nineteenth century, which sought unity through bureaucratic state building, German Catholics embraced tremendous diversity and autonomy in worship and church governance. The uprooting of thousands of Germans to Cincinnati was problematic, accompanied by lay anticlericism, irreligion, and disregard of church discipline. Even as Catholic clergy succeeded in consolidating Germans, discipline remained a challenge. "The Catholic religion thrives here," complained Franciscan Wilhelm Unterthiner to an Austrian colleague, "but still there are very lax people who do not receive the sacraments for years."[74] Purcell himself never mastered German, but he developed pragmatic policies. He avoided foisting temperance on German Catholics, for example, and encouraged lay initiative. Of the dozen German Catholic churches in Cincinnati by the time of the Civil War, only one (Immaculate Conception) was founded directly by the diocese, the rest by parochial subscription.[75]

Purcell's espousal of two controversial policies shaped his diocesan tenure. The first was trusteeism: granting lay Catholics supervisory trust over ecclesiastical property, subject to canon law. This practice originated from necessity due to shortage of diocesan clergy but continued throughout the antebellum period, reflecting the democratic sensibilities of the Queen City. Encapsulating the distance and autonomy of the American Catholic Church from Rome, trusteeism also lent itself to the idea of "Americanism," summarized in Orestes Brownson's 1856 essay "The Mission of America." Brownson, a New England–born convert, became American Catholicism's leading public intellectual, albeit a contrarian voice. Like Lyman Beecher, he championed national redemption, but unlike Beecher, he advocated the Catholic faith as the means of salvation. "It is but simply truth to assert," he wrote, "that ours, at present, is the country towards which Catholics throughout the world should turn their hopes." He warned against American Catholics separating "from the great current of American nationality," urging them to "take their position as free and equal American citizens, with American interests and sympathies, American sentiments and affections," or risk becoming "helot[s]."[76]

Brownson's call to Americanization, penned during the rise of Know-Nothingism, drew controversy within the Catholic Church in Cincinnati and elsewhere. Some, like Archbishop John Hughes of New York, urged greater ethnic pride and strengthening of European traditions. In Cincinnati, as well,

German and Irish Catholics contested Brownson's nationalistic assertions. Redemptorist F. X. Weininger was moved by parishioners to write Brownson (in Latin) against the assertion that "after God, our first and finest love has always been, and we trust, always will be, for our *country*." Such impertinence, Weininger believed, bordered on idolatry.[77] Unchastised, Brownson maintained that the nation's German and Irish immigrant populations required shepherding to avoid evangelical wolves in sheep's clothing. He described "the lowest stratum of our Catholic population" as "a very ill-instructed class of people, whose temptations are great, whose religious advantages are few, and who are plunged in many miseries both of soul and body."[78] To retain them in the fold, Brownson argued, the church must Americanize and embrace republican society. Ever the pragmatist, Purcell adopted Americanism but condemned Brownson for his bigoted views of immigrants. "That man," he wrote to his friend the bishop of New Orleans, "is destined to be our worst enemy in these United States."[79]

Under Bishops Fenwick and Purcell, the Diocese of Cincinnati developed a forceful presence in the public sphere, including print journalism. "We Catholics are not much disposed to speculate in Religion," conceded Purcell, "but as this is a speculating age we might speculate for it."[80] Recognizing the struggle for religious toleration, Fenwick established the *Catholic Telegraph* as the official journal of the diocese just one year prior to his death in the cholera epidemic of 1832. Only the second diocesan newspaper in the United States—after Boston's *Jesuit or Catholic Sentinel* (1829)—the *Telegraph* had two objectives. According to its first editor, Jesuit father James Mullon, "the primary object in issuing the Catholic Telegraph, is to aid in diffusing a correct knowledge of the Catholic faith." Second, the newspaper proselytized for the church's mission in redeeming America, its first edition highlighting news of local Protestants converted to the "bosom of the One Holy, Catholic, and Apostolic Church."[81]

The advent of a Catholic press tested the boundaries of toleration. Castigating the "new *papal* paper in this city," Rev. Amos Blanchard, Presbyterian editor of the *Cincinnati Journal*, asserted that "the right of every denomination in this country, to publish magazines, pamphlets, books and newspapers, in defense of their own peculiar tenets, is the beneficial result of protestant principles."[82] By 1837, the *Journal* exhibited even less tolerance of its Catholic counterpart, reflecting rivalries between the Catholic Church and the Benevolent Empire. "Popery is among us," the paper declared:

> The monarchs and monarchists of Europe supply its advocates with funds. They are anxious for its success. The Pope, who is a foreign

temporal prince has his agents and his subjects among us, who have sworn allegiance to his government. . . .

Let it be remembered that these men—the Jesuits and other popish priests and their followers—are determined opponents of our Missionary, Bible and Tract Societies; the constant opposers of Sabbath-schools; the clamorous advocates of "Sabbath Mails;" and are first and loudest, unless the infidels may be considered their equals, in raising the cry about "church and state."[83]

In defense of their faith, the editors of the *Telegraph* reprinted anti-Catholic editorials of local and national journals. By presenting multiple perspectives and engaging with critics, the newspaper challenged accusations of dogmatism. Reprinting critical material also highlighted the paper's significance as the first diocesan journal west of the Alleghenies. For its part the Protestant press took note of the *Telegraph*. "Here is a paper," alleged the *Boston Whig*, "circulating extensively among the great mass of emigrants who are flooding the West, which openly avows hostility to our form of government, and which is poisoning minds already besotted by ignorance, against the institutions which are affording them shelter and protection." In response, the *Telegraph* marveled at "the astonishing degree of misconception of every thing connected with Catholicity."[84]

A Call to Arms

The Mexican-American War (1846–1848) was a particular challenge for American Catholics, testing loyalty to nation against sympathy for coreligionists south of the border. Territorial disputes simmering since the Texan Revolution of 1836 culminated in a blundering raid across the Rio Grande by American forces. This skirmish prompted President James K. Polk to declare that the Mexicans had "passed the boundary of the United States, . . . invaded our territory and shed American blood upon the American soil."[85] The nativist tenor of Polk's war message to Congress obscured the fact that the Mexicans had not crossed the border; it had crossed them. Still, American belligerence reflected fears of foreign invasion at a time of massive Catholic immigration while imputing the superiority of an industrial, Protestant, and urban United States over rural, Catholic, and agrarian Mexico.

War with Mexico put American Catholics in an uncomfortable position. Responding to charges of disloyalty against "the Catholic citizen," the *Telegraph* rallied to their defense. While the editor regretted any compulsion for Catholics "to take up arms against brethren of the same faith," he compared the situation to the contemporaneous Oregon dispute over America's northern border, which might easily have placed "our Protestant fellow citizens . . . in the same position which we occupy at present." The analogy was strained, in the absence of any sectarian conflict with Great Britain, but the point was valid. At the same time, the *Telegraph*, having commented sparingly on the vexatious question of Texas, rushed to declare its support for the war effort: "The die is cast, the sword is drawn, and every man must enter with all his heart into the conflict with an unflinching determination to carry the flag of the union."[86]

If nothing else, war with Mexico allowed Cincinnati Catholics to vaunt their patriotism. Nativists, one declared, waved the flag, but when it came to action, they were "a used up faction." One local militia company, the Citizens' Guards, was formed "for the express purpose of protecting our good citizens from the d—d Irish and Dutch in the time of peace; but when their services were likely to be needed on the Rio Grande, they dissolved, and are now lying low until peace is restored." By contrast, some 450 of the 850 or so Cincinnatians responding to the first call for volunteers were "adopted citizens," mostly Catholics.[87] Many, such as Lieutenant Matthew Hett of the First Ohio Regiment of Volunteers, paid the ultimate price. The priest at Hett's funeral eulogized his death at the Battle of Monterrey:

> [Hett] proved through his deeds that a German can also die for his adopted fatherland. The deceased was also a Catholic. Through his death he punished again other lies . . . that a Catholic in the true sense of the word cannot be a good citizen of this republic because he would not be allowed to fight against Mexico due to the principles of his religion.[88]

In covering the fighting, the *Catholic Telegraph* contrasted the deeds of German and Irish volunteers with the duplicity of Cincinnati nativists. While "Catholic soldiers are shedding their blood at the call of their country," it noted, "a fashionable store-keeper on Fourth Street in this city has been busy recruiting for some secret society, whose object is to keep down the Roman Catholics."[89] Without question, the military service of Cincinnati Catholics subverted nativist claims to exclusive republican virtue. War also "Americanized" foreign-born Catholics—a fact not lost on political candidates. General Winfield Scott, stumping in his presidential election bid of 1852, praised immigrant voters in Cincinnati. "I am proud to have recognized, as I passed along your crowded streets," he proclaimed, "the familiar accents of your Irish and German citizens. . . . I always saw them fighting with admiration, and I shall always speak of them with praise."[90]

The Mexican-American War allowed immigrants to fight for their country but did little to stanch anti-Catholicism. At the war's height in 1847, nativists formed the Cincinnati chapter of the American Protestant Association, expressly "to resist the Catholic Church because of its enmity to American institutions." Members flanked the entrance to St. Peter in Chains, handing out nativist pamphlets.[91] Local nativists even produced a short-lived journal, the *Anti-Papist*, "devoted to the defense of Protestantism, promotion of evangelical religion and the diffusion of useful knowledge and intelligence generally."[92] Correlated with such activity was rising anti-Catholic violence. In 1848, for example, four nativists attacked a German tailor in Over-the-Rhine. Accusing him of underselling the competition, the assailants "*basted*" him, "*sheared* his hair, branded him on the seat with a *goose*, and finally *sewed him up* in a piece of muslin."[93]

Ironically, Catholic identification with territorial expansionism emboldened critics questioning the national character of the church. In terms of tribalism, it was fitting that John L. O'Sullivan, an Irish-American editor of New York's *Democratic Review*, coined the term "Manifest Destiny," celebrating America's right "to overspread and to possess the whole of the continent which Providence has given us."[94] Yet not everyone embraced this new ideal. Massachusetts Congressman Anson Burlingame, for one, portrayed Catholic promotion of westward expansionism thus:

> Slavery and Priestcraft . . . have a common purpose: they seek [to annex] Cuba and Hayti and the Mexican States together, because they will be Catholic and Slave. I say they are in alliance by the necessity of their nature,—for one denies the right of a man to his body, and the other the right of a man to his soul. The one denies the right to think for himself, the other the right to act for himself.[95]

Rather than acknowledge Catholic support for territorial expansion as proof of assimilation, some detected a conspiracy to dilute America's racial purity. According to a quotation reprinted in the nativist *Cincinnati Gazette*, the *Catholic Telegraph* maintained that "that the permanency of our republican institutions was dependent on the supremacy of the Catholic religion." By contrast, the *Gazette* insisted: "a glance at the map of the World shows that where free Governments exist, the Protestant religion is the prevailing religion." Quoting Edwin Vose Sumner, a veteran colonel of the Mexican-American War, the *Gazette* denounced Catholic designs to bastardize the American body politic. Sumner viewed mestizo populations, such as those of New Mexico, as "debased and incapable of self-government." Unable to make "respectable citizens," they were polluted with "more Indian blood than Spanish" and were scarcely capable of reproduction, "owing to their gross depravity." The results of integrating mixed-race populations "into our political household" attracted "little attention," added the *Gazette*, "from the believers of 'manifest destiny.'"[96]

Slowly and insensibly the nation slid toward Civil War, as old animosities of ethnicity, religion, race, and sectionalism worsened. Controversies such as the failure of the Wilmot Proviso seeking to eliminate slavery from territories seized during the Mexican War, and passage of the federal Compromise of 1850 introducing the notorious Fugitive Slave Act, played into anti-Catholicism. Critics tied the Catholic Church to southern slavocracy. They condemned the Catholic faith of Adele Cutts Douglas, the slave-owning, aristocratic wife of Democratic statesman Stephen Douglas.[97] They argued that America's Catholic Church had turned a blind eye to slavery in the interests of ecclesiastical unity and was complicit in great sin. Some leading Catholics spoke against slavery, however, chief among them Bishop Purcell. Writing in the *Catholic Telegraph* (the only antislavery Catholic newspaper in the United States), he lamented: "When the slave power predominates, religion is nominal. There is no life in it. It is the hard working man who builds the church, the school house, the orphan asylum, not the slaveholder, as a general rule."[98] Yet Purcell's antislavery stance did little to quiet critics of the Catholic Church.

Know-Nothingism and the Nativist Nadir

By November of 1853, organized political nativism obtained the form in New York City by which it became known more widely. Horace Greeley's *New York Tribune* (America's most circulated daily newspaper) reported the defeat of the Whig frontrunner for the city's district attorney "through the instrumentality of a mongrel ticket termed the 'Know-Nothing.' . . . This ticket is the work of the managers of a secret organization growing out of the Order of United Americans, but ostensibly disconnected therefrom."[99] While Greeley did not coin the term "Know-Nothing," he popularized its use, and its spread in the 1850s reflected the virulence of political nativism. More than any time before the Civil War, Catholics feared for their safety. "We are in the midst of all manner of threats from all manner of sects & infidels," complained Bishop Purcell, "no one knows how soon they may ripen into open, violent, and prolonged persecution."[100]

While anti-Catholicism animated Know-Nothingism, nativist attitudes to the foreign born in general were surprisingly conflicted. Nativism implied hostility to all things foreign, but foreignness varied depending on context. In

New Orleans, for example, a Know-Nothing chapter flourished among French Creole Catholics, who looked down on the Germans and Irish.[101] Ethnic and sectarian politics in the Queen City was equally ironic. Thus, the *Cincinnati Daily Times*, edited by James D. "Pap" Taylor, the American Reform ticket candidate for mayor, warned readers against all foreigners—Protestant or Catholic—who lacked patriotic fervor. Approving attempts in Massachusetts to ban foreign-born candidates from public office, the *Daily Times'* editorial stated: "If Protestant foreigners, permitting themselves to be humbugged by demagogues, voluntarily array themselves on the side of Popery, they have nobody but themselves to blame, if they are classed with them, as of the same genus, by Americans."[102] In a cruder vein, "A. Know-Nothing" wrote the *Cincinnati Enquirer* in July 1855: "'Americans should rule America' is my motto . . . it is far better than consorting with black Dutch, red-mouthed Irish and pussey John Bulls."[103]

For all the xenophobia of Cincinnati nativists, they depended on foreign-born allies in their anti-Catholic coalition. As the Democratic *Cincinnati Enquirer* argued in 1845, nativism was less concerned with ethnicity than with sectarian identity: "Natives hate a Native Catholic more than a foreign Calvinist."[104] In 1854, the *Enquirer* went so far as to blame "the foreign vote" for shoring up support for the American Party. It affirmed the worst fears of its Catholic readers by characterizing these unlikely voters as "IRISH ORANGE-MEN, SCOTCH AND ENGLISH TORIES, INFIDEL GERMANS, and lastly, the CHRIST-KILLING JEWS."[105] The editorial pointed to a spectrum of ethnic and sectarian groups whose grievances cemented a formidable bloc against Catholic interests. Elsewhere, the *Enquirer* complained: "We who combatted Native American intolerance against our adopted fellow citizens, years ago, little expected . . . such specimens of foreign nativism as we have lately seen manifesting itself among that class of our population."[106]

Who were these foreign nativists? Some, such as Hugh Kirkland, were Irish Protestants. Most were Germans. Many, like Emil Klauprecht, brimmed both with nationalistic fervor for their fatherland and patriotism for an adopted America. They came to America in two waves: first during the 1830s (the Dreissigers, or Thirtiers) and then following the political uprisings of 1848 (the Forty-Eighters). Most were highly educated, sophisticated, and politically engaged. Although only a small percentage of the city's overall German population, they compensated by their influence. The Forty-Eighters, especially, had a disproportionate impact on civic life. German nationalist émigrés, they were "a foreign radical element, destined to 'out-knownothing' the Know-Nothings" in Cincinnati.[107] Like their English-speaking nativist counterparts, these Germans vaunted anti-Catholic credentials. To them, opposition to Rome was not bigotry but liberty.

When, in December 1853, Pope Pius IX dispatched an emissary to tour the United States, German radicals reacted with rage. The mission to present a letter of goodwill to President Franklin Pierce, to cement Vatican relations in America, and to gather religious intelligence raised hackles in any event, but the pope's choice of Cardinal Gaetano Bedini as nuncio was especially galling. Bedini, a former governor of Bologna, was notoriously complicit in the 1848 executions of several revolutionaries, including Umberto Bassi, a renegade Catholic priest turned Garibaldini. Bedini's brutality was more vivid in contrast with the romantic martyrdom of Bassi, betrayed by his former church to an Austrian firing squad. Bedini's reputation was even problematic among fellow prelates in the United States. The bishop of St. Louis wrote Bishop Purcell that "the Nuncio's visit . . . is anything but agreeable, being one thing in appearance and another in effect." It was, he warned, "likely to have unfavorable results for religion."[108] If nothing else, such chariness gave the lie to claims such as Rebecca Reed's that the pope himself planned to visit American shores.

Compounding its fraught reception, Bedini's tour of the United States coincided with the North American tour of another controversial Italian, Alessandro Gavazzi, a defrocked Barnabite friar turned Protestant preacher. In addition to Cincinnati, Gavazzi's whistle-stop tour took in such cities as New York, Boston, Washington, Baltimore, Louisville, and Columbus and culminated in Canada, where his incendiary remarks were blamed for deadly rioting in Montreal.[109] Gavazzi's outspoken appearances were the conduit by which Bedini's alleged abuses were disseminated in the American press, transforming the cardinal from relative obscurity into a reviled interloper "received everywhere by Protestants with the greatest disgust . . . a known enemy of republican principles and the spread of political freedom."[110] Building on lurid propaganda, Gavazzi inflamed sensibilities in Cincinnati, such as when he accused the Sisters of Charity (the city's largest female Catholic order) of being "prostitutes the world over."[111]

Bedini's notoriety grew from his arrival in the United States in June 1853 to his December 1854 visit to Cincinnati, yet it remained strongest among émigré German republicans. Cincinnati's leading German radical paper, *Die Hochwaechter*, denounced Cardinal Bedini's Christmas Day appearance in the Queen City: "Is there no ball, no dagger, for this monster, whose equal was never on earth?" asked editor Friedrich Hausaurek.[112] Given the mood, violence between city police and protesting German Freemen was predictable.

As Purcell recalled, some five hundred to one thousand Freemen descended in nocturnal procession from their lodge on Vine Street to the vicinity of St. Peter in Chains, "with execrable charivari music, transparencies, a gallows, a stuffed and ready for hanging Nuncio, Mottoes infernal, clubs, dirks, pistols, &c." Many Germans were injured—one protestor, Karl Eggerling, died— while a police officer was shot in the leg, sixty-three protestors were arrested, and one of Bedini's retinue suffered a gashed head.[113] Alongside his fellow newspaper editor Hausaurek, Emil Klauprecht also witnessed the havoc, later describing how police ambushed the protestors at the corner of Ninth and Plum Streets, where they "broke and scattered wildly, accompanied by the screams of women and children."[114] The editors of the *Catholic Telegraph*, meanwhile, denounced this melee as "the first public fruit in Cincinnati, of Gavazzi's calumnies against the papal nuncio."[115]

The Cincinnati riot was not an isolated incident but the grim climax of a disastrous urban itinerary. In New Orleans, as in Cincinnati, German radical Freemen rather than Anglo-Americans led the opposition to Bedini. The bishop of New Orleans commiserated with Purcell over the "disgraceful Excitement of the savage and Infidel *freemen!*" yet noted, "Thanks to the *Engine* of the *Telegraph*, the affray was soon known, here." Although German radical anti-Catholics were "comparatively few" in the Crescent City, "the Riot was soon discussed in their Conventicles." New Orleanians awoke within days of the Christmas riot in Cincinnati, finding "*Placards . . .* at the Corners of every street, of very large dimensions," while "the most horrible, and savage-like sentiments, and threats," were aimed at Bedini, "in *English* (of the worst sort) *French, Italian,* and *German.*"[116] Although these handbills threatened life and limb for the Butcher of Bologna, local police removed them as swiftly as they went up, and Bedini judiciously avoided New Orleans toward the end of his tour.

The Bedini riot showed how fast the smoke of sectarianism engulfed rational discourse. In its aftermath Bishop Purcell denounced the radical press, but nativist and anti-Catholic newspapers defended their German counterparts, blaming the city's Irish-dominated police force. The *Western Christian Advocate* characterized the Cincinnati police as "hyenas . . . some are the most sensual, whisky-filled, brutal and ferocious-looking things that we have ever beheld."[117] One letter in the *Cincinnati Enquirer* reflected nativist attitudes to the Cincinnati police, decrying the force as "made up of Roman Catholics, bound . . . and ready, too, to do the bidding of the Jesuit Priests, even to the shedding of blood."[118] In the wake of the Christmas riot, Catholic unease was understandable. Bishop Purcell wrote the bishop of Baltimore: "For many years I have never felt secure of my life in this city, a single night. The martyrdom of our bodies will be a trifle."[119] Purcell's brother Edward, editor of the *Telegraph*, described the atmosphere as "violently excited . . . the Catholics are all armed, [and] resolutely determined to submit to no wrong." He lamented that several police officers were "likely to be bound over to the criminal court to be tried for doing their duty."[120]

Despite apparent imbalance in the ethnic profile of Cincinnati's small police force (more than half of whom were Irish, compared to some 15 percent of the total population), one outcome of the Bedini riot was to expose police authority to accountability.[121] A court of enquiry was established, its two-weeks-long proceedings detailed in the local press. The *Daily Gazette* denounced the conduct of the police as "one of the most flagitious outrages ever perpetrated by men holding the place of conservators of the peace."[122] Friedrich Hausaurek, editor of *Die Hochwaechter*, was acquitted of inciting violence. Police Chief Thomas Lukins was the highest profile scalp. While spared criminal indictment, Lukins was ridiculed for ordering his officers to "pitch in!" and faced accusations of brutality from several of those arrested. At the urging of the police court judge, Lukins resigned on January 19, 1854.[123]

Although only dimly comprehending the vehemence of the German mobs that sought to lynch the cardinal, American-born nativists in Cincinnati deemed the protest worthy of emulation. Three weeks after the Christmas riot, on the evening of January 14, 1854, a crowd of some four thousand protestors gathered at the corner of Carr and Sixth Streets—four times as many people as turned out against Bedini's visit. They marched to the house of Purcell with brass bands and banners pronouncing "DOWN WITH BEDINI," "NO POPERY," and "LOVE, LIBERTY, AND HUMANITY." There they burned an effigy of the cardinal in view of the police. This time the protest passed almost without incident (the city marshal was punched by a rowdy, leading to a minor scuffle). According to the *Daily Gazette*, almost everyone present was Anglo-American. The German Freemen stayed away. Nevertheless, their example was hailed for having "nerved the American liberals" to take to the streets.[124]

Anti-Catholic nativism in Cincinnati was part of a chaotic nativist groundswell that culminated in the unsuccessful 1855 mayoral run of James D. "Pap" Taylor, an unlikely figure for political office. Taylor was rotund, loudmouthed, combative, and intemperate, and many of his own supporters considered him an embarrassment. His critics mocked him mercilessly. The *Cincinnati Enquirer* delighted in exposing him as the child of foreign-born Irish immigrants. A campaign cartoon appeared in the March 18, 1855, issue depicting Taylor bawling with dismay as his drunken father booted him in the backside and his mother chased him away from home with a broom.[125]

A figure of fun, Taylor's politics were no laughing matter. During the cholera epidemic of 1849, he sided with German homeopaths and quack physicians against the perceived medical Jesuitism of Daniel Drake and the Board of Health. Taylor was quick to denounce police brutality in the aftermath of the Bedini riots, defending the German Freemen and co-opting their cause for Know-Nothingism. Wherever Taylor looked he saw conspiracies of power and corruptions of liberty, and he resolved to fight back.

In 1855, as Taylor prepared his mayoral run, his *Daily Times* harked back to Bedini's visit: "The spirits of the martyred BASSI and EGGERLING will doubtless hover about those who, on Monday next, have sworn to vindicate the cause for which they died!"[126] Associating the Know-Nothing banner with an executed Catholic priest (a renegade from papal authority, admittedly) and the German protestor who died in the Bedini riot exemplified nativist martyrology. But while Bassi in Bologna and Eggerling in Cincinnati were martyrs of a sort, their cause was European nationalism, not American nativism.

The Catholic clergy themselves misread the significance of ethnic and sectarian riots such as occurred in Cincinnati. On the eve of his departure, Bedini remarked to the brother of Bishop Purcell "that he had come to this country ten years too soon." Reflecting on Bedini's comment, Purcell interpreted it to mean Catholicism's "condition ten years hence" might improve given economic and community developments in the city, though he admitted that this was "hard to predict."[127] True, had Bedini come ten years later, he would have landed amid the Civil War and upheavals of a nature neither he nor Purcell anticipated. Yet the reaction against Bedini from German nationalists and radicals in Cincinnati would have been similar, given ongoing struggles in Europe and America. Reaction to Bedini's visit, while overlapping with Know-Nothingism, continued the anticlerical struggles of the Italian Risorgimento and anticipated the German nationalist Kulturkampf against Catholicism. Nor did the squalid circumstances of Eggerling's death in a street brawl with police diminish its significance in the eyes of his comrades.

Cincinnati's election of 1855 marked a nadir of sectarian relations in the city and across the country. Stoking national anti-Catholicism, the *Boston Bee* alleged that Bishop Purcell had flaunted a list of names in front of local Democratic bigwigs, demonstrating his control of some 6,200 Catholic votes.[128] In the wake of the Bedini riot, one resident complained that Cincinnati was "in a state of wild anarchy" and conditions for fellow Catholics had declined. Even the Democratic city government pandered to nativist bigotry. "They have disbanded all Catholic & foreign laborers who were at work on the new court house," he wrote, "and advertised for 350 hands—'Protestants and Americans preferred.' This is throwing a firebrand into society."[129]

The shrill tone of Cincinnati's nativist press encouraged the violence that erupted on polling day. Even when papers such as Taylor's *Daily Times* called for restraint, the tone was disingenuous. In the weeks leading into the April election, Taylor urged his supporters in emphatic uppercase to "VOTE EARLY! . . . BE VIGILANT! . . . STAY AT THE POLLS! . . . RALLY YOUR FRIENDS!" and "BEWARE OF LYING POSTERS!" that were "put out to catch simpletons and credulous people." Above all, he told them to "KEEP COOL!" and to be "conciliating, pacific, and slow to anger."[130]

Levelheadedness was never Taylor's hallmark. In print, he complained of the "strange combination" arrayed against him and the American Party. From his description, this conspiracy included every unlikely stripe: "leading Whigs, with the remnant of the Old-Line Democratic party . . . the Romish Church, with the German Freemen—a combination of every degree of foreign influence."[131] Taylor's denunciation of German Freemen was particularly odd, accusing the same émigré fraternity that protested Bedini's arrival in Cincinnati of siding with the Catholic Church. It is tempting to infer that one immigrant was as foreign as any other to the average Know-Nothing, who perceived that America was unraveling amid organized foreign immigration and invisible cabals of disparate factions.

Come the election, fighting between Know-Nothings and Irish and German immigrants left many injured and several killed. Several ballot boxes were destroyed in the eleventh and twelfth wards, bastions of the German Catholic vote. The result was nevertheless a declared triumph for Democratic candidate James J. Faran.

Pap Taylor's run for mayor was a fiasco, leading to three days of anarchy. His supporters assaulted immigrants and Catholics, attacking German neighborhoods and harrying police. Know-Nothings were aided and abetted by Kentucky ruffians, who mysteriously showed up at the polls at election day. Characteristically, the city papers gave only vague casualty numbers. The day after the election saw a dramatic invasion of Over-the-Rhine, checked by the hastily mustered German militia companies. A single artillery shot repelled the incursion, aimed above the heads of armed nativists storming the canal bridge over Vine Street. This immigrant demonstration of Second Amendment rights dispersed the nativists, though straggling rowdies roamed the streets in search of softer victims.

Cincinnati's riots were part of a wider spasm of ethnic and sectarian disorder tied to nationwide elections in 1855. In nearby Louisville, locals remembered "Bloody Monday," when over twenty were killed and hundreds were wounded in an anti-Catholic protest through the city's German district—a casualty rate eclipsing that of the Queen City.[132] The following year, fourteen died amid sectarian clashes in the Irish wards of Baltimore; similar incidents were common in every major immigrant city.[133] Nevertheless, Cincinnati's strategic location at the crossroads of the Ohio Valley magnified incidents of violence, imprinting them in the minds of foreigners recently arrived in America. Writing in broken English from Rockford, Connecticut, to his German family in 1855, for example, immigrant factory worker Martin Weitz illustrated anxieties prevailing among the German diaspora. He described "serious fighting . . . in the state of Ohio, in Cincinnati there was a blood-bath, the Germans won, there were many dead and wounded on both sides. The *Jenkeamerikaner* [Yankees], they call themselves *Nounorthing* yankees, they want to have control, but [if] democracy wins, it looks like there's going to be a revolution."[134]

Accustomed to political violence in their homeland, German immigrants like Weitz might imagine the worst, witnessing bloody upheavals on their American doorstep. Yet the ethnic violence of the 1850s should be seen in context. Though deadly, the Know-Nothing riots paled in comparison to other outbreaks in the city, notably the antiblack riots of 1829. Cincinnati was hardly an aberration in terms of unrest, viewed alongside eastern cities such as New York and Philadelphia. And for many German immigrants, the Queen City remained welcoming: "Here in Cincinnati," boasted one newcomer, "[we] have such good food and drink like the best burgher in Lengerich."[135]

Cincinnati was a focus of nativism in the United States, but the rise of Know-Nothingism pointed to a broader national crisis of political authority, brought about by the implosion of the Whig Party. Historians identify the Kansas-Nebraska Act of 1854 as the trigger of this collapse, which furthered discord over the question of slavery in America's territories and its legitimacy in admitting new states. Cincinnati Whigs quickly denounced the Kansas-Nebraska legislation, authored by the mercurial Chicago politician Stephen Douglas (cosponsor of the 1850 Compromise). The act abolished the 1820 Missouri Compromise (excluding slavery north of the 36th parallel), replacing existing law with the principle of "popular sovereignty," a euphemism for devolving federal power to popular referenda in the admission of prospective states such as Kansas and Nebraska. By allowing citizens a free vote over slavery in their state constitutions, noted the *Daily Gazette*, this law threatened sectional strife. As well as promising "a renewal of the slavery agitation," it struck at the heart of the Whig Party and its constitutional ideals, violating "a solemn compact made more than thirty years ago between the free and the slave States, a compound with which is indissolubly bound the great name of HENRY CLAY."[136] Protest as they might, Whigs were torn between North and South, slavery and free-soil factions. The door was open for a new national party combining nativist and anti-Catholic sentiment with free-soil, anti-Kansas-Nebraska politics.

The demise of the venerable Whig Party—hastened by the deaths of elder statesmen Daniel Webster and Henry Clay in 1852 and the party's disastrous showing in the presidential election that year—signaled open season for American voters. Know-Nothingism attracted many Cincinnatians as a rejoinder to the "Old Fogeyism," or unreconstructed Federalism, embodied by mainline Whigs. Nativists accused the Whig establishment of pandering to Catholics in the elections of 1852 and enabling the erosion of republican institutions, notably public schools. At the same time, the Know-Nothings regarded all politics with feverish mistrust. Their state platform promised deliverance from "the blighting influence of Papacy, Priestcraft, and Kingcraft" while adding that "there shall henceforth and forever more be no Slave States."[137]

"Americanism and Freedom are synonymous terms," declared Ohio Know-Nothing leader Thomas Spooner. "Foreignism and slavery are equally so, and one is the antipodes of the other."[138]

Under Spooner's presidency, membership of the Ohio order reached "epidemic" proportions. Between October 1854 and June 1855 alone, Spooner boasted that Know-Nothing membership in his home state had grown 160 percent from 50,000 to 130,000 members, organized into over one thousand chapters.[139] Incredibly, Ohio Know-Nothings counted themselves almost double the entire Catholic population of the Diocese of Cincinnati. Despite their expansion, however, they struggled to translate popularity into lasting success. The failure to communicate a clear message doomed the American Party and Know-Nothingism, just as it had doomed the Whigs. The Republican Party emerged as the natural successor to both the Whigs and the Know-Nothings, embodying a more coherently free-soil ideology than the former while tempering the xenophobic excesses of the latter. By appealing to the ideological center in the North and Midwest, the Republicans secured a broad coalition opposing slavery, secession, and intemperance. Yet for all their moral high ground, Republicans reflected common prejudices. Lincoln detested Know-Nothings and other nativists but kept his criticisms private for fear of alienating a core constituency.[140] And the Republican platform of 1856 declared "the duty of Congress to prohibit in the territories those twin relics of barbarism, polygamy and slavery."[141] The former institution was the preserve of the Latter-day Saints, precariously ensconced under the federal jurisdiction of Utah. While most Republicans saw polygamy as sinful, its practice remained widespread among the Mormons, America's most persecuted religious minority. Identification of polygamy with the evils of slavery therefore revealed the Republican Party as a complex vehicle, with multiple concerns and prejudices.

While Lincoln became the national face of the Republican Party, much credit belonged to his Cincinnati ally, Salmon Portland Chase. Born in New Hampshire, Chase was orphaned in 1817 and grew up in Cincinnati with his uncle Philander Chase, Episcopal bishop of Ohio. Before entering politics as a Cincinnati councilor in 1840, Chase was a radical attorney, defending runaway slaves and abolitionists such as Birney. Between early years as a Whig and joining the Republicans, Chase affiliated with various antislavery parties and factions, notably the Liberty Party (led by Birney) and the Free Soil Party (fusing Whigs and Liberty Party members with antislavery Democrats). Such shifting alliances indicated the chaos in which Know-Nothingism rose and fell and the Republican Party was born. Although his abolitionism was an electoral liability, Chase's massive intellect and deal-making skills enabled his rise as Ohio's Republican governor in 1855 and United States senator for Ohio in 1860 (resigning soon thereafter to become Lincoln's secretary of the treasury). Second only to Lincoln, Chase was the most brilliant Republican statesman. Like Lincoln he was also capable of Machiavellian ruthlessness, despite his antislavery convictions.

With characteristic bluntness, Chase advised Oran Follett, Republican editor of the *Ohio Columbian*, how best to appeal to Protestant Ohioans: "It would be better if you admitted that there was some ground for the uprising of the people against papal influences & organized foreignism, while you might condemn the secret organization & indiscriminate proscription on account of origin or creed." A fellow Republican, Ohio senator Benjamin Wade, echoed Chase, condemning the intrigue of Catholic clergy and immigrants as "justly censurable & calculated to provoke the hostility which has embodied itself in the Know Nothing organization."[142] Nativism, then, if not always condoned by Ohio Republicans, was ripe for their apologies.

As the *New York Tribune*'s Horace Greeley foretold, Know-Nothingism was "as devoid of the elements of permanence as an anti-Cholera or anti-Potato rot party would be."[143] But despite its spectacular efflorescence in the 1850s, Know-Nothingism was subsumed by the rise of the Republican Party and the cataclysm of the Civil War, becoming just one more convolution in the ever-evolving American party system.

The last words in this chapter belong to John Baptist Purcell, whose defense of toleration promoted Catholic assimilation in Cincinnati. "Our civil constitution," he wrote, "grants perfect liberty to every denomination of Christians. . . . I verily believe this was infinitely better for the Catholic religion, than were it the special object of the state's patronage and protection . . . all we want is a fair field and no favor. Truth is mighty and will prevail."[144] Anti-Catholics, however, found much that seemed intrinsically anti-American. Though papal infallibility was not enshrined as doctrine until the First Vatican Council (1869–1870), its idea had long been debated within the Catholic Church. Critics, including the Protestant controversialist Alexander Campbell, invoked the audacity of this idea to tarnish the faith. But Purcell would have none of it. Challenged by Campbell in the fall of 1836 to publicly defend the authority of the Catholic Church, the bishop accepted, engaging in a well-publicized and fiercely contested series of debates hosted by the Baptist Church on Sycamore Street from January 13 to 21, 1837. Purcell spent much effort denouncing the heresy of Martin Luther but spared some breath on his own account. "No enlightened Catholic," Purcell asserted, "holds the Pope's infallibility to be an article of faith. I do not; and none of my brethren, that I know of, do. The Catholic believes the Pope, as a man, to be as liable to error, as almost any other man in the universe. Man is man, and no man is infallible, either in doctrine or morals."[145] Though essentially a stalemate (both sides claiming victory), the Purcell-Campbell debates were as much public entertainment as theological interrogation, driven by "the novelty of a Roman Catholic bishop occupying a Protestant pulpit."[146]

It would be misleading to represent Purcell in simple terms as a Jeffersonian democrat, although few spoke as eloquently for the Americanist wing of his church. With his elevation in 1850, he attained the rank of Catholic archbishop. While his private opinions were one thing, his public opinions rested exclusively—in theory at least—on church doctrine. That said, the issues were all too pressing to be resolved outside the political sphere. Chief among them was the question of education. As the Catholic Church grew, schoolhouses became as much a part of Cincinnati's landscape as houses of worship. The parochial system not only coexisted with public schools but actively competed with them. While public education was nominally secular, as noted, both defenders and detractors of public schools saw them as de facto Protestant institutions. No question in Cincinnati became more controversial than mandatory scripture readings and what form (if any) religious instruction should take in the classroom.

5

"A Young Empire of Mind"

Education and the Bible War

Religion, morality, and knowledge being necessary to good
government and the happiness of mankind, schools and the means
of education shall forever be encouraged.

—THE NORTHWEST ORDINANCE (1787)

On September 28, 1869, an immense crowd swelled into the auditorium of Pike's Music Hall in downtown Cincinnati. "In numbers; in deep intense feeling; in earnest, bounding enthusiasm, and more than all, in character," reported the *Cincinnati Gazette*, "it was one of the most remarkable that ever assembled." Not since the Civil War, when patriotic Cincinnatians "lost all thought of old antagonism," was such apparent unanimity on display. Advance notice of the meeting had been placed in the local press and announced in the Protestant pulpits of the city three days earlier. The *Daily Commercial* reported that "the main hall, both galleries, and all the aisles and lobbies were densely packed, the rush being so great that hundreds of people failed to gain even standing room." Hundreds more people were turned away for want of space. The crowd included men and women of "all classes of society" and "[n]early every religious denomination."[1]

What inspired such passion? The issue that animated the Pike's Hall protestors was no less than the use of the Protestant King James Bible in the city's public schools. The controversy became known as "the Bible War" and shaped understanding of the boundaries between church and state in the United States. What, if anything, was the role of religious education in state-supported common schools? Should students be assigned the Bible as holy scripture or merely an instructional resource? What was the proper place of sectarian instruction in a republic? To understand how the Bible question evolved in its urban context, this chapter first considers the formation of education in Cincinnati, a development rooted in the religious landscape.

Foundations of Education

In its bill of rights, the Northwest Ordinance (1787) encouraged "schools and the means of education" but did not require future states to supply public education.[2] The idea of free public education had yet to germinate when Ohio's state constitution (1803) promoted the right of education for all, asserting "that no law shall be passed to prevent the poor in the several counties and townships within this state from an equal participation in the schools, academies, colleges, and universities within this state." The constitution linked this right of education to "a natural and indefeasible right to worship Almighty God according to the dictates of conscience," stating that because "religion, morality and knowledge [are] necessary to good government and the happiness of mankind, schools and the means of instructions shall forever be encouraged by legislative provisions not inconsistent with the rights of conscience."[3] Such optimism anticipated a flourishing educational landscape, but without the catalyst of sectarian competition, its realization took decades to emerge.

Cincinnati's commercial origins on the Ohio River encouraged bold ambition but only modest growth in education at first. Like other western cities, however, the Queen City depended on cultural growth to attract immigration. As early visitors observed, lots were cleared for the construction of churches before anything else.[4] Formal schooling, presumably, would follow in the footsteps of an educated ministry drawn to the urban frontier. Meanwhile, some modest private attempts filled the gap. An Irish schoolmaster named Lloyd established the first log cabin school near the public landing in 1792. Another teacher, one "Mr. Stuart," opened a second school two years later.[5] Early newspapers advertised popular demand for education. One subscriber in 1801, for example, offered to instruct "a few boys in the *Latin* and *Greek* languages, and some other parts of literature nearly connected with them." The would-be schoolmaster apologized, however, that the opening of his school was delayed for want of "suitable books" and that he could accept no more than six students.[6]

Unsurprisingly, given its stalling first steps, Ohio trailed its more established southern neighbor in promoting learning. In April 1800, for example, the Commonwealth of Kentucky underwrote an academy at Newport, facing Cincinnati across the river, where students could learn "reading, writing and arithmetic, at eight dollars per annum." The first president of the Newport

Academy was Rev. Robert Stubbs, an Episcopal minister.[7] This early endeavor drew no sharp distinctions between the pulpit and the classroom at a time when most educators were clergymen. Kentucky's Catholic Church also played a key role, with the introduction of female religious orders including the Sisters of Loretto (1812), the Sisters of Charity of Nazareth (1812), and the Dominican Sisters at Springfield (1822). These sisterhoods became synonymous with teaching, as well as health care and other social services, and their proximity to Cincinnati proved significant.[8]

Not until 1815 did Cincinnati boast an educational flagship beyond the small-scale private schoolhouse ubiquitous to the region. After much campaigning, Presbyterian minister Joshua Lacy Wilson realized his ambition of establishing a school based on the fashionable Lancaster Seminary model imported from industrial England. Local subscriptions contributed some $12,000, including generous donations from prominent citizens such as General William Lytle and Judge Jacob Burnet. As with many civic enterprises, the Lancaster (or Lancastrian) Seminary developed under religious aegis, in this case led by the Presbyterian and Methodist Churches. Not everyone endorsed the scheme, however, despite being promised "an assemblage of schools, in one edifice, where a child may enter in its alphabet, and come out with an education equal to that afforded by many of our colleges."[9]

Higher education in Cincinnati began in 1819, the year of the Queen City's incorporation. Chartering Daniel Drake's Medical College of Ohio, the state legislature also elevated the Lancastrian Seminary as the first "literary institution" in the city (thereafter known as Cincinnati College). The 1819 *Cincinnati Directory* noted this college was "not yet in complete operation" but emphasized its geographical advantages. "It must be obvious to every one acquainted with the Western Country," wrote the editor, "that Cincinnati is a very eligible situation for a seat of learning. Its location on the Ohio renders the communication with distant parts of the country easy and frequent. It is a healthy, populous city, and can afford the wealth and talents necessary to endow and foster an institution of the kind." With the selection of "learned and liberal-minded professors" and the establishment of "proper discipline," Cincinnati College promised "to rival the colleges of the East."[10]

Like other ventures in the Ohio Valley, Cincinnati College's fortunes were short lived. The institution enjoyed generous support from boosters of the Lancaster Seminary but struggled to enroll students. Its governance reflected a Presbyterian bias under the presidency of Rev. Elijah Slack, a former professor of chemistry at Princeton University. Faculty included the ubiquitous Joshua Lacy Wilson, who taught logic and moral philosophy, apparently without compensation.[11] Despite its aspirations, Cincinnati College was overly ambitious, given the nascent educational demands of the Queen City. The institution folded in 1826 amid financial troubles, but expectations persisted that Cincinnati would become a major seat of learning.

Cincinnati's commercial growth made demand for schooling inevitable; less certain was the form this schooling would take. The idea of publicly funded common schools originated in the early nineteenth century with New England reformers such as Horace Mann and Henry Barnard, becoming fashionable in the reform-minded city. Nevertheless, progress was lackadaisical. Hoping to stimulate education, the State of Ohio passed a law in 1825 requiring an annual one-half-mill property tax to provide "instruction of youth of every grade and class without distinction, in reading, writing, arithmetic, and other necessary branches of common education."[12] That same year, Cincinnati created "The Board of Trustees and Visitors" (officially renamed "The Board of Education" in 1868). The board's foundation pointed toward future policy, even if there were not yet any schools for its members to govern or visit. Four years later, in 1829, the city established its school district as "The Common Schools of Cincinnati."[13]

Less is known about Cincinnati's first common schools, which began in 1829 after the city charter was amended to provide for taxpayer-funded education. Their earliest embodiment was a pair of unassuming buildings housing seventy to eighty students in total: one by Sycamore and Fifth Streets, the other by the river near the future site of the city waterworks. In 1831 Cincinnati's oldest extant public school, Woodward High School, opened its doors, promising a "higher" or more comprehensive curriculum. Even with the establishment of the city school district, some forty years after the first white settlers in Ohio, private bequests and subscription funded most common schools. Organization of resources was painfully slow. In December 1824, for example, eccentric local farmer Thomas Hughes bequeathed twenty-seven acres "for the education of poor, destitute children whose parents are unable to pay for their schooling." The school that bore his name would not open until March 1845, twenty years after his death.[14] Above all, the quality of public schools was mixed. An early report declared them "poorly lighted and situated in unhealthful localities, and . . . patronized by those only who had not the means to study elsewhere."[15] To supporters, however, they were cornerstones of civilization. "Although they have not yet realized all the anticipations of their enlightened and patriotic founders," reported the Board of Education in 1833, "in a soil lately rescued from the savage, and among a people gathered from every clime, (scarcely even amalgamated in the use of a common language,) these noble institutions are yet slowly but surely advancing."[16]

Catholic Competition

Makeshift as it was, public education was spurred by the arrival of Catholic competition. Cincinnati's first Catholic seminary opened in May 1829, predating the city's public school by several months. Bishop Fenwick, a Dominican, named this institution after St. Francis Xavier, cofounder of the Society of Jesus. On the face of it, this was an odd choice. No Jesuits operated in Cincinnati at the time, but in dedicating the seminary, Fenwick signaled his determination to recruit Jesuit teachers, an ambition fully realized by his successor, Purcell. The choice of patron for the city's first Catholic seminary alarmed many Protestants, given the Jesuits' image as shock troops of the Catholic Church. The diocese went on to establish its first parochial and religious schools in the city, beginning with the St. Peter Academy in the fall of 1829. Governed by the newly transplanted Sisters of Charity, the first permanently founded tuition-free school in the state was yet another alarm bell to Cincinnati's nativists.[17]

The growth of Catholic schooling in Cincinnati reflected a more assertive national leadership within the church. In 1829, as Cincinnati's first public and Catholic schools were founded, James Whitfield, archbishop of Baltimore, convoked a series of provincial councils to consolidate the American Catholic hierarchy. Bishop Fenwick, for one, applauded this move, trusting that "much good . . . will be effected, many salutary regulations adopted, abuses corrected, and uniformity adopted."[18] The First Provincial Council advised Fenwick and other American prelates on various issues, but especially education: "Since it is evident that many of the young, the children of Catholic parents, especially the poor, have been exposed and are still exposed . . . to great danger of the loss of faith or the corruption of morals, on account of the lack of such teachers as could safely be intrusted with so great an office, we judge it absolutely necessary that [Catholic] schools should be established."[19] With ensuing decades of Catholic immigration, such demands only grew.

Fenwick's successor, John Baptist Purcell, rose to national attention as a spokesman for Catholic parochial education. His influence reflected the growth of American Catholicism, now established as the nation's largest denomination. Following the creation of additional archdioceses in St. Louis (1847), New Orleans (1850), New York (1850), and Cincinnati (1850), the Plenary (formerly Provincial) Council at Baltimore spoke with amplified authority on behalf of the American church. In an 1852 pastoral letter, the archbishop of Baltimore urged Catholic parents to "give your children a Christian education, that is an education based on religious principles, accompanied by religious practices and always subordinate to religious influence. Be not led astray by false and delusive theories. . . . Listen not to those who would persuade you that religion can be separated from secular instruction."[20]

Purcell's elevation gave him authority over the suffragan dioceses of Cleveland, Detroit, Louisville, and Vincennes, and between 1852 and 1866, he convened his own series of Provincial Councils at Cincinnati. There he asserted the rights of Catholic parents to demand religious instruction for their sons and daughters and warned against the perils of public education. Cautioning his flock, Purcell outlined "our most sacred and our most solemn duty to rear up children in the knowledge, fear, and love of God," warning that since "religious training is not possible in the Public Schools as at present organized and conducted, our children are necessarily excluded from them as effectively as they would be by locks and bolts."[21]

Antebellum public schools in the Queen City and their Catholic parochial competitors jostled for cultural influence, not to mention enrollment and retention. In 1832, when Lyman Beecher came to Cincinnati, just 2,252 students attended the city's common schools, founded three years before. By 1850, when he returned to New England, public enrollment had risen to 11,544. This enrollment continued to rise, by 1875 numbering 27,822.[22] But the parochial system was catching up. By 1848, ten Catholic schools operated in Cincinnati, educating some two thousand students. On the eve of the Bible War in 1869, that number had risen to twelve to fifteen thousand parochial students, gaining on the public schools' tally of nineteen thousand students. Catholic schools thus became the catalyst for development in the educational landscape.[23]

In *A Plea for the West* (1835), Lyman Beecher warned of "floods of pauper emigrants . . . filling our prisons, and crowding our poorhouses," but it was the schoolhouse and not the poorhouse that most concerned Cincinnati nativists and Catholics alike.[24] As competition between parochial and public schools mounted, sectarianism intensified. In 1848, the *Western Christian Advocate* warned readers that the Jesuits planned to open a free primary school in the city "to pervert the minds of the poor, as they now do the children of the wealthy in their higher seminaries."[25] Prominent Catholic convert Don Piatt rejoindered that public schools were "the devil's nurseries" and taught students to "commit murder for five dollars."[26] Meanwhile Rev. Charles Peabody, Cincinnati agent of the American Tract Society, hoped that common schools would check parochial education in the Ohio Valley. "Presbyterian influence then, must of course predominate," he predicted. "Romanism . . . cannot grow except in the soil of ignorance. I see in the presentation of common schools—in the growing intelligence of the people—in the habits of independent thinking in this western country, a fatal barrier against the influence of Rome."[27]

Those like Peabody who hoped public education might extinguish Catholic influence were disappointed. The high numbers of Protestant students in the parochial system (a majority in some schools) testified to its reputation of excellence.[28] Education furnished both sorely needed income and valuable propaganda: "One of the chief consolations of the Catholic community of this city," declared the *Telegraph*, "is derived from the immense number of children who are receiving a thorough Catholic education in our flourishing schools."[29]

As enrollments suggested, Catholics heeded the clergy's calls to keep their children in parochial schools, where they increasingly encountered Protestant peers. Despite sectarian loyalties, outright separation of Catholic and public education was not yet regarded as inevitable, while the church still had a voice on the city's public school board. In 1869, for example, ten of the thirty-seven board members were Catholic—hardly a token representation.[30] And as his later utterances indicated, Archbishop Purcell hoped the public school system might accommodate Catholic demands. When objections proved insurmountable, however, the doors of public education closed on the Catholic Church, just as Purcell had feared. Use of the King James Bible in the public schools proved a stumbling block for integration.

"A Young Empire of Mind": Beecher, McGuffey, and "Unsectarian" Religion

Education was key to Protestant and Catholic conceptions of national character and good citizenship, but it was also ambivalent, capable of instilling both cultural integration and fostering ethnic and sectarian separatism. Cincinnati's Catholic Church trod cautiously, viewing public schools as competition but still seeking dialogue with the city's Board of Education. If the common schools enrolled Catholic children, church leaders reasoned, Cincinnati Catholics should enjoy some say over access to funding and other issues. By contrast, many Protestants and nativists regarded public education as a bulwark against the influence of Rome. They warned that Catholic schools were designed less to educate than to indoctrinate the children of Protestant families.

Sectarian tensions between Catholic and Protestant in Cincinnati were more cultural than theological. Upheavals caused by overseas immigration raised questions of identity and assimilation, moreover, for which education provided the only plausible solutions. Lyman Beecher stated the case with typical force in *A Plea for the West*: "If we do not provide the schools which are requisite for the cheap and effectual education of the children of the nation," he wrote, "it is perfectly certain that the Catholic powers of Europe intend to make up the deficiency."[31] Echoing his father-in-law the following year, Lane Seminary professor Calvin Stowe warned: "Unless we educate our immigrants, they will be our ruin." Emphasizing the value of English language instruction and patriotism, Stowe deemed it "altogether essential to our national strength and peace, if not our national existence, that foreigners who settle on our soil, should cease to be Europeans and become Americans."[32]

The sort of education Beecher and Stowe envisioned was nonsectarian but hardly secular. It flattened distinctions between religion and ethnicity, transmuting civic republicanism into the sort of homogenized Protestantism that defined Manifest Destiny. Its representative text (besides the King James Bible) was *McGuffey's Eclectic Reader*, first issued in 1835 by Cincinnati publishing house Truman & Smith. These inexpensive readers were the brainchild of William Holmes McGuffey, a Miami University professor, Presbyterian minister, and colleague of Lyman Beecher. McGuffey moved on from Miami in 1836 as president of Cincinnati College (forerunner of today's University of Cincinnati) and in 1839 was appointed president of Ohio University in the southeastern part of the state.[33] Despite his relative transience in the Queen City, his *Readers* were a direct product of Cincinnati's assertive Presbyterian evangelicalism. Popular in every state, they shaped the educational culture of the nation for generations to come. Blending memorable but didactic verse, generically Calvinist morality, and strident nationalism, they cemented popular Protestant identification of Christianity with secular republican values. Just as Presbyterian historians rebranded the colonial revivals of eighteenth-century New England the First Great Awakening, McGuffey's books centered the faith of the Pilgrims and their Puritan contemporaries. "Every settler's hearth was a school of independence," declared one passage, "the scholars were apt, and the lessons sunk deeply; and thus it came that our country was always free; it could not be other than free."[34]

For all their nostalgia, the success of the *Eclectic Readers* (122 million copies sold in various editions from 1836 to 1920) confirmed the Queen City as a flourishing center of publishing, commerce, and cultural influence. In his preface to the 1838 revised edition, Cincinnati publisher Winthrop Smith even noted that some New England textbook publishers were seeking legal redress, "aggrieved that our books contained a portion of matter similar to our own." This early example of copyright litigation prompted Smith to complain that his competitors wished "not only to force their own books in the Western market, but to wrest from Western talent, and Western enterprise, the legitimate fruits of preserving [sic] toil."[35] Such grievances suggested the influence of geographic sectionalism in antebellum educational publishing, just as major local markets still dominate the textbook industry today.[36]

Questions of sectarian identity were inseparable from the sectional politics of the early American republic. While many northern Protestants identified slavery with the Catholic Church, anti-Catholicism focused more on the West, seen as more vulnerable to foreign corruption. Fears proliferated that the Catholic Church was conspiring to make Cincinnati the Vatican of the New World, even that the Ohio Valley might secede from the United States under Catholic influence. When the *Eclectic Reader* came out just four years after Lyman Beecher's arrival in Cincinnati, tensions in the Ohio Valley between Protestants and Catholics rivaled those stirred by race and slavery—doubly so for Beecher and McGuffey, who, in addition to sharing the same publisher, shared backgrounds and beliefs concerning the millennial destiny of the United States.

In *A Plea for the West*, Beecher depicted immigration as a hindrance to the salvation of mankind. "The religious and political destiny of our nation is to be decided in the West," he warned. "There is the territory, and there will soon be the population, the wealth, and the political power." Though Beecher dreaded Catholicism, he remained optimistic—in fact, intoxicated—by opportunities for growth and salvation. "The West," he declared, "is a young empire of mind, and power, and wealth, and free institutions, rushing up to a giant manhood." Above all, he insisted, "the destiny of the West will be a conflict of institutions," adding: "I am pressing upon republican America that it is better for her to educate her population by her own sons and money, than to rely on the school masters and charitable contributions of the despotic governments of Europe."[37]

The challenge was daunting, but Beecher remained convinced that German and Irish immigrants could assimilate. "Let the Catholics mingle with us as Americans," he insisted, "and come with their own children under the full action of our common schools and republican institutions . . . and we are prepared cheerfully to abide the consequences."[38] Clearly, public schools loomed large in the struggle for hearts and minds, though they remained, in his mind, *our* schools—Protestant in all but name. Their values were steeped in the Bible, their ideology American Christianity writ large. What better vessels for such an education than the *Eclectic Readers*, penned by his friend

McGuffey? Introducing one edition, Beecher proclaimed himself "not a little gratified to know that our youth have access to so perfect a series of Reading Books. They are excellent for educational purposes—their religion is *unsectarian*, true religion—their morality the morality of the gospel."[39]

The Western Literary Institute and College of Professional Teachers: A Lens on Antebellum Cincinnati

Education was the arena in which Cincinnati's sectarian tensions most intensified, witnessed by the rise and fall of the influential Western Literary Institute and College of Professional Teachers (W.L.I.C.P.T.). Although the W.L.I.C.P.T. was intended as a forum for ecumenical dialogue, such dialogue brought unintended consequences. Historian Daniel Aaron identified the association as "the greatest single influence in shaping Cincinnati's educational policies and, indeed, the educational policies for the Ohio Valley."[40] Founded in 1831 to encourage cultural and educational interests, the W.L.I.C.P.T. sought to improve teaching standards and foster dialogue on education west of the Appalachians. This association was short lived, but it united educators, clergy, and literary authors from across sectarian boundaries in the belief that "the glory of this age is its educational spirit." In addition to John Baptist Purcell, who was most active in his membership, the W.L.I.C.P.T. included such luminaries as Lyman Beecher, Alexander Campbell, Calvin Stowe, Daniel Drake, Catherine Beecher, and Lydia Sigourney.[41]

Nothing better indicated the progress of society than who was welcomed and who was excluded. Female education, especially, indicated cultural and economic growth. The prominence of women highlighted the W.L.C.I.P.T.'s progressive ethos, education being one field where gender boundaries yielded to change. Education of immigrants, especially German speakers, was also a priority. But the W.L.C.I.P.T. was socially and racially exclusive and jealous of its prestige. To the extent that nativists such as Beecher and Campbell found common ground with the Catholic Church, it lay in their conviction that leadership was the prerogative of social elites. Under the umbrella of the W.L.I.C.P.T., considerations of gender, race, and ethnicity thus shaped the educational politics of Cincinnati and the Ohio Valley. These politics, in turn, reflected conflicts among elites, torn between paternalistic attitudes and the shifting foundations of a commercial, multiethnic, democratic society.

The annual *Transactions* of the W.L.I.C.P.T. revealed fine lines between paternalism and progress. In an "Essay on Female Education," local teacher Almira Phelps acknowledged "that intellectual enjoyments do, in some degree, cause a disrelish for the common toils of life, such as fall to the lot of most females." But, she insisted, "the same argument may be urged in relation to male education." What mattered more was "the vista of the future," in which "*female seminaries,* or institutions of a permanent and elevated character . . . must be regarded as a most important step." Such schools were "fast multiplying" in Cincinnati, she reported, and gaining such renown that "*Europe is now looking to us as pioneers in female education.*"[42]

Phelps recognized that academically rigorous instruction was once virtually unknown in Cincinnati but was becoming the norm. Nevertheless, the inroads of the Catholic Church heightened concern among many Protestant leaders, including W.L.I.C.P.T. stalwart Rev. David Root, Lyman Beecher's predecessor at the Second Presbyterian Church. Root wrote a colleague in 1830, expressing his alarm at the state of female schooling. "You know what the Papists are doing," he warned, "or trying to do; & you can easily foresee the probable consequences, if they should get this department of education into their hands." He called for "*immediate* efforts to establish [Protestant] schools for young ladies." He noted that such schools would lend "as much to moral, religious, & general character, as to intellectual culture."[43]

Traditional girls' schools focused on accomplishments such as needlework, dancing, French, and music, designed to enhance the eligibility of young unmarried women. These skills were taught in a variety of institutions, but many taught more rigorous offerings on the curriculum. These included the prestigious "Female Academy" founded by Dr. John Locke in 1823. Englishwoman Fanny Trollope visited the school's "annual public exhibition" five years later, encountering Dr. Locke, "a gentleman who appears to have enlarged and liberal opinions on the subject of female education." Trollope approved of Locke's pedagogy but expressed astonishment "that the higher branches of science were among the studies of the pretty creatures I saw assembled there." The curriculum included mathematics as well as moral philosophy. Trollope described the "method of letting young ladies graduate, and granting them diplomas on quitting the establishment," as "quite new to me."[44]

Much as Locke's academy startled Trollope with its bold curriculum, female education in the Queen City remained rooted in ideas of social order. Women were seen as the conscience of society and were disproportionately represented among the churchgoing population.[45] Many Protestants championed female education, regarding it as inoculation against both the pitfalls of enthusiasm and the allure of Roman Catholicism while bolstering ideals of feminine domesticity. John W. Pickett, coprincipal of a girls' academy in

Cincinnati, for example, delivered an 1836 address on "Female Education" to the W.L.I.C.P.T., elaborating upon the connection between religion and pedagogy:

> Since Christian revelation—that great charter of women's rights!—has pointed out her elevated duties, we can see no reason why the female mind should be trifled with; why instead of science, it should be taught to deal with gewgaws; why instead of thought, accurate and deep, it should be taught its opposite; and instead of devoting attention to the graces of mind and heart, it should be inducted into the follies of the passing day.[46]

Similarly, Protestant ministers including Lyman Beecher and Caleb Atwater (both active in the W.L.I.C.P.T.) promoted rigorous standards of female education. And while women were excluded from the clergy, education was one field in which women such as Catharine Beecher could minister with the approval of the church. Thus, Lyman Beecher's eldest daughter channeled her zeal into the Western Female Institute (1833), having previously established the Hartford Female Seminary in Connecticut (1823). She shared her father's enthusiasm on the Ohio Valley, regarding the region as "so capable of being rendered a Paradise."[47] And though not technically affiliated to the Lane Seminary, the Western Female Institute was identical in its missionary outlook, dedicated to transforming the American frontier in the image of Christ.

Education also provided women's leadership in the Catholic Church, albeit within a context of patriarchy. Female religious orders proliferated throughout the Queen City and its hinterlands. "Protestants are forced to acknowledge the solidity of instruction given by these ladies," wrote Bishop Purcell. "Consequently a goodly number of them have confided to them their children." These religious orders were behind every development in Catholic education, including coeducational parochial schools, Sunday schools, private all-girls boarding schools, and even adult education. The most significant orders in Cincinnati included the Sisters of Notre Dame de Namur (1840, arriving from Belgium), the Ursuline Sisters (1845), the Sisters of Charity (arriving 1850 and establishing seventeen schools in Ohio over the next two decades), and the Sisters of Mercy (1858). In addition to their role as educators, these women religious were central to Cincinnati's social infrastructure, providing health care, orphanages, and other charitable services.[48]

While Cincinnati educators, voluntary societies, and religious orders promoted female education, concern for the city's black population was lacking among white citizens. Policy underwrote indifference and hostility, excluding black children from public schools and denying black taxpayer representation from the common schools fund.[49] Admittedly, segregated schools were permitted under the 1829 charter amendment and could be funded using taxes from black citizens. Yet such schools required approval from the Ohio legislature, and state lawmakers consistently blocked the path forward. In the early 1830s, the State of Ohio snubbed a petition to fund a free black school in Cincinnati, despite acknowledging the heavy tax burden of black citizens. "The decision might," they wrote, "at first appear unnatural, and unbecoming a charitable, high-minded and intelligent community . . . [but] the security of our government rests in the morality, virtue, and wisdom of our free white citizens." In providing for the education of Ohioans, they clarified, "the common school fund is not the offspring of the offices of charity."[50]

Overt prejudice forced black Cincinnatians to rely on their own resources. Fanny Trollope was among those who observed the segregation of the Queen City, noting how the black population was "greater than the appearance of the town would lead one to expect . . . owing to the number of free Negroes who herd together in an obscure part of the city, called little Africa."[51] Such obscurity extended, naturally enough, to the schoolroom. The question of black education was hardly addressed in the proceedings of the W.L.I.C.P.T.. And when Purcell asked the archbishop of Baltimore, "Can anything be done . . . to provide for the religious instruction and general amelioration of the colored population of the United States?" he posed his question in the abstract, more concerned with an imagined end to slavery than the needs of free black Cincinnatians.[52] In a similar vein, the Lane rebels who scandalized Beecher in 1834 stirred more objection by teaching in the black community than by agitating for abolition.

Organized religion did little to redress imbalances of education. Most black churchgoers in Cincinnati identified as Protestant, belonging to segregated congregations. Though these churches supported education, they lacked the wealth and clout of the mainline Protestant congregations within the Benevolent Empire. White politicians, educators, and religious leaders neglected black Cincinnati. Some black churches were literally erased from maps printed in the Queen City.[53] Racial integration was little better from the Catholic Church. Although the *Telegraph* publicized instances of black converts, outreach was limited, and parochial schools were hardly less segregated than their public counterparts.[54]

The slow growth of Cincinnati's black population through the 1830s and 1840s reflected a city scarred by race riots in 1829 and limited access to social services, including education.[55] A handful of privately funded black schools operated through the 1830s, despite obstacles. One school met in the basement of a Baptist church on Western Row that was described as "cold, and damp, and out of repair."[56] Yet even this modest schoolhouse attracted local mobs. One eyewitness recalled: "The howling of the rowdies around the church, chiming with the rattling of the window shutters and the whistling of the winter winds through the vacant panes and cracks of the door, the rattle of stones and brickbats against the house, while the little ones within would gather up close to the teacher, and huddle closer together, trembling with fear and not knowing . . . whether to stay and await the fire of the assailants, or rush out and brave the curses of the drunken rabble."[57] Hostility to black education only compounded matters. Even when petitioning and legal challenges led the Ohio legislature to relent on the question of black public schools in 1849, provisions were far from equitable, resulting in segregated and underfunded "colored schools."[58]

Despite segregation and persecution, as historian Nikki Taylor argued, the situation for black Cincinnatians was not hopeless. Institutions such as the African American Episcopal Church on Sixth Street and Broadway "provided a platform for political action, a site for fellowship, and a place to fulfill the spiritual needs of the black community." Despite challenges of racism and underfunding, black private schools furnished additional resources to the black community. Years of oppression resulting from racial violence, Black Laws, exclusion from tax-funded services, and denial of citizenship bred resilience. By 1829, black Cincinnatians "were making strides toward self-determination" and laying down roots despite efforts to isolate them.[59] Nevertheless, the race riots of that year threw back these strides considerably. Though well below one thousand black citizens (2.6 percent of Cincinnati's population) were recorded in a city directory of 1834, its white editor passed no comment on their decline.[60]

In contrast to prevailing silence on black education, the schooling of immigrant children, especially Germans, inspired interest in the W.L.I.C.P.T. and beyond. "There are no less than 10,000 Germans in Cincinnati, and its immediate vicinity," noted Calvin Stowe in 1835, "including those only, who live so near the city as to attend church here on the Sabbath." Over two-thirds of these immigrants were Catholics, he emphasized. "Not more than a fourth part of them can speak English well, and many do not understand it at all." On top of language barriers, German children were "in many instances deterred from attending the English schools, because their foreign garb and accent expose them to the ridicule of the native scholars." Stowe applauded the efforts of students at Lane Seminary, who had spent the past two years running a Sunday school in Over-the-Rhine "instructing the German children in the English language, and the principles of the Christian religion."

(Unlike Lane students' earlier outreach to the black community, this project enjoyed official sanction.) According to their tutors, moreover, these young foreign students were "uncommonly apt at learning, and much more attentive than American children." Stowe advocated assimilation, insisting that children of German immigrants learn English in the common schools. "Now," he argued, "we have no choice left. These people are in our midst; they are coming among us more and more." Like his father-in-law, Stowe saw opportunity as well as dangers in immigration. Germans were industrious and intelligent. Their contributions could and should enrich the United States. "To sustain an extended republic like our own," he warned, however, "there must be a *national* feeling, a national assimilation."[61]

The rigid Anglicization championed by Stowe proved impracticable, but his concern for immigrant education was widely shared. Beginning in 1840, Cincinnati's Board of Education took up the challenge of expanding its services to the city's German population. Again, the public system fell behind parochial schools, which had offered German-language schooling since 1835. Cincinnati's first dedicated bilingual school, the German-English Primary School of the Catholic Church, enrolled 150 students in its first year on West Fifth Street, including "the children of many Protestant families." In response, the Presbyterian-led Emigrants' Friends Society (supported by Beecher) attempted to establish its own German-language school but struggled to compete with the ethnocentric outreach of the Catholic Church. After much lobbying, the Board of Education thus voted on August 3, 1840, to allow "schools to be organized to teach children of German parentage orthographie and grammar in their native language." The city's first German-English public school opened the following month in the basement of the North German Lutheran Church on Walnut Street. Its inauspicious location highlighted both the limited resources and continuing religious overtones of the new German schools.[62]

Heavy demand for German-language public schooling survived many challenges. By 1848 the Board of Education's corresponding secretary, Bellamy Storer, reported that German public schools were "among the most interesting and important departments of our system. They are thoroughly instructed and governed; the teachers and pupils are emulous to excel, and . . . that liberality of sentiment which should ever exist between the native and adopted citizen, is not only exhibited, but practically illustrated. Whatever doubts may have heretofore existed as to the policy of establishing these schools, there is now, we believe, no ground to indulge them." While such schools continued to expand, they labored under shortages of funds and faculty. An 1855 report counted 1,883 German-language public students in the city but only 18 teachers. Naturally, with some 105 students per teacher, rooms were "crowded to excess." Lacking pens and paper, many classes had only slates for writing. Several districts struggled to find qualified teachers. Little wonder they remained vulnerable to competition.[63]

Education was the key to success in nineteenth-century Cincinnati, its legacy passed down through generations. Issues of language, religion, and ethnicity influenced assimilation, but speaking German at home was no barrier to advancement in the classroom. Cincinnati Germans associated through a host of cultural, business, and sporting organizations, including singing societies, *Bauvereinen* (savings and loan societies), and rifle clubs, which nurtured a sense of ethnic belonging. But educational success ensured the emergence of German Cincinnatians as a respected community in the public sphere.[64] Barriers of race, by contrast, proved more problematic in this regard. Lack of educational opportunity, especially, ensured that black Cincinnatians faced an uphill struggle for decades to come.

Antebellum Discord

In the years leading up to the Civil War, sectarian tensions overshadowed the educational politics of Cincinnati. Admittedly, dialogue persisted. Bishop Purcell's membership of the W.L.I.C.P.T., for example, signaled his commitment to ecumenical ideals. Likewise, Cincinnati's Board of Education represented the city's ethnic and religious (if not racial) diversity, composed of Protestants and Catholics, Jews and freethinkers, native-born and immigrant citizens. And although many Cincinnatians regarded public education as a bulwark against Catholicism, Purcell hoped that Catholics and Protestants might seek common ground. Specifically, he hoped that parochial schools might receive subsidy from the common schools fund to which Catholic taxpayers contributed. In the 1840s, the consolidation of Catholic schools into the public system was even considered, though Catholics insisted their schools should maintain autonomy over religious curriculum and appointment of faculty. These outcomes seemed unlikely in retrospect, and their frustration produced a hardening of attitudes on both sides.

Even more than partisan politics, religious identity was crucial to social formation in antebellum Cincinnati. But among Cincinnati Catholics in particular, ethnic and ideological divisions complicated adherence to faith. Among the city's leading public figures, John Baptist Purcell embodied tensions between Americanized Catholicism and the all-encompassing, universal authority of Rome. Both sides of this equation were on display during the Purcell-Campbell controversy, the historic series of public debates that absorbed Cincinnatians in 1837. Purcell and his equally outspoken opponent, Alexander Campbell, were both natives of Ireland, born on opposing sides of the confessional divide. Both men were renowned orators in Cincinnati. Campbell resided in Bethany, Virginia, but the Queen City was practically his second home on the itinerant preaching circuit, as evidenced by his active involvement in the College of Teachers. Apparently, Campbell challenged Purcell to debate after hearing the latter's "tirade against the Protestant modes of teaching," including use of the King James Bible, before an audience at the W.L.I.C.P.T.[65]

Purcell and Campbell entertained antagonistic understandings of history. For Campbell, as for many Protestants in Cincinnati, the Reformation was not just a religious event but the foundation of liberty from which American democracy sprang. By contrast, he insisted that Roman Catholicism, "if infallible and insusceptible of reformation, as alleged, is essentially anti-American, being opposed to the genius of all free institutions, and positively subversive of them." He conceded to Purcell:

> In one sense, we both may be called foreigners; yet we are not foreigners in the same sense. I claim a very intimate sense with the Protestant family. I am one of that family. It was then my family, that first settled this country. The bishop's family settled Roman Catholic America. He is a foreigner here as I would be a foreigner in Mexico or South America.

Campbell's flagrant appeal to nativism undermined any semblance of civility. Though the authority of other religious faiths (including the city's growing Jewish minority) was not debated, he identified Protestantism with true Americanism, foreshadowing the xenophobia of the Know-Nothing movement of the 1850s.[66]

As the bishop of a mostly immigrant congregation, Purcell refused to be drawn into a nativistic slugging match. Instead, he appealed to history, arguing that the reforms of Martin Luther had yielded division and anarchy rather than republican liberty. Purcell disparaged "the disastrous principle of mental emancipation, so highly eulogized when it was first proclaimed, and received with so much enthusiasm, until it was found to be a very Babel of the confusion of all creeds." From this assertion, he concluded "that every society formed on Protestant principles, being essentially fallible, none should assert the inconsistent pretension of controlling faith by authority, or of regulating creeds, under pretense of superior wisdom."[67] While not quite conceding that America was a Protestant nation, Purcell insisted on the separation of church and state to maintain religion alongside republican democracy. By extension, Purcell's dual allegiance to the pope and the United States reflected this ideal of separation, rather than conflicting loyalties.

The Purcell-Campbell debate was a study in contrasts, highlighting the discourse of religion amid the growing "climate of distrust" in early Cincinnati.[68] By submitting to debate, Purcell acceded to the democratic spirit of his adopted city, but his defense of Catholicism was highly traditional, rooted in the Catholic Church's exclusive claims to legitimacy. Campbell, on the other hand, was unabashedly populist, at times calling directly on the audience for demonstrations of support. Campbell and Purcell both claimed victory from their debate, which foreshadowed controversies over the role of religion and religious authority in education. At the same time, both men agreed to split the proceeds from the copyright of the debate between Catholic and Protestant benevolent institutions in Cincinnati, advancing the work of religion in the life of the city.

As Campbell and Purcell jousted, the question of the King James Bible grew more contentious. Though well intentioned, the diverse composition of the W.L.I.C.P.T. and the city Board of Education only exacerbated sectarian politics. Once again, Purcell's involvement with the former group embroiled him in controversy following his debates with Campbell. At issue were two W.L.I.C.P.T. addresses defending the use of the King James Bible in the common schools: the first by Joshua Lacy Wilson and the second by Benjamin P. Aydelott, a local Episcopalian minister and president of Woodward College. Purcell took umbrage at the latter's insistence that assigning the King James Bible was the best means to promote religion in public schools. This led Purcell and Aydelott to engage in heated debate. Both men agreed to report on the Bible question to the W.L.I.C.P.T. in the fall of 1837. Purcell's submission marked his strongest criticism yet of the city school board, which he regarded as displaying an increasing "sectarian bias." In consequence, the bishop recommended what amounted to religious streaming within the public school system "that the students of different creeds be assembled together, to be instructed in the Bible and in their religious and moral duties generally, by their own pastors." Aydelott, by contrast, scoffed at such accommodation, insisting to the W.L.I.C.P.T. that the Bible should be taught unmediated and unexpurgated, by which he meant "the common English version, or that effected by the public authority in the reign of James the First."[69]

Purcell's exasperation with his Protestant colleagues only mounted. As he cautioned the archbishop of Baltimore the previous year: "If any of our city papers reach the Metropolis (of our Church)," he wrote, "you will perceive that I wd. not let their immense new lever, the Western Literary Institute & College of Teachers, have it all their own way this time."[70] He sensed, as Fenwick before him, that the city's Protestants were "united against the Catholics" and he came to regard the W.L.I.C.P.T. as just one more instrument of sectarian power.[71] More than ever he feared the ruinous effects of public education on Catholicism. Concern over cultural influence led him to establish the Roman Catholic Society for the Diffusion of Knowledge (1839), which aimed both to underwrite the *Catholic Telegraph* and to develop parochial education. "If the Society . . . is conducted with energy and wisdom," he wrote, "it will be the instrument of much good. I recommended to it the preparation of a suitable series of elementary and other school books, where the Catholic youth of our Church would see nothing to weaken their faith, or taint their morals, but much, on the contrary, to improve both."[72]

Purcell defended the separation of church and state, but like most nineteenth-century American separatists, his ideology was pragmatic. Despite dismay at the direction of public education, he remained committed (in theory at least) to cooperating with city schools. While advocating Catholic education for Catholic children, he lobbied for a portion of the common schools fund to be set aside for parochial schools. Against claims for common religion (or no religion) in the common schools, Purcell countered that Catholics had as much right to tax-funded education as any citizens. Intriguingly, the idea of partially consolidating the public and parochial schools was floated as early as June 1840, despite Purcell's ongoing concern surrounding use of the King James Bible. The Board of Education's annual report for that year especially identified "the Charity School supported by the Catholic Church, but not confined by any means to the children of Catholics," as a candidate for public merger. Though detailed discussion of consolidation was not included in the report, and the subject was dropped the following year, the authors confided that the Catholic Church might continue supplying faculty to the consolidated school. This, in turn, implied a continuing willingness to compromise across denominational bounds.[73]

The King James Bible remained a stumbling block to school integration. In 1842, Purcell lodged a formal objection to the Board of Education against the usage of Protestant scripture and the allegedly offensive content of other assigned textbooks. Surprisingly, the board responded with resolutions inviting the bishop "to examine the books used in English Common Schools, and the German Common Schools," and point out (but not necessarily censor) "all obnoxious passages." Even more strikingly, the board resolved "that no pupil of the Common Schools be required to read the Testament or Bible, if its parents or guardians request that it be excused from that exercise."[74] Whether or not these resolutions placated Purcell, neither apparently was put into practice.

In the summer of 1852, Dr. Jerome Mudd, a Catholic member of the city school board, revived the Bible question. Mudd introduced resolutions proposing that teachers be allowed free choice in the reading and assigning of different versions of scripture. He insisted that parents should have the last word on what version of the Bible—Protestant, Catholic, or Jewish—their children took to school. After some deliberation, the board chose to keep the King James Bible for exclusive use in the classroom. In summarizing its decision, the board insisted that public school students must be educated "in such a manner as to prepare them to protect and defend the laws and institutions. Our country is republican, morally, politically, and religiously."[75]

Stung by the Board of Education's implicit anti-Catholicism, the newly elevated Archbishop Purcell weighed in. In a pastoral letter of March 26, 1853, he railed against the charge that Catholicism was less republican, less democratic, and less American than other faiths and restated his commitment to working with the school board in good faith. Looking ahead to the city elections of 1853, however, he urged fellow Catholics to elect candidates "who will fairly represent the wishes and requirements of their constituents in the halls of legislation, the Council Chamber, and the School Board," even going so far as to recommend certain candidates standing "on the right side of the questions at issue."[76] This was a bold endorsement from an archbishop only too cognizant of the hostile climate in Cincinnati. Most strikingly, his hard line on the question of public schools resembled that of his New York counterpart and fellow Irishman John Hughes, a Catholic apologist with a flair for agitation.[77] Purcell concluded his letter in the third person, presumably to deflect accusations of political meddling: "We are only beginning to agitate these questions . . . [and] have never sought to influence the votes of Catholics."[78]

As the 1853 elections played out, Purcell looked on in dismay. Though this political cycle avoided the violence that broke out two years later, the same voices were raised. The question of school taxation grew in significance, one newspaper describing it as the "all-absorbing topic" of the spring campaign. James D. Taylor of the *Daily Times* ran on a "free school" ticket to oppose Catholic access to the common schools fund. Though a dark horse candidate, Taylor came second with 35 percent of the vote. Two other anti-Catholic candidates together scored around 25 percent of the remainder, ensuring the narrowest plurality for Democrat David Snelbaker. Moreover, Taylor's campaign underlined parallels between anti-Catholicism ("free schools") and antislavery ("free soil"). Mounting political opposition alarmed the archbishop and fellow Catholics. "We are in the midst of all manner of threats from all manner of Sects & infidels," Purcell wrote. "No one knows how soon they may ripen into open violent and prolonged persecution."[79]

"The Vexed School Question"

Only in light of the sectarian landscape of Cincinnati can the protest meeting at Pike's Music Hall be revisited. The protestors who clamored in 1869 for the King James Bible's restoration in public schools revealed the weight of religion in nineteenth-century Cincinnati. A series of preachers and lawyers addressed the audience at length. At stake, insisted local attorney Rufus King, was not merely the question of the Bible but whether the system of public schools could continue at all. The Bible was, he continued, "the corner-stone of our American institutions, as every man knows who has ever read the Declaration of Independence, or even the Constitution of our own State." Notwithstanding such questionable assertions, no one could doubt the protestors' faith in their Protestant religion and public institutions. In the two weeks since the Board of Education floated the idea of withdrawing the Bible, 8,713 citizens (some 4 percent of Cincinnati's population) had already petitioned the board. Public sentiment bolstered the Pike's Hall protest. "Does the reading of the Bible," asked speaker George R. Sage, "in simple decent recognition of its divine authority—reading it without note or comment—transform the school house into a church? Does it make the school house a place of worship? It costs nothing." Noting prayer at the 1787 Constitutional Convention in Philadelphia and religious invocations in the statehouse at Columbus, Sage echoed the sentiments of many: "This is a Christian land; ours is a Christian civilization. Whatever is commendable in our form of Government, or commendable in our social state, is due to the influence of the religion of Jesus Christ. Our seminaries of learning, our hospitals of mercy, our asylums for the distressed and the unfortunate, our common schools, are its offsprings and monuments."[80]

The protest at Pike's Hall garnered much attention but failed to perturb the anti-Bible wing of the Cincinnati Board of Education. On November 1, 1869, board members forged ahead with their proposed withdrawal of the King James Bible from the curriculum. Just two days later, in response, a group of thirty-seven Cincinnati citizens filed a petition with the Hamilton County Superior Court demanding an injunction. The plaintiffs noted "that the reading of the Holy Bible without note or comment" had been accepted practice since the city's first common school was founded in 1829 and complained that the board's new policy denied students "instruction in the elemental truths and principles of religion." They argued the prohibition would extend to "a large number of the textbooks" containing "selections and passages from the Holy Bible." They insisted that "the corporate authorities of the city of Cincinnati" were "authorized and requested by law" to safeguard religious education in the public schools. Finally, they accused the Board of Education of exercising improper authority, asserting that its 1853 charter (establishing "The Board of Trustees and Visitors of Common Schools") was "a 'special law conferring corporate powers,' forbidden by the Constitution of Ohio."[81]

The resulting court case, *Minor v. Board of Education of Cincinnati*, set the stage for the so-called Bible War, a prolonged legal struggle over the meaning of church-state separation that helped define its practice across the nation. The practice of reading scripture in the classroom was rooted in the colonial "common schools" of New England, the ideological antecedents of nineteenth-century common or public schools.[82] Although the Bible War played out on the national stage, the first legal action began over the reading of scripture in Cincinnati's common schoolrooms and originated in the ethnic, sectarian, and ideological tensions of the nineteenth-century Queen City. The Bible War continued into the twentieth century, with legal actions in Ohio and numerous other states for many decades. True, there is a danger in compounding church, state, and religion in light of present-day secular ideology. And the secularization of public education was more haphazard than the outcome of legal test cases suggested.[83] Nevertheless, the constitutional question was resolved in 1963, when the United States Supreme Court determined that "no state law or school board may require that passages from the Bible be read or that the Lord's Prayer be recited in the public schools."[84] This ruling outlawed a practice of religious instruction stretching back to the beginnings of public education. In so doing, it conflicted with nineteenth century perceptions of the schoolhouse as the seedbed of religion, "the sacred temple of the American nation."[85]

The United States Supreme Court's 1963 conclusion that the Bible is a sectarian text, unfitted for public education, would have dismayed early champions of American common schools. Horace Mann, the nation's leading advocate for public education, particularly approved of the use of the King James Bible in the classroom. "That our Public Schools are not Theological Seminaries, is admitted," he wrote. "But our system earnestly inculcates all Christian morals; it founds its morals on the basis of religion; it welcomes the religion of the Bible, and in receiving the Bible, it allows it to do what it is allowed to do in no other system,—*to speak for itself.*"[86] Mann's faith was rooted in the idiosyncratic Unitarianism of New England, but his brand of civic religion spoke to a broad spectrum in the Ohio Valley, including

Beecherite Presbyterians, evangelical Baptists and Methodists, and even some within the Jewish community.

To Cincinnati Catholics, use of the King James Bible in public schools betrayed a crusade against their faith. Mandatory reading of the Protestant scripture, insisted John Baptist Purcell, went hand in hand with anti-Catholic propaganda. Since the 1830s the bishop had warned against "sectarian free-schools . . . where, under the pretext of Charity . . . unsuspecting children have tracts placed in their hands, insinuating the vilest and most malicious slanders of our real principles." Such corrupting knowledge, he lamented, "reminds us of the price first paid for it in Eden."[87] Like others of his faith, Purcell insisted that Catholic children received scriptural instruction under church supervision. In this context, Horace Mann's insistence on the Bible speaking *for itself* was alarming. Worse, Mann emphasized that the common schools "bear upon their face, that they are schools which the children of the entire community may attend."[88]

The use of the Bible in public schools became the most divisive political issue in Cincinnati. Questions of ethnic and sectarian relations that had once seemed relatively open became increasingly fraught. The Bible War confirmed the dominance of two separate educational systems, public and parochial, and drew increasingly sharp distinctions between nonsectarian and sectarian modes of education. It was no coincidence that this controversy began when and where it did, in the immediate aftermath of the Civil War and in a city long regarded as a cultural laboratory for the nation. The Bible War was the result of sectarian accretions on the religious landscape. Its outcome, however, was the accommodation of religious and ethnic differences that had long threatened tumult. Whereas the Civil War culminated a bloody legacy of racial and sectional divisions in America, Cincinnati's Bible War was fought out in the courts. After the rioting and disorder of the Know-Nothing years of the 1850s, the judicial resolution of such matters indicated at least some moderation.

A Controversial Proposal

The American Civil War, ironically, was a moment of relative détente in the sectarian politics of Cincinnati. Though threatened by armed invasion from Confederate forces in neighboring Kentucky, the Queen City was tranquil compared with many cities on the urban Atlantic Seaboard. In places like Boston and New York, Irish Catholics rioted against the draft, their clergy calling in vain for peace. But under the leadership of John Baptist Purcell, an outspoken opponent of slavery, Cincinnati's Catholic Church rallied against Confederate rebellion. The *Catholic Telegraph* called for "the fervent cooperation of our Catholic citizens in upholding the flag of our country," noting that "the President has spoken, and it is our duty to obey him as the head of the nation."[89] Underlining his message, Purcell boldly flew the Stars and Stripes from the spire of his cathedral. In Cincinnati, he insisted, no one should suffer any doubt where the church's loyalty lay—or that of the Catholic community. For the duration of the war, it sent a powerful message.

Despite popular anti-Catholicism, Purcell and his fellow religionists persisted in working with the city's Board of Education over the ensuing years. Thus, in the summer of 1869, board member F. W. Rauch revived the idea of consolidating the parochial and public schools. This proposal embodied the centralizing tendency of the Board of Education (that same year, for example, the board formed a committee to discuss the unification of Cincinnati College with other institutions, anticipating the 1870 establishment of the University of Cincinnati by the city).[90] Moreover, Rauch's proposal appealed to both Catholics who hoped it might serve the long-term interests of parochial education in the city and Protestants who hoped that bringing the parochial system under the jurisdiction of public schools by legislative incorporation would dilute the influence of Rome. Both factions favored sectarian compromise while gambling on pragmatic self-interest. At the same time, many Cincinnatians, especially evangelical Protestants, opposed Rauch's proposed innovation, with the Presbyterian *Cincinnati Gazette*, for example, referring to it as a "Jesuitical scheme on foot."[91]

Undeterred by nativist opposition, Rauch joined with other Catholics on the board, notably Edward Purcell (the archbishop's younger brother and editor of the *Catholic Telegraph*), to draft a six-point proposal for the merger. Under their proposal, the city would purchase existing parochial schools with the understanding that they would be exempt from religious instruction altogether. At Edward Purcell's urging, the plan was modified to allow these consolidated schools to offer religious instruction on weekends. These proposals met with internal as well as outside opposition, particularly from German Catholics who feared their distinctive schools would become unduly Americanized. Notwithstanding such misgivings, the vicar-general's editorials in the *Telegraph* continued to maintain that public-parochial merger was both inevitable and desirable. Catholics, he insisted, "can not push back Niagara, and if we cannot be of one religion, we can, which is the next best thing, be of one *nation*."[92]

The architect of the merger proposal, F. W. Rauch, was an upstanding German-American citizen, a Republican activist, and an amateur composer of patriotic music.[93] Although Rauch's faith would have alarmed many Cincinnatians, the Board of Education proved conciliatory at first. Negotiations forged ahead with Rauch's fellow Catholic board members and Vicar-General Edward Purcell, who closely advised his brother the archbishop. At last it seemed as though consolidation of the Catholic and public school systems was imminent.

On September 6, Cincinnati's Board of Education met to discuss consolidation issues under Rauch's proposals, but these discussions took a twist when board member Samuel A. Miller proposed a motion that went even farther than the Catholic plan. He proposed two resolutions aimed specifically at the objections of Catholic parents, many of whom remained hostile to the city schools. First, he recommended "that religious instruction and the reading of religious books, including the Holy Bible, are prohibited in the common schools of Cincinnati . . . to allow the children of parents of all sects and opinions to enjoy alike the benefits of the common school fund." Second, he urged repeal of the policy that "the opening exercises in every department shall commence by reading a portion of the Bible by or under the direction of the teacher and appropriate singing by the pupils."[94]

Miller's proposals that city schools be purged of all religion entirely had an unsettling effect. A respected scientist and educator, Miller was of no declared religious faith. The taint of infidelity subjected him to the suspicions of Protestants and Catholics alike. Critics accused him of belonging among the "gentlemen [who] have found their way into the School Board" who regarded the Bible as "a cheat and a delusion" and represented their views "in singular disproportion to their number in the community."[95] Alongside Rauch's earlier proposals, which had applied only to any merged parochial schools, Miller's proposals broke any consensus toward consolidation. And when the board met again on September 13, a letter from Archbishop Purcell was read to assembled members, plunging matters into confusion. Events were taking a new turn. Purcell was readying to set sail for Rome to participate in the First Vatican Council, convoked by Pope Pius IX. Writing in the third person, the archbishop assumed a frosty tone:

The undersigned, in the interests, as he believes, of justice, charity, and patriotism, will be most happy to meet in conference on the vexed school question a committee appointed by the School Board of this city. He is perfectly satisfied with the Catholic schools as they now exist, but he thinks, as every honest man may, that it is unjust to impose restrictions, such as in conscience they and their natural guardians must ever resist on the rights of Catholic children to the benefits of the district schools. The public will then see who are the exclusionists and the intolerant.[96]

A second letter from Purcell was read before the board on September 20, protesting that the "entire government of Public Schools in which Christian Youth is educated could not be given over to the civil power." Purcell wanted to put off any firm decision until his return, which would delay the board's decision by six months. Worse, he insisted on referring the consolidation question to the pope himself. Not surprisingly, board members deplored Purcell's "ridiculous" procrastination. Why, complained one, must they "await the action of a representative of a church, who, without authority to act here at home, must go across the ocean and consult a foreign prince"?[97]

Three factors influenced Purcell's backpedaling. First, anti-Catholicism riled by the Cincinnati press exacerbated his skepticism. Local editors seized on the revived Bible controversy as evidence that the Catholic Church had infiltrated the city's common schools. Lumped in the public mind with Rauch's ill-fated consolidation scheme, their hostile voices represented Miller's proposal to remove the Bible from the public school classroom as "a Jesuitical scheme" and an attempt by the Catholic Church to gain "complete mastery" of the public schools. Purcell's appeal to public opinion, to see "who are the exclusionists and the intolerant," thus betrayed exhaustion at the constant sniping and criticism.[98]

Second, Miller's resolution to withdraw religion from the public schools (a resolution conflated in the local press with F. W. Rauch's more nuanced proposals) went beyond anything Purcell and his colleagues intended. Catholics specifically objected to the use of Protestant scripture and the perceived anti-Catholicism of other assigned texts, but they still maintained that religious instruction was essential. Even Rauch's proposal to prohibit religious instruction in publicly consolidated Catholic schools, though countenanced by Purcell's brother and appearing to bear the archdiocesan imprimatur, misrepresented the church's true interests. The archbishop's own misgivings were hardly a secret, moreover. He had long objected to the purportedly anti-Catholic nature of assigned classroom texts in public schools. But he also agreed with his Protestant peers that the Bible was foundational. His backpedaling, therefore, was not a change of heart but rather his confirmed opinion. He did not object to teachers assigning scripture (the parochial schools taught from the approved Douay Version) and balked only at the proposed expansion of the school board's civil authority. That said, Purcell's critics might have been right that "division of the school fund is the *ultimatum* of the Catholics." Whether Catholics demanded their entitled "portion" or only their fair "share" was the key question.[99]

Finally, unforeseen events across the Atlantic dictated Purcell's position. The First Vatican Council (1869), to which he was summoned, transformed relations between Rome and the American Catholic Church, subjecting the latter to unprecedented scrutiny. The ambitious Pope Pius IX was reasserting papal authority against an unprecedented tide of anticlerical nationalism sweeping through Europe. His papacy had endured the red-shirted socialist followers of Italian freedom fighter Garibaldi bombarding Saint Peter's Square. It was beginning to face the secularizing Kulturkampf of Bismarckian Prussia, which sought to root out Catholic influence from the newly unified German Empire. The Vatican response was a reactionary backlash not seen since the end of the Napoleonic Wars. "The Church," declared Pius, "is essentially an unequal society . . . comprising two categories of persons, the Pastors and the flock."[100] While Protestant and freethinking Cincinnatians, native and immigrant, rejoiced in the global progress of liberal nationalism, Catholics once more felt the chafing of religious authority in a pluralistic republic. Purcell had formerly dissented on papal infallibility, but now the ex cathedra authority of his pope was becoming unquestionable.[101] This authoritarian climate rendered Purcell's private opinions moot on such questions as consolidating parochial and public schools, no matter the support among his laity. Though the archbishop espoused Americanization, he now fell in line with the authoritarian climate in Rome.

Purcell's parting shots left the Board of Education in a quandary. In a fog of indecision at the September 13 meeting, the board tabled Miller's resolutions and opted to appoint another new committee to conciliate with the Catholic Church. In any event, Purcell's letter of September 20 laid rest to any eleventh-hour compromises.

On November 1, the Cincinnati Board of Education finally backed Miller's proposals, voting twenty-two to sixteen to remove the King James Bible from its curriculum. Ten of the twenty-two in favor were Catholics, but as the overall majority indicated, the picture was more complex than the simple sectarianism portrayed in the press. Despite overwhelming demonstration of pro-Bible public opinion, board members were motivated by other concerns. The board's annual report of the previous year emphasized the growth of parochial school competition, urging compromise to make the city's common schools "less objectionable to the Catholics" or else risk "irrepressible conflict."[102] The decision to withdraw the Bible from the classroom thus indicated willingness to accommodate Catholic demands, although, as Purcell's backpedaling indicated, these demands proved mercurial. Just two days later, moreover, the petition was submitted to the Hamilton County Superior Court demanding an injunction. The speed with which the petition was filed suggested the board's decision was anticipated. Adding insult to injury, the court also issued a restraining order, allowing Bible reading to continue unimpeded until the matter was resolved.[103] The stage was set for the Bible War to move from the Board of Education to the courthouse.

"The Spires Will Point to the Heaven"

The resulting case, *Minor vs. Board of Education of Cincinnati*, had far-reaching implications and raised strong passions. The plaintiffs condemned the Board of Education as being "in violation of law and against public policy and morality," with the Bible ban intended to make the city schools "deistical and infidel both in their purpose and tendency."[104] In response, the school board assembled one of the strongest legal defense teams Cincinnati had ever seen. It included three of the Queen City's most brilliant lawyers: attorney George Hoadly, later governor of Ohio; his colleague Stanley Matthews, a future justice of the United States Supreme Court; and John B. Stallo, a German-born intellectual eventually appointed United States ambassador to Rome. This noteworthy triad defended the board's corporate autonomy to act in the public interest while defending it in civil court against the imputations of irreligion. The significance of the case was thus twofold: testing to what extent Ohio was constituted along secular or religious lines and testing the bounds of authority between state and municipal government and incorporated entities, such as the Board of Education.

The record of *Minor v. Board of Education*, published in Cincinnati as *The Bible in the Public Schools* (not to be confused with the similarly titled account of the Pike's Hall meeting the preceding year), ran to over four hundred pages of argument and opinion. Two advocates stood out most vividly in defense of the school board's anti-Bible position. First was Stallo. He appealed to principles of religious liberty and personal conscience to argue against the use of the Bible from the classroom. In addition, he reminded the court of the upheavals that continued to shape Cincinnati: "The time is not far distant, when the Catholics in this city will be in the majority." A Catholic majority population surely undermined Protestant complacency. What if the school board were to insist that students make the sign of the cross, "the sacred symbol of Christianity" but widely perceived as a sectarian gesture? Stallo then asked: "Has not the Catholic the right, for the same reason, to say: reading the Bible without comment is the peculiar symbol of Protestantism, and it is not to be tolerated in the schools established by Catholics and Protestants alike?"[105] The outcome of introducing any kind of religion, he continued, was argument to the point of absurdity over what constituted, or did not constitute, sectarian privilege. Better to avoid such questions altogether. Removing the Bible from the public schoolroom, he insisted, would strengthen, not weaken, religion in Cincinnati. Should the Bible ban remain in force:

> The spires will point to the heaven, the unmuffled church bells will speak of God, as before; the "free Bible" will have free sway, but in a free State, in free churches or religious schools, by the side of free secular schools. And I hope my friend will not regard it as a calamity if the son of a Presbyterian or Methodist, after his intercourse with the child of a Jew, Catholic, or unbeliever, should turn to the Scriptures with the feeling that the truth is broader than the leaves of any book.[106]

Stallo's Germanic background colored his reception. Though nominally Catholic, he was steeped in the Hegelian thought of the secular enlightenment: a fitting amalgam of Romanism and infidelity in the eyes of his opponents. His arguments also reflected the influence of evolutionary science, not long after Charles Darwin published *On the Origin of Species* (1859). Thus, Stallo applied Darwin's argument "that nature produces the several genera and species of the vertebrates" to the religious landscape, where "denominational differences may be evolved by emphasizing or bringing into relief certain truths or doctrines taught or believed to be taught by the Bible."[107] Even reading the Bible without note or comment, sectarian emphases would emerge through the simple act of selection, shaped by the prejudices of adherents. Placing the Bible in the hands of public school teachers and their students thus produced "denominational schools, though of the poorest possible sort . . . for what religious culture can be imparted by the hurried mechanical 'dog-trot' . . . [and] mumbling of scriptural passages"?[108] Religion, Stallo insisted, flourished best amid houses of worship and the private sphere of conscience, not in the public schools.

Aside from Stallo, the most forceful advocate for the Bible ban was Judge Stanley Matthews, who argued exhaustively for the school board. Personally, Matthews was a devout Presbyterian. At times his argument cleaved almost as closely to theology as it did to legal reasoning. In contrast to his colleagues, he cut an anxious figure, admitting at the outset the toll this case demanded. "Except, the loss of dear children," he pleaded, "this is the most painful experience of my life—to be told that I am an enemy of religion, that I am an opponent of the Bible, that I have lost in this community my Christian character."[109] Although Matthews's concern for his reputation seemed exaggerated in light of his subsequent appointment to the United States Supreme Court, his concerns underlined the coercive force of religion and religious community in the nineteenth-century Queen City.

When pressed by Judge Storer, Matthews insisted that the reading of the King James Bible amounted to a sectarian act of worship. All citizens, he argued, remained "equally entitled to, not toleration—I hate that word, there is no such thing known in this country as toleration—but civil and religious equality, because it is right, and a right."[110] The spirit of religious freedom, rather than mere toleration, absolved Matthews from reining in his own prejudices. "The Bible, the Bible is the religion of Protestants," he confessed, while insisting that "the Church, the Church alone . . . is the doctrine of Catholics."[111] Matthews found the scriptural religion of the Jews closer to his own faith but noted the problem of forcing Jewish children to read the life of Christ: "The record of this divine life and death and resurrection is something more to the Jew than ordinary history: it is a blasphemy, sacrilege."[112] And unlike his liberal Catholic colleague J. B. Stallo, Matthews found it necessary to reiterate his doctrine. "If your Honors please, I do not know how often it may be necessary for me to disclaim that I am not a Roman Catholic and that I am not a Jew," he announced, to laughter in the courthouse. "I am a Calvinistic Protestant. I believe in the doctrines of election and predestination."[113]

As a Calvinist Protestant, Matthews rejected the doctrines of Catholicism, and as an attorney, he appealed to the sectarian prejudices of the presiding bench. His clinching argument for eliminating the King James Bible from the public schools, ironically, lay in the competition from parochial education. Once Catholic parents no longer feared Protestant indoctrination of their children, might they not flock to the city schools? "The day that your Honors decree the dismissal of this petition," Matthews contended, "you write upon these walls the destruction of every denominational parish school in the city of Cincinnati." Underlining his Protestant credentials, Matthews quoted the autobiography of the late Lyman Beecher on New England in the wake of disestablishment. "And the fact is, we all felt our children would scatter like partridges," wrote Beecher, "if the [religious] tax law was lost." Instead, "we were thrown on God and on ourselves, and this creates that moral coercion which makes men work."[114]

In equating the Board of Education's anti-Bible stance to disestablishment in the early American republic, Matthews provided sound logic but fell short of the historical consensus of his audience. While the argument for religious freedom was plausible, it was precisely the need for "moral coercion" in a pluralistic society that first led Beecher and his allies to support the public schools. In the end, the plaintiffs' lawyers won the day by re-claiming "the religion and morality which the Constitution seeks to inculcate through the common schools." Siding with the petitioners, the superior court overruled the Board of Education in February 1870. The court's two-to-one decision to restore the Bible reflected the sectarian leanings of magistrates Marcelus Hagans (a Methodist Sunday school crusader) and Bellamy Storer (an evangelical Presbyterian). Storer once served as both corresponding sec-retary and president of the Board of Education, in which capacity he ap-proved "the principles of the Bible" as "the only reliance for the safety of the individual as well as the masses; they alone can infuse strength and power into the social system, fully expand the intellect, and teach . . . that by elevat-ing the minds of our fellow men, we have in the highest sense exalted our own."[115] Remarkably, Storer's bias attracted little adverse criticism, much less calls for his recusal.

To opponents of the Bible in public schools, the court's decision des-ecrated the separation principle of the United States Constitution, enshrined by Jefferson as the "wall of separation between Church & State."[116] Asserting the pluralism of Cincinnati's religious landscape, the board's initial resolu-tion prohibited Bible reading on the basis of toleration and equal access to the common school fund. Dissenting justice Alphonso Taft (father of future United States president William H. Taft) parted with his two judicial col-leagues on the constitutionality of Bible reading in a powerful opinion. The use of scripture "was and is," he maintained, "sectarian. It is a Protestant wor-ship, and its use is a symbol of Protestant supremacy in schools, and as such offensive to Catholics and to Jews." A liberal Unitarian, Taft insisted that Protestant Christianity was no more entitled to privileged treatment than the faith of "the Pagan and Mormon, the Brahmin and the Jew, the Swedenbor-gian and the Buddhist, the Catholic and the Quaker."[117]

To supporters of Bible reading in the common schools, the superior court's ruling vindicated a decades-long concordance between Christianity and public education. The court's majority cited section seven of Ohio's state constitution's bill of rights (adapted from the Northwest Ordinance), which stated: "Religion, morality, and knowledge, however, being essential to good government, it shall be the duty of the General Assembly to pass suitable laws to protect every religious denomination in the peaceable enjoyment of its own mode of public worship, and to encourage schools and the means of instruc-tion." The connection between religion and education was clear, they argued. By contrast, the autonomy of the Board of Education was questionable. Its existence was contingent on the mandate of the State of Ohio. Thus, the court ruled that board members had overstepped their authority, regardless of whether it was otherwise advisable to keep the Bible out of the classroom. "Our common schools," concluded the ruling, "can not be secularized under the Constitution of Ohio. It is a serious question whether as a matter of policy merely, it would not be better that they were, rather than offend conscience. With this, however, we have now nothing to do."[118]

Revealingly, Storer, Hagans, and Taft all reflected on the likelihood of public offense. As the recent public meetings illustrated, sectarian passions rode high and were likely to erupt into violence. But Taft called out his colleagues on the constitutional link among religion, government, and education. "The religion of the Bill of Rights," he emphasized, "is not sectarian religion." Nor did he believe the courts had the right to regulate public schools. "If the Board of Education have not power to say, whether the schools shall be opened with the reading of Bible and singing, who has that power? It is not claimed that the Legislature has prescribed any such opening of the schools. The Board itself made the rule, which no other person or body, under the laws, could do, and now has repealed it."[119]

Religious Landscape

The resolution of *Minor v. Board of Education* boiled down to what did, or did not, amount to "sectarian" religion. This question mattered greatly in Cincinnati. The Queen City's diversity made it as much of a cultural laboratory as any other city in the United States in 1869, with over one hundred congregations representing around twenty-five denominations. This diversity included twenty-three Roman Catholic churches, six Jewish houses of worship, and a bewildering variety of Protestant sects.[120] How to bring "religion, morality, and knowledge" into the classroom without constituting an establishment of religion was a thorny problem. How to forge consensus among religious conservatives, liberals, and freethinkers of varying stripes, meanwhile, was an almost impossible conundrum. Few if any religious leaders openly opposed civic and religious freedom, but these concepts meant radically different things to different traditions and individuals.

The Queen City's religious landscape was by no means exclusively Christian. On the eve of the Civil War, perhaps ten thousand Jews resided in the city, or around 6 percent of the total population. Cincinnati was especially important, not only as the oldest Jewish community west of the Alleghenies but also as the cradle of American Reform Judaism. Nineteenth-century observers described the city as "a sort of paradise for the Hebrews" and "the pioneer Jewish city of the world." The earliest documented Jewish Cincinnatian, English-born Joseph Jonas, settled in the city in 1817. Though Jonas thrived in the dynamic urban economy, it was several years before any fellow Jews joined him in the city. Yet he remained undaunted by what he regarded as an Errand into the Wilderness, albeit a wilderness integrating into the economic fabric of the young nation. Assimilation would preserve Jewish identity, he predicted: "The almighty will give his people favour in the eyes of all nations, if they only conduct themselves as citizens in a moral and religious point of view."[121]

For Jonas, as for most Jewish Cincinnatians, moral and religious citizenship entailed separation of private conscience and public life. And although anti-Semitism existed in the Queen City, interdenominational cooperation prevailed as a new generation of mostly German-speaking Jews arrived. The city's first synagogue, for example, received donations of twenty-five dollars each "from fifty-two gentlemen of the Christian faith." The Reform movement within Judaism originated in central Europe, emphasizing ethical teachings and cultural assimilation, often at the expense of more traditional liturgical concerns. Its principal founder in Cincinnati, Bohemian-born Isaac Mayer Wise, served as rabbi of the Bene Yeshurun congregation from 1854, forging strong relations with a wide array of gentile leaders. Wise cultivated friendships with Unitarian ministers Moncure D. Conway and Thomas F. Vickers, calling them "our allies" in the pursuit of religious liberty. Rabbi Max Lilienthal, who led the Bene Israel congregation, joined Wise in Cincinnati the following year. As Wise later appreciatively wrote, Lilienthal epitomized American Jewish citizenship, donating liberally to benevolent causes and serving on a plethora of civic boards, including the Board of Education and the Board of Examiners. Together, Rabbis Wise and Lilienthal shaped the development of Cincinnati's religious and civic landscapes.[122]

Rabbi Wise extended his influence in 1854, founding the English-language newspaper *The Israelite* (renamed the *American Israelite* in 1874). Through the pages of his journal, Wise spoke on a variety of theological and public issues, including the Bible War. In a characteristically colorful editorial of October 1869, he extrapolated the question of religious liberty from the Bible controversy, using the built environment of the Queen City by way of illustration. The junction of Eighth and Plum Streets, he noted (somewhat hyperbolically), formed "a correct and concrete idea of civil and religious liberty . . . a picture to which the world at large can offer no parallel, no precedent, no comparison." At the northwestern corner sat city hall, housing the police court and the mayor's office, among other functions. Here, wrote Wise, "the Board of Education fights the battles of the Lord for or against the Archbishop of Cincinnati . . . [and] the Board of Health feels quite well and healthy, notwithstanding the dead fish and the miserable meats sold in market." Immediately adjacent from this "broad representation of civil liberty and uncivil liberties" stood "the archbishop's cathedral with its magnificent porch and tower," which Wise imagined in dialogue with city hall:

"I alone can save you from the claws and paws of the devil and the terrible caldron of hell," that cathedral maintains, "unless you go to heaven in my particular fashion, you can not go there at all. Unless you give the superintendency over the state, school and society into the hands of the priest, and unless you believe and obey him, you are wicked and ungodly libertines and infidels, whom the Lord will punish in due time."

On the southeastern corner of Eighth and Plum was Wise's own house of worship, "the gorgeous temple of K.K. Benai Yeshurun, a monument of three thousand years of history, pointing heavenward with its two minarets, Boaz and Joachin, nodding compliance to the emblem of liberty and the progress of humanity, and disputing the claims of the cathedral on the monopoly of religion." And crossing the corner northeast to the junction of Eighth and Plum, Wise lauded "the new and radical Unitarian Church, in which Rev. Thomas Vickers will preach. This church stands nearer to the temple than to the cathedral; and in doctrine too, it approaches Judaism much closer than Roman Catholicism."[123]

Cincinnati's landscape was an apt metaphor for Wise's conceptions of religious liberty, thrown into relief amid the Bible War. Despite its fanciful tone, the rabbi's editorial struck to the core of the Reformed Jewish perspective, most notably in comparison of his temple's two Moorish towers to the bronze columns—"Boaz and Joachin"—adorning the biblical Temple of Solomon. The Bene Yeshurun temple (1865) was built at considerable expense just after the Civil War. Wise's commissioning of a fashionable non-Jewish architect, James Keys Wilson, and the temple's location opposite the Catholic cathedral and city hall indicated Reform Judaism's claims to acceptance in Cincinnati.[124] Even the styling of Bene Yeshurun as a "temple" was significant. It underlined the Reformed belief that America might become a permanent resting place for Jews to partake in full religious and civic liberty. Wise's theology was controversial within Judaism as a whole, where the term "synagogue" denoted a temporary house of assembly and "temple" was reserved for the ancient seat in Jerusalem. But Wise believed in the promise of American liberty for his people. His mistrust of Roman Catholicism, however, reflected the historically reactionary politics of Rome in his native Europe. Notwithstanding the bloodshed of the French Revolution, its secularizing influence was a blessing for European Jews burdened by centuries of anti-Semitic canon and civil law. While Pope Pius IX sought to turn back the clock to the ancient regime, America's revolutionary freedom of religion was alive and well, reflected Wise, personified in the cheerful pragmatism of preachers like his Unitarian colleague Thomas Vickers.

The Doctrine of "Hands Off!"

Expressing disappointment in the wake of *Minor vs. Board of Education*, the *Catholic Telegraph* assured readers that the decision to restore the King James Bible was "a transient, momentary victory of the Evangelicals; a victory of popular prejudice over religious liberty."[125] Certainly, the Bible issue was not yet laid to rest, and within a few years the *Telegraph*'s assurances were vindicated. Another cycle of bitterly contested city elections took place, resulting in the 1870 reelection of eight anti-Bible school board members at the expense of their opponents. And the legal struggle continued. In June 1873, the Ohio Supreme Court unanimously overturned *Minor vs. Board*, reasserting the chartered authority of local boards of education and insisting that "the courts have no rightful authority to interfere by directing what instruction shall be given or what books read" in the public schools.[126] The court unanimously ruled that "religious freedom . . . can best be secured by adopting the doctrine of the Seventh Section of our own Bill of Rights . . . summarize[d] in two words by calling it the doctrine of 'Hands Off!' Let the state not only keep its own hands off, but let it also see to it that religious sects keep their hands off each other."[127]

The Ohio Supreme Court's 1873 ruling (confusingly entitled *Board of Education v. Minor et al.*) was just one chapter in a broader national controversy surrounding the place of religion in education. Nevertheless, it reflected the crowded religious landscape of Cincinnati. In particular, the 1869 injunction against the King James Bible, and the subsequent uproar and legal wrangling, resulted from sectarian divisions within the Cincinnati Board of Education and from the challenges of accommodating the city's large Catholic population. And while other cities and states faced similar challenges to remove the Bible from the classroom, *Board vs. Minor* became a notable test case, cited in several state supreme court decisions. These included a 1926 ruling in New York, denouncing a private school's efforts to compel a Jewish student to attend Christian worship "in violation of his constitutional rights."[128] Similar challenges culminated in the United States Supreme Court's 1963 decision that ruled mandatory reading of scripture in public schools unconstitutional.

While the Cincinnati Bible War highlighted the limits and possibilities of religious toleration in nineteenth century America, it was not simply a battle between secularists and enthusiasts. Rather, it was a conflict between concepts of toleration, championed for different reasons. To its supporters, Bible reading in public schools was part of America's capacious civic religion. These advocates maintained that sectarianism (in the narrow denominational sense) was incompatible with a free public sphere, but that religion in general was essential to social wellbeing. Their partial definitions of these categories enabled them to discriminate sharply against Catholicism by claiming that it was as much an anti-republican ideology as a mere religion. They railed against secularism or irreligion on the grounds that public religion was essential to national liberty.

Those who supported removing the King James Bible, meanwhile, represented complex lines of partisanship. The Catholics, of course, were the largest bloc, and felt themselves discriminated against the most directly. Led by Archbishop Purcell, the Catholic Church proposed an alternative common schools system, allowing both Catholic and Jewish scripture in the classroom. After this plan came to nothing, the Catholic members on the Board of Education joined with liberal Protestants and others to back F.W. Rauch's proposal for consolidated public-parochial schools. But Samuel Miller's proposal to entirely eradicate religious instruction threw matters into confusion. It enabled supporters of the King James Bible to call out conspiracy between Catholics and freethinkers designed, in the words of one protestor, "to make the schools of Cincinnati schools of atheism."[129] Such charges were absurd. Despite unanimous support among Catholic board members for the Miller resolution, Cincinnati's Catholic Church was averse to secularizing the public schools.[130] As board advocate Stanley Matthews admitted, there was "no doubt the Catholics held precisely the same views that were held by the gentlemen of the other side,—that the state should provide religious instruction."[131]

The Bible War divided Cincinnatians along ethnic as well as sectarian lines. The city's German population regarded the King James Bible with mistrust, regarding it as an instrument of Anglicization. German papers such as the *Volksfreund* and the *Volksblatt* denounced "the dark spirit of intolerance." Even the *Courier*, an English language newspaper for German readers, considered the King James Bible "an artifice to cover sectarian designs."[132] And while German nationalists opposed English scripture in public schools, German Catholics had comparable scruples regarding the eradication of scripture from the public classroom. Though they sought access to the common schools fund, they refused to do so at the expense of sectarian identity.

The amalgamation of ethnic and sectarian identities underlined the complexities of the Bible War. Two minority religious groups particularly exerted influence in this regard: Cincinnati's Jewish and Unitarian communities. Cincinnati Jews were among the staunchest supporters of public education, with an estimated eighty percent of Jewish children attending the city's common schools.[133] "They make the education of their children a sacred duty," observed journalist Lafcadio Hearn, "and in this they patronize the Public Schools and the Public Library. They are the most firm supporters of our public educational system."[134] Yet support took different forms within the community. While some Jews supported use of the King James Bible, the liberal and Reform Jewish leadership overwhelmingly opposed it. Memory of persecutions in Europe and a consequent urge to assimilate in American society influenced leaders such as Max Lilienthal, a seasoned member of the Board of Education, who considered the Bible question part of a bigger constitutional picture. During the deliberations before the superior court, Lilienthal wrote a December 1869 article in New York's *Jewish Times*: "If decided . . . in favor of our nonsectarian school system, then the agitation of inserting an acknowledgement of God into our constitution will be silenced, the aspiration of the Catholics for the supremacy of their church will be at least legally frustrated; the separation of state and church will be gloriously vindicated, and the brightest gem in the American diadem, 'Religious liberty and freedom of conscience,' will have been put beyond the reach of any kind of fanaticism and bigotry."[135]

Isaac Mayer Wise similarly denounced scripture teaching as "sectarian," adding that "the main moral of the schools is, to educate citizens to perfect equality and friendship. You cannot throw the seed of religious discord into the schools without upsetting the system."[136] Wise championed the city's public schools, despite having inherited a Jewish day school (Talmud Yelodim, founded 1849) when he assumed the pulpit of Bene Yeshurun in 1854. In 1867, he dissolved the sectarian school, against some protest. Wise insisted that Jewish parents instead enroll their children in the common schools, which he extolled as engines of social integration and patriotic Americanization.[137]

Though small, Cincinnati's affluent and educated Unitarian population enjoyed disproportionate influence in the Bible War, including two of the most militant partisans on the Board of Education. Theologically liberal but socially conservative, Rev. Amory Dwight Mayo insisted the United States was a Christian nation. Addressing his fellow citizens at Pike's Hall, he asked: "Has America ceased to be a free republican country?" Meanwhile, Mayo's liberal colleague Rev. Thomas Vickers was outspoken in the anti-Bible camp, insisting: "If there is any fighting to be done, there are young men and old men in this country who are ready to shoulder the knapsack and the musket and fight for their religious freedom."[138] In the end, however, the last word belonged to Unitarian layman Alphonso Taft, whose 1870 dissenting opinion laid the foundation for restoring the Bible ban in Cincinnati public schools. Taft summarized his view of civil religion, which resembled that of Rabbi Wise. "The Religion of the Bill of Rights," Taft asserted, "is not sectarian religion . . . [but] reverence and love toward God and charity toward men—a sentiment cultivated in many ways, among which are, undoubtedly, the various sectarian forms of public worship, and, as I think also, all forms of useful secular education."[139]

Cincinnati's Bible War reflected changes on the American religious landscape, culminating in gradual acceptance of sectarian differences. Earlier attempts to consolidate the city's Catholic schools within the common schools funding system only highlighted divergent interests of different communities, even as they attempted to resolve conflict. The outcome ensured separation of the public and parochial systems, confirming the former in its secular identity. Though many Cincinnatians suspected the Bible controversy was a Catholic ploy, the relative enrollments of public and parochial schools in the Queen City suggested the public schools flourished without the King James Bible. In 1870, they counted 27,182 students, against 12,944 in the parochial system. By 1900 public enrollments rose to 44,285, while Catholic schools counted 13,080 students after three decades of almost static enrollment levels. The Catholic schools became sectarian enclaves while the public schools broadened their outreach. Black students finally integrated into the public system in 1887 with the advent of school desegregation in Ohio.[140] Ultimately, the Bible War yielded accommodation, as the ramifications of ethnic, sectarian, and racial pluralism entered the twentieth century.

Epilogue

> The spires will point to the heaven, the unmuffled church bells
> will speak of God, as before.
>
> —STALLO (1870)

In Cincinnati, the spires still point to heaven, but the landscape has changed since *Minor v. Board of Education* came before the city's superior court. Two upheavals proved momentous. The first was the First World War, when Cincinnati nativists attacked the identity of their German-American neighbors. German-language instruction was dropped from the public schools curriculum, German books were removed from city libraries, and businesses were pressured to change German-sounding names. Even German street names fell: in one hasty stroke, for example, German Street became English Street. Nativism returned to the pulpit. One minister even preached that "German Huns" ought to be hanged from city lampposts.[1] Such vitriol did more than encourage jingoistic fervor. In the context of war, Cincinnati Germans faced a crisis of identity even more acute than the Know-Nothing violence of the 1850s. Anti-German sentiment died down by the 1930s, but following the Second World War, urban renewal and infrastructure projects wrought a subtly pernicious toll. This next upheaval was illustrated by the fate of Holy Trinity Church, or Heilige Dreieinigkeit. Occupying the corner of West Fifth and Mound Streets since 1834, the oldest German Catholic house of worship west of the Alleghenies (complete with murals by renowned local artist Frank Duveneck) was torn down in 1958 to make room for the I-75 highway. Much of the city's historic West End was similarly razed, displacing urban residents.[2] Material progress thus erased historical memory, but the process of forgetting was as old as the city, the site of Holy Trinity standing within the shadow of indigenous mounds destroyed by early white settlers.

Despite the erosion of its history, Cincinnati has retained much of its distinctive character rooted in the religious landscape. The city's German and Catholic influence remains preserved in its architecture, foodways, language, and more. But popularity does not equal authenticity. For example, Cincinnati's celebrated German festival, Oktoberfest, founded as recently as 1976, no more represents ancient custom than the St. Patrick's Day parades in Boston or New York City. Cincinnati's enduring cultural innovations, however, have always meshed the diverse traditions of its population with the demands and opportunities of its urban landscape. The city's parochial school system is a case in point, having evolved alongside the public schools in the antebellum period. Though scorned by many Cincinnatians, the parochial system belied its sectarian origins by catering to non-Catholic families. The success of its model ensured Catholic representation on the city Board of Education and other policy-making forums. Similarly, Jewish, Unitarian, and other faith traditions outside mainline Protestantism played a disproportionate role in creating the educational and cultural landscape of the city. Such diversity reflected the young foundations of the city. Moreover, the lack of any entrenched religious establishment (despite the assertive cultural influence of evangelical Protestantism) ensured the freedom of religion enshrined in the Northwest Territory Ordinance and Ohio's bill of rights flourished in practice as well as in theory.

Despite the determined opposition of nativists, the Catholicization of Cincinnati's religious landscape proved irreversible. Today, Catholicism remains by far the single-largest religious denomination in greater Cincinnati, with over two hundred thousand adherents in Hamilton County (2010).[3] But the Queen City cannot simply be understood as an urban Catholic buckle in the Protestant Bible Belt. As shown in recent data from the Public Religion Research Institute (P.R.R.I.), a nonprofit, nonpartisan survey organization, demographic change and sectarian decline mark the Queen City's twenty-first-century religious landscape. And in the United States as a whole, organized religion is waning. More Americans identify as unaffiliated than at any time in living memory. In Cincinnati, this decline is particularly bad news for the Catholic Church. Although Catholics accounted for some 19 percent of Cincinnatians surveyed for the P.R.R.I. census in 2019, this total was down from 21 percent in 2014, while the numbers of unaffiliated rose from 19 to 26 percent in the same short period. This drop was even sharper among non-Hispanic Catholics in the Queen City, whose share of the surveyed population fell from 19 percent in 2014 to 16 percent in 2019. Cincinnati's Hispanic Catholics grew from 2 to 3 percent of the total population in the same period. Across the nation, Hispanic worshipers have been vital in filling the pews of the American Catholic Church, having long since overtaken Catholics of German, Irish, Italian, and eastern European descent in many American cities. Counting adherence in ratio to overall population, greater Cincinnati is no longer exceptional in its Catholicism, coming joint twenty-first out of thirty United States metro areas surveyed in the 2019 P.R.R.I. poll. Though Cincinnati's Hispanic population increases, numbers remain low compared to other American cities. The city's white Catholic population (estimated at 15 percent of total population), meanwhile, is dwindling. Similar decline prevails among white evangelical and black Protestant communities, down from 24 and 9 percent of all Cincinnatians surveyed in 2014 to just 18 and 8 percent respectively in 2019. At the same time, pockets of diversity point to the influence of global immigration. Buddhists, Hindus, and Muslims are small but distinct minorities, each accounting for less than 1 percent of the city's total 2019 population. Cincinnati's Jewish population is larger, at roughly 1 percent, though less than half mid-nineteenth-century levels in proportion to overall population.[4]

Headcounts of affiliation tell only a partial story, and Cincinnati's religious landscape continues to shape the institutional life of the city. This remains especially true in the field of education. Cincinnati's Catholic Schools, for example, are the eighth largest such system in the United States, placing the archdiocese's influence beyond the relative size of its jurisdiction across social, sectarian, and racial boundaries.[5] Notably, the Catholic Inner-city Schools Education Fund (C.I.S.E. Fund) serves nearly two thousand students in eight inner-city Catholic schools. Of these students, 93 percent count below the poverty line and 83 percent are classed as "minority" population. Only 24 percent are themselves Catholic.[6] Although the Archdiocese of Cincinnati no longer covers vast geographic extent, it contains much diversity. It also enjoys the means to support four institutes of higher education, as well as the longest continually published Catholic newspaper in the United States.[7] Comparably, American Reform Judaism exerts great influence, despite humble beginnings in nineteenth-century Cincinnati. Under the leadership of Isaac Mayer Wise, Reform Jewish families sent their children to the public schools, and assimilation into the broader American community was urged. Nevertheless, Reform Judaism spread far beyond Cincinnati. The city's Hebrew Union College (established 1875) today has branches in New York, Los Angeles, and Jerusalem, while the *American Israelite* (founded in 1854 as *The Israelite*) is the nation's oldest English-language Jewish newspaper. Such examples of cultural longevity demonstrate the weaving of religious diversity into the social fabric following Cincinnati's Bible War.

In the contrast to the sustained influence of the Archdiocese of Cincinnati or the lasting appeal of Reform Judaism, the Protestant Benevolent Empire, or Evangelical United Front, lost influence over the Queen City and the nation. Its flagship institution, Lane Theological Seminary, closed its doors in a 1930 merger with Chicago's McCormick Seminary, ending operations just over a century since its founding.[8] From early years, the seminary never quite recovered following the Lane rebellion of 1834, when abolitionist students feuded with the socially conservative Lyman Beecher. More importantly, its fortunes waned with the decline of the A.H.M.S., for which it provided hundreds of young preachers. Although the A.H.M.S. continued through most of the nineteenth century, demand for frontier ministers dwindled with the American frontier itself, and the organization became increasingly dominated by a sectarian elite in the urban Northeast. By 1893, the A.H.M.S. renamed itself the Congregational Home Missionary Society, having long since abandoned its interdenominational foundations and its seat of influence in Cincinnati.[9] Efforts to transcend the provincial and sectarian origins of American Protestantism thus came full circle, shedding ecumenical plumage in the process.

In the end, the nineteenth-century evangelical vision of the Queen City as a millennial metropolis receded. Cincinnati became one more midwestern city among many. Today, Protestants of various stripes nominally account for roughly half of all Cincinnatians, but no denomination holds sway. If the Beecherite nightmare of a second Vatican in the Ohio Valley proved to be a fever dream, so too hopes for Protestant cultural dominance proved illusory.

At the time of writing, our world faces a new pandemic. Though COVID-19 is less deadly than cholera and more readily treated, its impact on everyday life is no less disruptive. Moreover, like cholera, today's pandemic has accelerated social changes already discernible prior to the pandemic. Though it may be problematic to assign agency to organisms as primitive as *Vibrio cholerae* or coronavirus, in terms of social evolution, they embody a collective agency as powerful as any voluntary human association. Throughout the nation, in cities such as Cincinnati, businesses struggle to remain open, social distancing is enforced, and images of protest and conflict overshadow political discourse. Though twenty-first century Cincinnati has not witnessed refugees fleeing the city, as happened in 1849, its downtown is at times eerily quiet, as businesses, shoppers, and commuters retreat into the virtual quarantine of the Internet. But the mostly quiet summer of 2020 was also punctuated by mask-wearing crowds gathered to protest racial injustice. Public spaces such as Washington Park, the former site of Presbyterian and Episcopal cemeteries, and Fountain Square, home of the old Fifth Street Market where itinerant evangelists once preached, were transformed anew by demonstrations. Such quasi-revivalistic enthusiasm suggests the city remains meaningful as a focus of the public sphere, albeit in a secular context. Yet parallels between phenomena such as Black Lives Matter and the Benevolent Empire are at best superficial. Where faith and sectarian identity once animated crowds in the Queen City, old boundaries have shifted. Religion no longer enjoys a privileged role in civic life. And even where public spaces offer a backdrop to politics and religion, the virtual nature of society decenters geography in unprecedented ways. Thus, in an age of online worship and electronic advocacy, the city's significance as a regional center of competing cultural and religious projects diminishes.

Cincinnati's future is no more set in stone today than in 1788, when its first surveyors platted its streets on the banks of the Ohio. Demographically, at least, some signs of revival are apparent. The 309,317 Cincinnatians recorded by the 2020 United States Census mark a 4.2 percent increase over the last decade, ending seventy years of declining population. The city's 125,443 black residents, by contrast, signal a 5.7 percent decline in Cincinnati's African American population, whose modern foundations arose with the southern Great Migration of the twentieth century.[10] Patterns of gentrification and displacement tell a particular tale in the Queen City, while in the United States as a whole, the population is increasingly racially and ethnically diverse and more urban. Cincinnati may no longer be twenty years behind the times, as Mark Twain contended, but with the relative declension of its religious landscape and the accompanying shift of its cultural identity, it has in a sense become a place out of time, far removed from the millennial horizons of nineteenth-century boosters. While Cincinnati's prospects as a regionally significant American city seem secure, the meaning of the city in the twenty-first century is less certain.

Notes

INTRODUCTION

1. On Twain's sojourn in Cincinnati, see: Dale Patrick Brown, *Literary Cincinnati: The Missing Chapter* (Athens: Ohio University Press, 2011), 80–85.

2. Calvin Colton, *Manual for Emigrants to America* (London: F. Westley & A. H. Davis, 1832), 111, 113.

3. J.W.S., "Appendix A": in Charles Cist, *Cincinnati in 1841: Its Early Annals and Future Prospects* (Cincinnati: Charles Cist, 1841) 275. William Cronon argued that boosters in Cincinnati anticipated "the model of urban growth—central place theory—that has dominated twentieth-century thought about this subject." Cronon highlighted S. H. Goodin's essay, "Cincinnati—Its Destiny," which regarded midwestern metropolises such as Cincinnati, St. Louis, and Chicago as "competing cities of the same grade of circles." Each, insisted Goodin, vied for accession to *"the next circle beyond . . . a central city—a city which shall have all these cities as satellites or outposts—Where shall that city stand?"* William Cronon, *Nature's Metropolis: Chicago and the Great West* (New York: W. W. Norton, 1991), 38–39.

4. Daniel Aaron, *Cincinnati: Queen City of the West, 1819–1838* (Columbus: Ohio State University Press, 1992), 318.

5. Henry C. Binford, *From Improvement to City Planning: Spatial Management in Cincinnati from the Early Republic through the Civil War Decade* (Philadelphia: Temple University Press, 2021), 5.

6. Andrew Heath, *In Union There Is Strength: Philadelphia in the Age of Urban Consolidation* (Philadelphia: University of Pennsylvania Press, 2019), 4; and Dominic Pacyga, *Chicago: A Biography* (Chicago: University of Chicago Press, 2011), 27.

7. Adam Arenson, *The Great Heart of the Republic: St. Louis and the Cultural Civil War* (Cambridge, Massachusetts: Harvard University Press, 2011), 4–5.

8. D. W. Meinig, *The Shaping of America: A Geographical Perspective on 500 Years of History*, vol. 2, *Continental America 1800–1867* (New Haven, Connecticut: Yale University Press, 1986), 361.

9. Tyler Anbinder, *City of Dreams: The 400-Year Epic History of Immigrant New York* (New York: Houghton, Mifflin, Harcourt, 2016), 172–173.

10. Heath, *In Union There Is Strength*, 24.

11. Catherine C. Cleveland, *The Great Revival in the West, 1797–1805* (Chicago: University of Chicago Press, 1916).

12. Daniel Drake, *Natural and Statistical View, or Picture of Cincinnati and the Miami Country* (Cincinnati: Looker & Wallace, 1815), vii.

13. Jonathan Edwards, "Five Sermons on Different Occasions," in *The Works of Jonathan Edwards A.M.*, vol. 2, ed. Henry Rogers (London: F. Westley & A. H. Davis; New York: Daniel Appleton, 1835), 30.

14. Stephen Chapin, *The Duty of Living for the Good of Posterity: A Sermon, Delivered at North Yarmouth, December 22, 1820, in Commemoration of the Close of the Second Century from the Landing of the Fore-fathers of New England* (Portland, Maine: Thomas Todd, 1821), 40.

15. Alexis de Tocqueville, *Democracy in America*, vol. 1 (New York: Alfred A. Knopf, 1963), 306.

16. Randall Balmer and John R. Fitzmier, *The Presbyterians* (Westport, Connecticut: Greenwood, 1993), 47–48.

17. Daniel Walker Howe, "Religion and Politics in the Antebellum North," in *Religion and American Politics: From the Colonial Period to the Present*, ed. Mark A. Noll and Luke E. Harlow (New York: Oxford University Press, 2007), 130.

18. Clifford Stephen Griffin, *Their Brothers' Keepers: Moral Stewardship in the United States, 1800–1865* (New Brunswick, New Jersey: Rutgers University Press, 1960), x–xi.

19. Trustees of Lane Seminary to Lyman Beecher, n.d., Lane Theological Seminary Records, 286-1-13, folder 19, Presbyterian Historical Society, Philadelphia.

20. Lyman Beecher, *A Plea for the West* (Cincinnati: Truman & Smith, 1835), 11.

21. Per the United States Census in 1840, New York was the largest city, with 312,710 inhabitants. Next came Baltimore with 102,313 inhabitants; New Orleans (102,193); Philadelphia (93,665); Boston (93,383); and Cincinnati (with 46,338 inhabitants, the sixth-largest city in the nation).

22. Charles Cist, *Sketches and Statistics of Cincinnati in 1851* (Cincinnati: William H. Moore, 1851), 47–48. Prior to German unification in 1870, German immigrants identified with the German-speaking diaspora included Swiss and Austrians. Irish immigration figures are similarly problematic. The United Kingdom governed nineteenth-century Ireland, and most Cincinnatians listed as natives of Great Britain were, in fact, Irish.

23. Andrew R. L. Cayton, *Ohio: The History of a People* (Columbus: Ohio State University Press, 2002), 21.

24. Frances Trollope, *Domestic Manners of the Americans*, 5th ed. (London: Richard Bentley, 1839), 56.

25. Timothy L. Smith, *Revivalism and Social Reform: American Protestantism on the Eve of the Civil War* (New York: Harper & Row, 1957), 9.

26. Richard Wade, *The Urban Frontier: The Rise of Western Cities, 1790–1830* (Cambridge, Massachusetts: Harvard University Press, 1959), 1.

27. Frederick Jackson Turner, "The Significance of the Frontier in American History," in *Frontier and Section: Selected Essays of Frederick Jackson Turner*, ed. Ray Allen Billington (Englewood Cliffs, New Jersey: Prentice Hall, 1961), 39.

28. Dickson Bruce, *And They All Sang Hallelujah: Plain-Folk Camp-Meeting Religion, 1840–1845* (Nashville: University of Tennessee Press, 1974), 51.

29. Roger Finke and Rodney Starke, *The Churching of America, 1776–2005: Winners and Losers in Our Religious Economy* (New Brunswick, New Jersey: Rutgers University Press, 2005), 1–2.

30. John D. Buggeln, "A Marketplace for Religion: Cincinnati, 1788–1890" (Ph.D. diss. Indiana University, 2002), 155.

CHAPTER 1

1. "An Ordinance for the Government of the Territory of the United States Northwest of the Ohio River" (1787), section 14, article 1.

2. The standard measurements prescribed by the Northwest Ordinance outlined the rectilinear grid of Cincinnati's central streets before the first block was laid. The surveyor's square betrayed the "stadial" model of progress, which segregated civilization from savagery, city from the wilderness. This eighteenth-century segregation of nature and civilization remained evident in the twentieth-century writings of revisionist historians, including Richard Wade, who emphasized the role of cities—notably Cincinnati—in colonizing the frontier but minimized the cultural influence of rural hinterlands in a pendulum swing away from the earlier agrarian view of history championed by Frederick Jackson Turner. See: Turner, "Significance of the Frontier"; and Wade, *The Urban Frontier.*

3. Cincinnati's original name derived from its position diametrically opposite the mouth of the Licking River, which fed into the Ohio River from Kentucky. Hence: *L*[icking]; *os*, from the Greek (mouth); *anti*, from the Latin (opposite); and *ville*, from the French (town).

4. Kentucky's moniker, "the dark and bloody ground," mistranslated the original Iroquois name, but its reputation was apt, with 3,600 Kentuckians and thousands more American Indians killed in twenty years of conflict. Ellen Eslinger, ed., *Running Mad for Kentucky: Frontier Travel Accounts* (Lexington: University Press of Kentucky, 2004), 50.

5. John Cleves Symmes to Jonathan Dayton, July 17, 1789, in: Francis W. Miller, *Cincinnati's Beginnings: Missing Chapters in the Early History of the City* (Cincinnati: Peter G. Thomson, 1880), 124–125.

6. Charles Fenno Hoffman, *A Winter in the West*, vol. 2 (New York: Harper & Brothers, 1835), 130.

7. Miller, *Cincinnati's Beginnings*, 124.

8. James E. Lewis, Jr., *The American Union and the Problem of Neighborhood: The United States and the Collapse of the Spanish Empire, 1783–1829* (Chapel Hill: University of North Carolina Press, 1993), 14.

9. François Furstenberg, "The Significance of the Trans-Appalachian Frontier in Atlantic History," *American Historical Review* 113, no. 3 (June 2008): 648.

10. William R. Shepherd, "Wilkinson and the Beginnings of the Spanish Conspiracy," *American Historical Review* 9, no. 3 (April 1904): 497.

11. George Washington to Benjamin Harrison, October 10, 1784, in: W. W. Abbot and Dorothy Twohigh, eds., *Papers of George Washington: Confederation Series* (Charlottesville: University of Virginia Press, 1992–1997), 2:92.

12. William Henry Harrison, *A Discourse of the Aborigines of the Ohio Valley* (Chicago: Fergus, 1883), 12.

13. John Kobler, MSS journal, 1798, quoted in: Buggeln, "A Marketplace for Religion," 24.

14. Lorett Treese, *A Serpent's Tale: Discovering America's Ancient Mound Builders* (Yardley, Pennsylvania: Westholme, 2016), 60.

15. Drake, *Natural and Statistical View*, 208.

16. Rick Nutt, *Contending for the Faith: The First Two Centuries of the Presbyterian Church in the Cincinnati Area* (Cincinnati: Presbytery of Cincinnati: 1991), 8.

17. Henry Knox to George Washington, December 26, 1791, in: Mary Stockwell, *Unlikely General: "Mad" Anthony Wayne and the Battle for America* (New Haven, Connecticut: Yale University Press, 2018), 70.

18. R. Douglas Hurt, *The Ohio Frontier: Crucible of the Old Northwest, 1720–1830* (Bloomington: Indiana University Press, 1998), 188.

19. Samuel P. Chase, ed., *The Statutes of Ohio and of the Northwestern Territory, Adopted or Enacted from 1788 to 1833 Inclusive*, vol. 1 (Cincinnati: Corey & Fairbank, 1833), 101.

20. Jacob Burnet, in: Daniel Hurley, *Cincinnati: The Queen City* (Cincinnati: Cincinnati Historical Society, 1982), 21.

21. John Gano, in: Patrick Griffin, *American Leviathan: Empire, Nation, and Revolutionary Frontier* (New York: Hill & Wang, 2007), 265.

22. Wade, *The Urban Frontier*, 101.

23. Francis Baily, *Journal of a Tour in Unsettled Parts of North America in 1796 and 1797* (London: Baily Brothers, 1856), 228.

24. The Northwest Territory imposed corporal punishment for various crimes and misdemeanors, including public drunkenness, for which citizens could be placed in the stocks. Chase, *Statutes of Ohio and the Northwestern Territory*, 100.

25. James Flint, "Letter from America," in *Early Western Travels, 1748–1846*, vol. 9, ed. Reuben Gold Thwaites (Cleveland: Arthur H. Clark, 1904), 155.

26. William Warren Sweet, *Religion on the American Frontier, 1783–1850*, vol. 2, *The Presbyterians: 1783–1840* (New York: Harper & Row, 1936), 394.

27. Henry A. Ford and Kate B. Ford, *History of Cincinnati Ohio with Illustrations and Biographical Sketches* (Cleveland: L. A. Williams, 1881), 148.

28. "Northwest Ordinance (1787)," National Archives, accessed May 20, 2022, https://www.archives.gov/milestone-documents/northwest-ordinance.

29. Francis Trollope, *Domestic Manners of the Americans* (New York: Penguin Classics, 1832, 1997), 60–61.

30. Griffin, *American Leviathan*, 97.

31. In placing stock in the rule of law, Heckewelder likely sought to salve his conscience, preferring the authority of the United States to the vigilantism that befell Gnadenhutten. Johann Heckewelder, *The First Description of Cincinnati and Other Ohio Settlements (1792)*, trans. Don Heinrich Tolzmann (Lanham, Maryland: University Press of America, 1990), 45.

32. Trollope, *Domestic Manners*, 34.

33. September 8, 1803. Francis Asbury, *Journal of the Rev. Francis Asbury, Bishop of the Methodist Episcopal Church*, vol. 3 (New York: Lane & Scott, 1852), 127.

34. Charles F. Goss, *Cincinnati: The Queen City, 1788–1912*, vol. 1 (Cincinnati: S. J. Clarke, 1912), 488.

35. Like the Methodists, Catholic priests competed for converts, prayed for the faithful, slept on hard floors, wore rough coats, and endured hunger, cold, and disease. Like the Catholics, Methodist itinerants also practiced celibacy, being largely recruited among young single men. Martin John Spalding, *Sketches of the Early Catholic Missions of Kentucky, from Their Commencement in 1787, to the Jubilee of 1826–7* (Louisville: J. Webb & Brothers, 1844), 70.

36. Stephen Badin to John Carroll, March 2, 1797, in: Margaret DePalma, *Dialogue on the Frontier: Catholic and Protestant Relations, 1793–1883* (Kent, Ohio: Kent State University Press, 2004), 36.

37. Samuel Thomas Wilson to John Carroll, 1806, in: Anne M. Butler, Michael E. Engh, and Thomas W. Spalding, eds., *The Frontiers and Catholic Identities* (Maryknoll, New York: Orbis Books, 1999), 11.

38. Article IX of Kentucky's 1792 constitution declared: "The Legislature shall have no power to pass laws for the emancipation of slaves without the consent of their owners."

39. David Rice, *Slavery Inconsistent with Justice and Good Policy* (Philadelphia: M. Gurney, 1792), 24.

40. David Barrow, "Diary," June 15, 1795, Filson Historical Society, Louisville, Kentucky.

41. John Cleves Symmes to Charles W. Short, April 9, 1810, in: John Craig Hammond, *Slavery, Freedom, and Expansion in the Early American West* (Charlottesville: University of Virginia Press, 2007), 128.

42. "The Northwest Ordinance of 1787," in: Phillip R. Shriver and Clarence E. Wunderlin, Jr., eds., *The Documentary Heritage of Ohio* (Athens: Ohio University Press, 2000), 62.

43. According to the United States Census, Ohio's 1820 population was 581,434 versus 564,317 for Kentucky. Moreover, Ohio's population growth already eclipsed its southern neighbor between 1800 and 1810: increasing 408.7 percent for Ohio versus 84 percent for Kentucky.

44. "Constitution of the State of Ohio—1802," in: Shriver and Wunderlin, *The Documentary Heritage of Ohio*, 100.

45. Cincinnati's race riots (1829) saw violence between white working-class and black citizens, triggered when the city attempted to enforce its Black Laws. It produced an exodus of some 1,100 to 1,500 refugees—over half the city's free black population. Nikki Taylor, *Frontiers of Freedom: Cincinnati's Black Community, 1802–1868* (Athens: Ohio University Press, 2005), 14.

46. Alice Felt Tyler, *Freedom's Ferment: Phases of American Social History to 1860* (New York: Harper & Row, 1962), 1.

47. "The Whigs could easily have been replaced by the nativist Know-Nothing Party. Catholics and immigrants might have displaced black slaves as the hot topic of national politics. . . . After all, anti-slavery sentiments and racism often resided comfortably in the same mind." Thomas Bender, *A Nation among Nations: America's Place in World History* (New York: Hill & Wang, 2006), 164.

48. The term "America's Pentecost" from: Paul Conkin, *Cane Ridge: America's Pentecost* (Madison: University of Wisconsin Press, 1990).

49. Charlotte Ludlow to James Chambers, July 7, 1797, in: Lewis H. Garrard, *Memoir of Charlotte Chambers, by Her Grandson, Lewis H. Garrard* (Philadelphia: T. K. & P. G. Collins, 1856), 35.

50. While Ludlow remained within the Presbyterian fold, she attended sermons by revivalists of various denominations, a common practice among evangelicals. Following her husband's death in 1804, she cofounded the Ohio Bible Society and joined other voluntary societies in Cincinnati, organized by local women. "Charlotte Ludlow to Mrs. Chambers," n.d., and "Charlotte Ludlow to Mrs. Dunlop," n.d., in: Garrard, *Memoir of Charlotte Chambers*, 47, 48.

51. James McGready, "Narrative," *New York Missionary Magazine* 3 (1802), 156.

52. Barton Stone, "A Short History of the Life of Barton Warren Stone, Written by Himself (1847)," in *Voices from Cane Ridge*, ed. Rhodes Thompson (St. Louis: Bethany, 1954), 67.

53. In 1801, the *Kentucky Gazette* gave detailed demographic data for Lexington based on the latest census. The total population was just 1,795, including 1,333 white inhabitants, 439 slaves, and 23 "free people of color." *Kentucky Gazette*, April 27, 1801.

54. Stone, "Life," 64.

55. John B. Boles, *The Great Revival, 1787–1805: The Origins of the Southern Evangelical Mind* (Lexington: University Press of Kentucky, 1972), 70.

56. McGready's "Narrative" can be found in: James McGready, *The Posthumous Works of the Reverend and Pious James M'Gready* (Nashville: J. Smith, 1837), vii–xi, and excerpted in: *Western Missionary Magazine* 1 (February 1803), 27–28; (March 1803), 45–54; (April 1803), 99–103; (June 1803), 172–172; and *New York Missionary Magazine* 3 (1802), 156–159. Of McGready's "Narrative," Paul Conkin wrote: "No simple description of religious events, save possibly Jonathan Edwards' *Faithful Narrative*, had as profound and lasting an effect." Conkin, *Cane Ridge*, 55.

57. Timothy L. Smith, *Revivalism and Social Reform: American Protestantism on the Eve of the Civil War* (New York: Harper & Row, 1957), 9.

58. "The roadside along the beaten path was a landscape shaped by the natural environment. Rows of townhouses jammed along a main street looked little like the singular farmhouses that freckled the countryside, but strangely, observers noted repeatedly how the rural landscape blended in to the villages and vice versa." Craig Thompson Friend, *Along the Maysville Road: The Early American Republic in the Trans-Appalachian West* (Knoxville: University of Tennessee Press, 2005), 58.

59. Drake, *Natural and Statistical View*, vi–vii.

60. Boles, *The Great Revival*, 67.

61. Levi Purviance, *The Biography of Elder David Purviance* (Dayton: B. F. & G. W. Ells, 1848), 300.

62. Boles, *The Great Revival*, 58.

63. Barton Stone, *The Biography of Eld. Barton Warren Stone* (Cincinnati: J. A. & U. P. James, 1847), 39.

64. Richard McNemar, *The Kentucky Revival; or, a Short History of the Late Extraordinary Out-Pouring of the Spirit of God, in the Western States of America* (Pittsfield, Massachusetts, 1808), 34–35.

65. James B. Finley, *Autobiography of James B. Finley; or, Pioneer Life in the West* (Cincinnati, 1853), 166.

66. Peter Cartwright, *The Autobiography of Peter Cartwright, the Backwoods Preacher* (New York: Carlton & Porter, 1857), 38.

67. Conkin, *Cane Ridge*, 86.

68. Terah Templin to Joshua Lacy Wilson, February 2, 1802, Joshua Lacy Wilson Papers, Reuben T. Durrett Collection, Special Collections, University of Chicago Library.

69. Stone, *Biography*, 38.

70. Robert Breckinridge McAfee, "The History of the Rise and Progress of the First Settlements on Salt River & Establishment of the New Providence Church" (handwritten MSS), Filson Historical Society, Louisville, Kentucky, 16.

71. William Walls Woodward, *Surprising Accounts of the Revival of Religion in the United States of America* (Boston: William Walls Woodward, 1802), 36–37.

72. Beverly W. Bond, Jr., ed., *The Correspondence of John Cleves Symmes, Founder of the Miami Purchase* (New York: Macmillan, 1926), 299–302.

73. John Lyle, "Journal of a Missionary Tour within the Bounds of the Cumberland Presbytery Performed in the Year 1805," MS, 3, 5, 8, 20, Kentucky Historical Society, Frankfort, Kentucky.

74. George Washington Ranck, *History of Lexington Kentucky: Its Early Annals and Recent Progress* (Cincinnati: Robert Clarke, 1872), 109.

75. Adam Rankin, *Review of the Noted Revival in Kentucky, Commenced in the Year of Our Lord, 1801* (Lexington, Kentucky: John Bradford, 1803), 24, 20.

76. Woodward, *Surprising Accounts*, 35–36.

77. Spalding, *Sketches*, 104.

78. Stephen Badin to John Carroll, April 11, 1796, in: Spalding, *Sketches*, 8.

79. DePalma, *Dialogue on the Frontier*, 37.

80. Edward Fenwick to Father Concanen, March 3, 1807, in: Ambrose Coleman, "The Foundation of the Dominican Province in the United States," in *Historical Records and Studies, United States Catholic Historical Society of New York*, part 2 (October 1900), 372–373.

81. Stephen J. Stein, *The Shaker Experience in America* (New Haven, Connecticut: Yale University Press, 1992), 58.

82. Stein, *The Shaker Experience*, 57–58.

83. Conkin, *Cane Ridge*, 145.

84. Tom Kanon, "Seduced, Bewildered, and Lost: Anti-Shakerism on the Early Nineteenth Century Frontier," *Ohio Valley History* 7 (2007): 25n10.

85. Stone, *Biography*, 51.

86. The Cumberland Presbyterian Church continues to this day. McGready remained in good fellowship, although he returned to the mainstream Presbyterian Church. Rev. George Lewis wove a short history of the Cumberland Presbyterians around his encounter with one Mr. Smith, a Glasgow-born preacher traveling to Cincinnati who, "though not enjoying the advantages of a classical education," benefited from his "excellent Scottish education." George Lewis, *Impressions of America and the American Churches* (Edinburgh: W. P. Kennedy, 1845), 307–308.

87. Goss, *Cincinnati: The Queen City*, 484.

88. Andrew Carr Kemper, *A Memorial of the Rev. James Kemper for the Centennial of the Synod of Kentucky* (s.l., 1899), 15–17.

89. Lewis, *Impressions of America*, 309.

90. Caleb Swann Walker, "Diary," MSS VP 2307, Cincinnati History Library and Archives.

91. Walker, "Diary." At one Kentucky revival, a Presbyterian minister described a physician arriving with his friends to mock proceedings. The doctor, "a professed deist," swooned and was joined on the ground by dozens of his companions. "I humbly hope," added the preacher, "that most of them have experienced saving change." Ellen Eslinger, *Citizens of Zion: The Social Origins of Camp Meeting Revivalism* (Knoxville: University of Tennessee Press, 1999), 220–221.

92. Walker, "Diary."

93. Drake, *Natural and Statistical View*, 162, 164.

94. "From its beginnings to 1828, the United States spent nearly $3.6 million on internal improvements . . . in that same span of years, the thirteen leading benevolent societies, overwhelmingly Protestant in constituency and purpose, spent over $2.8 million to further their goals." Robin Klay and John Lunn, "Protestants and the American Economy in the Postcolonial Period: An Overview," in *God and Mammon: Protestants, Money, and the Market, 1790–1860*, ed. Mark A. Noll (New York: Oxford University Press, 2002), 41.

95. "Charlotte Ludlow Riske to Bella [Dunlop]," June 19, 1816; journal entry, September 28, 1816; and "C.L.R. to Nathaniel White," February 1817, in: Garrard, *Memoir of Charlotte Chambers*, 77, 79, 87.

96. Sam Haselby, *The Origins of American Religious Nationalism* (New York: Oxford University Press, 2015), 232–233.

97. William Henry Venable, *Beginnings of Literary Culture in the Ohio Valley: Historical and Biographical Sketches* (Cincinnati: Robert Clarke, 1891), 171.

98. Arthur J. Stansbury, *Trial of the Rev. Lyman Beecher, D.D. Before the Presbytery of Cincinnati on the Charge of Heresy* (New York: New York Observer, 1835), 3.

99. Wilson's First Presbyterian Church occupied a lot between Main and Walnut Streets; Beecher's Second Presbyterian sat between nearby Vine and Race Streets.

100. Aaron, *Cincinnati*, 29.

101. Oliver Farnsworth, *The Cincinnati Directory* (Cincinnati: Oliver Farnsworth, 1819).

102. "A Citizen," in: Farnsworth, *The Cincinnati Directory*, 32–34.

103. F. Gerald Ham, "The Prophet and the Mummyjums: Isaac Bullard and the Vermont Pilgrims of 1817," *Wisconsin Magazine of History* 56, no. 4 (Summer 1973): 295.

104. *Western Spy*, April 15, 1818.

105. Ham, "The Prophet and the Mummyjums," 296.

106. *Western Spy*, April 15, 1818.

107. *Home Missionary and American Pastor's Journal* 12, no. 4 (August 1839).

108. *Cincinnati Daily Times*, March 2, 1855.

109. *Western Spy*, April 15, 1818.

110. Timothy Flint, *Recollections of the Last Ten Years, Passed in Occasional Residences and Journeyings in the Valley of the Mississippi* (Boston: Cummings, Hilliard, & Co., 1826), 275, 277–278.

111. Flint, *Recollections*, 37–38, 41.

112. Unlike the Shakers, Bullard and his followers left little record, but similarities are revealing. Despite differences, both displayed millenarian enthusiasm and prophetic ideology. Both were outsiders from the rural Northeast: upstate New York and Vermont, respectively. This region became known as the Burned-Over District from the revivals sweeping its towns and valleys. It produced Shaker matriarch Ann Lee, Isaac Bullard, Mormon founder Joseph Smith, and self-styled prophet William Miller. It was a hotbed of resistance to urban networks of evangelical nationalism. In *The Burned-Over District*, Whitney Cross described how this "broad belt of land" connected west as far as the Ohio Valley via a "psychic highway," contiguous to the Erie Canal and other navigable waterways. Along this axis "congregated a people extraordinarily given to unusual religious beliefs, peculiarly devoted to crusades aimed at the perfection of mankind and the attainment of millennial happiness." Whitney R. Cross, *The Burned-Over District: The Social and Intellectual History of Enthusiastic Religion in Western New York, 1800–1850* (Ithaca, New York: Cornell University Press, 1950), 1.

113. *Cincinnati: A Guide to the Queen City and Its Neighbors* (Cincinnati: Wiesen-Hart, 1943), 160.

114. Teresa Ransom, *Fanny Trollope: A Remarkable Life* (New York: St. Martin's, 1995), 77.

115. Trollope, *Domestic Manners*, 55–56.

116. Trollope, *Domestic Manners*, 61–62.

CHAPTER 2

1. Alan I. Marcus, *Plague of Strangers: Social Groups and the Origins of City Services in Cincinnati, 1819–1870* (Columbus: Ohio State University Press, 1991).

2. Charles Fenno Hoffman, *A Winter in the Far West*, vol. 1 (London: Richard Bentley, 1835), 129. Usage of the term "melting pot" dates back to Israel Zangwill's 1892 play depicting New York immigrant life, *The Melting Pot*.

3. George Wilson Pierson, ed., *Tocqueville and Beaumont in America* (Baltimore: Johns Hopkins University Press, 1996), 566.

4. Michel Chevalier, *Society, Manners and Politics in the United States: Being a Series of Letters on North America*, trans. Thomas Gamaliel Bradford (Boston: Weeks, Jordan & Co., 1839), 200.

5. William Sherwood, 1848, in: Gregory Rhodes and Karen Regina, eds., *Cincinnati: An Urban History Sourcebook* (Cincinnati: Cincinnati Historical Society, 1988), 13.

6. Isabella Lucy Bird, *The Englishwoman in America* (London: John Murray, 1856), 125.

7. Charles Mackay, *Life and Liberty in America: or, Sketches of a Tour in the United States and Canada, in 1857–8*, vol. 1 (London: Smith, Elder, & Co., 1859), 201.

8. Andrew R. L. Cayton, "Artery and Border: The Ambiguous Development of the Ohio Valley in the Early Republic," *Ohio Valley History* 1, no. 1 (Winter 2001): 19. Cayton attributes the phrase "drainage is destiny" to Jack Kirby.

9. "An ordinance for preventing carrion from laying in the streets, lanes, allies, or commons of the town of Cincinnati, and for other purposes," targeted "person or persons" who would "cast, carry draw out or lay any dead horse or other dead carcase of cattle, sheeps, hog, dog, or any other animal, or any excrement, pelts or filth of any kind whatever" to be fined "a sum of money not exceeding three dollars." Unlicensed butchers and slaughterers were subject to fines of five dollars. *Western Spy and Hamilton Gazette*, July 24, 1802.

10. *Western Spy*, June 15, 1811.

11. *Inquisitor and Cincinnati Advertiser*, June 1, 1819, in: Aaron, *Cincinnati*, 89.

12. *Cincinnati Daily Gazette*, September 13, 1848, in: Marcus, *Plague of Strangers*, 107.

13. John P. Foote, *Memoirs of the Life of Samuel P. Foote* (Cincinnati: Robert Clarke, 1860), 174–175.

14. Marcus, *Plague of Strangers*, 55, 252n20.

15. J. P. Harrison, "Letter on the Sanitary Conditions of Cincinnati," in *The Transactions of the American Medical Association*, vol. 2 (1849), 619–621.

16. *Cincinnati Daily Gazette*, April 12, 1849.

17. *Daily Atlas*, January 1, 1849.

18. *Liberty Hall and Cincinnati Gazette*, March 30, 1849. The article listed thirty-two cholera deaths aboard three steamers at Louisville.

19. *Cincinnati Daily Gazette*, May 16, 1849.

20. Ken Emerson, *Doo-Dah!: Stephen Foster and the Rise of American Popular Culture* (New York: Simon & Schuster, 1998), 141.

21. A. E. Gwynne to [Cettie M.] Gwynne, July 5, 1849, in Ruth C. Carter, "Cincinnatians and Cholera: Attitudes toward the Epidemics of 1832 and 1849," *Queen City Heritage* 50 (1993): 43.

22. Margaret Haines Lytle to Elias H. Haines, May 12, 1849, Lytle Papers, Cincinnati History Library and Archives.

23. *Cincinnati Daily Gazette*, January 9, 1849.

24. Drake, *Natural and Statistical View*, 167.

25. In 1849 alone, Cincinnati newspapers included the *Catholic Telegraph*, the *Cincinnati Daily Gazette*, the *Cincinnati Daily Times*, the *Cincinnati Enquirer*, the *Cincinnati Volksblatt*, the *Daily Atlas*, the *Daily Dispatch*, *Der Wahrheitsfreund*, *Liberty Hall*, and the *Western Christian Advocate*.

26. *Liberty Hall*, May 24, 1849.

27. *Daily Cincinnati Gazette*, January 9, 1849.

28. Walter J. Daly, "The Black Cholera Comes to the Central Valley of America in the 19th Century—1832, 1849, and Later," *Transactions of the American Clinical and Climatological Association* 119 (2008): 145.

29. *Cincinnati Gazette*, August 8, 1849, and September 5, 1849. Eaton's population in the 1850 census was 1,346.

30. The leading local Presbyterian minister claimed foreigners accounted for 42 percent of all cholera fatalities, a fact he attributed to alcohol. Joan E. Marshall, "Cholera in an Indiana Market Town: 'Boosters' and Public Health Policy in Lafayette, 1849," *Indiana Magazine of History* 98, no. 3 (September 2002): 182–183, 199.

31. Walter Stix Glazer, *Cincinnati in 1840: The Social and Functional Organization of an Urban Community during the Pre-Civil War Period* (Columbus: Ohio State University Press, 1999), 72.

32. *Cincinnati Daily Gazette*, June 29, 1849.

33. David A. Tucker Jr., "Notes on Cholera in Southwestern Ohio," *Ohio Archeological and Historical Quarterly* 49 (October 1940): 383.

34. Donald A. Hutslar, "God's Scourge: The Cholera Years in Ohio," *Ohio History Journal* 105 (Summer–Autumn 1996): 182.

35. New York City's Board of Health recorded 5,017 cholera victims in 1849, or about 1 percent of the city population. In London around 15,000 people, some 0.5 percent of the 2.5 million inhabitants, died that year from cholera. Charles E. Rosenberg, *The Cholera Years: The United States in 1832, 1849, and 1866* (Chicago: University of Chicago Press, 2009), 114; and Philip Alcabes, *Dread: How Fear and Fantasy Have Fueled Epidemics from the Black Death to Avian Flu* (New York: Public Affairs, 2009), 65.

36. "Cincinnati being the home station of most of the steamers on the Ohio and lower Mississippi routes, the bed linen used upon them is usually washed by laundresses on shore. On the Nashville and St. Louis boats, such washing is generally done on board by laundresses from the shore, but at times the linen is taken on shore. Dr. Clenendin, through whose exertions, the light of truth shines on this local epidemic, states: 'These facts are certainly possessed of the most important bearing upon the history of the introduction of the disease, and from them the diffusion of cholera over the city of Cincinnati may be accounted for.'" Edmund Charles Wendt, *A Treatise on Asiatic Cholera* (New York: William Wood, 1885), 54.

37. Such conditions were typical. One physician noted: "Among the Germans especially, eight to ten families are seen to occupy the same house—a family in each room." Harrison, "Letter on the Sanitary Condition," 620.

38. Leonard Koester, ed., "Early Cincinnati and the Turners: From Mrs. Karl Tafel's Autobiography," *Historical and Philosophical Society of Ohio Bulletin* 7, no. 1 (January 1949): 19.

39. "Cholera is known by many names; thus the terms Asiatic, Indian, Malignant, Spasmodic, Eastern or Oriental, Algide, and epidemic cholera, and many others, have all been used to designate the same disease." L. M. Lawson, *Cholera: Its Nature and Treatment* (Cincinnati: Robinson & Jones, 1848), 2.

40. Orin E. Newton, *Asiatic Cholera as It Appeared in Cincinnati, O., in the Years 1849, 1850 and 1866* (Cincinnati: American Eclectic Review, 1867), 10.

41. Aaron, *Cincinnati*, 45.

42. Rosenberg, *The Cholera Years*, 26.

43. Cist, *Cincinnati in 1851*, 45.

44. John Lea, "Reprints and Reflections: 'Cholera, With Reference to the Geological Theory: A Proximate Cause—a Law by Which It Is Governed—a Prophylactic,'" *International Journal of Epidemiology* 42 (2013): 37.

45. Lawson, *Cholera*, 15.

46. S. A. Latta, *The Cholera in Cincinnati: or, A Connected View of the Controversy between the Homeopathists and the Methodist Expositor* (Cincinnati: Morgan & Overend, 1850), 3.

47. J. S. Chambers, *The Conquest of Cholera: America's Greatest Scourge* (New York: MacMillan, 1938), 221.

48. Glazer, *Cincinnati in 1840*, 93. Hailed as a man of "commanding talents" with "an unusual, almost prophetic vision," Drake embodied the coincidence of medical and civic interests. Physician and entrepreneur, urban booster, and property developer, he founded the Medical College of Ohio (1819), forerunner of today's University of Cincinnati College of Medicine. Emmet Field Horine, *Daniel Drake, 1785–1852: Pioneer Physician of the Midwest* (Philadelphia: University of Pennsylvania Press, 1961), 11.

49. Rosenberg, *Cholera Years*, 77–78.

50. *Daily Atlas*, January 5, 1849.

51. Edward S. Abdy, *Journal of a Residence and Tour of the United States of North America, from April 1833, to October, 1834*, vol. 2 (London: John Murray, 1835), 329.

52. Thomas C. Carroll, "Observations on the Asiatic Cholera, As It Appeared in Cincinnati during the Years 1849 and 1850," *Western Lancet* 15 (1854): 325–327.

53. Chambers, *Conquest of Cholera*, 223–224.

54. Edward D. Mansfield, *Memoirs of the Life and Services of Daniel Drake: With Notices of the Early Settlement of Cincinnati, and Some of Its Pioneer Citizens* (Cincinnati: Applegate, 1860), 220–222.

55. *Daily Cincinnati Gazette*, May 19, 1849.

56. Jonathan D. Sarna and Nancy H. Klein, *The Jews of Cincinnati* (Cincinnati: Center for the Study of American Jewish Experience, Hebrew Union College–Jewish Institute of Religion, 1989), 46; and Kevin Grace and Tom White, *Cincinnati Cemeteries: The Queen City Underground* (Charleston, South Carolina: Arcadia, 2004), 60–61.

57. Finley, *Sketches of Western Methodism: Biographical, Historical, and Miscellaneous* (Cincinnati: Methodist Book Concern, 1855), 110. Cincinnati's original Methodist burial ground, behind the Wesleyan Chapel on Fifth Street, was among those closed due to overcrowding. A newer, larger Wesleyan Cemetery opened in 1843 by the west fork of Mill Creek, five miles north of the city. Charles Theodore Greve, *Centennial History of Cincinnati and Representative Citizens*, vol. 1 (Chicago: Biographical Publishing, 1904), 713.

58. Grace and White, *Cincinnati Cemeteries*, 46.

59. Christine Quigley, *Skulls and Skeletons: Human Bone Collections and Accumulations* (Jefferson, North Carolina: McFarland, 2001), 76.

60. Cist, *Cincinnati in 1851*, 145.

61. "Incorporation of Spring Grove Cemetery and Laws Relating to Cemeteries," in: Adolphus Strauch, *Spring Grove Cemetery: Its History and Improvements* (Cincinnati: Robert Clarke, 1869), 84–90.

62. Strauch, *Spring Grove*, 28, 22.

63. One author counted Cincinnati church adherence at roughly 30,600, or some 66 percent of the 46,338 residents in the 1840 census. Estimated adherence was twelve thousand Roman Catholics, six thousand Presbyterians, five thousand Methodists, four thousand Baptists, two thousand Episcopalians, one thousand Unitarians, five hundred Universalists, and five hundred "Dunkards" [*sic*]. James S. Buckingham, *The Eastern and Western States of America*, vol. 2 (London: Fisher, Son, & Company, 1842), 393.

64. Margaret Lytle to Elias H. Haines, July 2, 1849, Lytle Papers, Cincinnati History Library and Archives.

65. See: Nathan O. Hatch, *The Democratization of American Christianity* (New Haven, Connecticut: Yale University Press, 1989).

66. By 1851 alone the city boasted five orphanages, various homes for widows and paupers, a poorhouse with its own farm, a "relief union," a tract depository, numerous domestic and foreign missionary boards and benevolent organizations, and over a dozen temperance societies. Cist, *Cincinnati in 1851*, 150–159.

67. Lyman Beecher, *Autobiography of Lyman Beecher*, ed. Barbara Cross (Cambridge, Massachusetts: Belknap Press, 1961), 2:226.

68. "Harriet Beecher Stowe to Eliza Cabot Follen, February 16, 1852," in: Charles Edward Stowe, *Life of Harriet Beecher Stowe, Compiled from Her Letters and Journals* (Cambridge, Massachusetts: Houghton Mifflin, 1890), 198.

69. John King Lord, *Sermons of Rev. John King Lord*, ed. Nathan Lord (Boston: Perkins & Whipple, 1850), 92.

70. *Cincinnati Journal*, June 29, 1832.

71. Rosenberg, *The Cholera Years*, 44.

72. *Catholic Telegraph*, July 12, 1832.

73. John A. McFarland to Francis P. McFarland, July 19, 1849, I-1-a ALS, Archdiocese of Cincinnati Collection, University of Notre Dame Archives.

74. Roger Fortin, *Faith and Action: A History of the Archdiocese of Cincinnati, 1821–1996* (Columbus: Ohio State University Press, 2002), 128.

75. Rosenberg, *The Cholera Years*, 146.

76. Fortin, *Faith and Action*, 128

77. Christopher J. Kauffman, *Ministry and Meaning: A Religious History of Catholic Health Care in the United States* (New York: Crossroad, 1995), 61.

78. *Louisville Journal*, August 21, 1849, in: Gail E. Husch, *Something Coming: Apocalyptic Expectation and Mid Nineteenth-Century American Painting* (Hanover, New Hampshire: University Press of New England, 2000), 126.

79. Fortin, *Faith and Action*, 82. Prior to the establishment of the orphanage, the St. Aloysius orphans were housed with German-speaking host families in the city.

80. Charles Theodore Greve, *Centennial History of Cincinnati and Representative Citizens*, vol. 1 (Chicago: Biographical Publishing, 1904), 588.

81. Cist, *Cincinnati in 1851*, 151.

82. *Western Washingtonian and Sons of Temperance Record*, October 31, 1845.

83. *Cincinnati Enquirer*, June 25, 1853.

84. Three murders were reported in Cincinnati in 1846 and twenty-two in 1854. Jed Dannenbaum, *Drink and Disorder: Temperance Reform in Cincinnati from the Washingtonian Revival to the WCTU* (Urbana and Chicago: University of Illinois Press, 1984), 76–77.

85. *Cincinnati Commercial,* July 20, 1853, in: Dannenbaum, *Drink and Disorder,* 74. Other notorious Cincinnati neighborhoods included "Rat Row" along the wharf and the German "Sausage Row."

86. Drake, *Natural and Statistical View,* 139.

87. *Daily Atlas,* May 18, 1849.

88. *Western Christian Advocate,* January 21, 1843.

89. Jed Dannenbaum, "Immigrants and Temperance: Ethnocultural Conflict in Cincinnati, 1845–1860," *Ohio History* 87, no. 2 (Spring 1978): 127.

90. *Cincinnati Gazette,* May 16, 1849.

91. *Western Christian Advocate,* November 13, 1850.

92. *Liberty Hall and Cincinnati Gazette,* May 24, 1849.

93. *Cincinnati Daily Gazette,* May 31, 1849.

94. *Western Christian Advocate,* January 9, 1850.

95. *Western Christian Advocate,* November 13, 1850.

96. *Western Christian Advocate,* February 12, 1844.

97. *Daily Atlas,* January 1, 1849.

98. *Cincinnati Journal,* May 25, 1837.

99. Jed Dannenbaum, "The Crusader: Samuel Cary and Cincinnati Temperance," *Cincinnati Historical Society Bulletin* 33, no. 2 (Summer 1975): 146.

100. *Proceedings in the Fifth Ward for Coffee House Reform* (Cincinnati, 1837), 9.

101. Dannenbaum, *Drink and Disorder,* 25.

102. Elizur Deming, *The Cincinnati Directory for the Year 1834* (Cincinnati: E. Deming, 1834), 258–259.

103. *Western Washingtonian,* March 14, 1846.

104. See: Dannenbaum, *Drink and Disorder,* 90.

105. Critics of William Henry Harrison's 1840 presidential campaign popularized the term "log cabin and hard cider" to deride its folksy populism. Howe, *What God Hath Wrought,* 574.

106. Glazer, *Cincinnati in 1840,* 76.

107. *Cincinnati Enquirer,* June 25, 1853.

108. *Proceedings,* 7.

109. *Proceedings,* 12.

110. William J. Rorabaugh, *The Alcoholic Republic: An American Tradition* (New York: Oxford University Press, 1979), 121.

111. *Journal of the American Temperance Union* 14, no. 8 (August 1, 1850): 120.

112. John G. Wooley and William E. Johnson, *Temperance Progress in the Century* (London: Linscott, 1903), 115.

113. *Report of the Executive Committee of the American Temperance Union, 1840* (New York: S. W. Benedict, 1840), 55–56.

114. Dannenbaum, *Drink and Disorder,* 33–34.

115. Dannenbaum, "The Crusader," 138.

116. One story had young George Washington rescue a drowning girl from a frozen river, his "self-sacrificing spirit" foreshadowing the later, "more august events of his life." *Western Washingtonian and Sons of Temperance Record,* August 30, 1845.

117. Jed Dannenbaum notes that of the seventy-four divisions outside Hamilton County, 77 percent "were on major canals, rivers, railroads, or the National Road.

Another thirteen (17.6 percent) were within seventy-five miles of Cincinnati." Dannenbaum, *Drink and Disorder*, 46.

118. A. B. Grosh, *The Washingtonian Pocket Companion, Containing a Choice Collection of Temperance Hymns, Songs, etc.* (Utica, New York: B. S. Merrell, 1842), 10.

119. Published collections of sermons were commonplace, but Finney furnished step-by-step instruction for the organization and conduct of revivals. Revivalism, he asserted, was "not a miracle, or dependent on a miracle in any sense. It is a purely philosophical result of the right use of the constituted means." Charles Grandison Finney, *Lectures on the Revivals of Religion* (New York: Leavitt, Lord, & Co., 1835), 12.

120. Dannenbaum, "The Crusader," 142.

121. Lyman Beecher to John Bartholomew Gough, January 21, 1845, in: John Marsh, *Temperance Recollections: Labors, Defeats, Triumphs. An Autobiography* (New York: Charles Scribner, 1866), 128.

122. *Western Christian Advocate*, March 8, 1844.

123. *Western Washingtonian and Sons of Temperance Record*, November 21, 1845.

124. *Western Washingtonian*, April 18, 1846.

125. *Western Washingtonian*, September 20, 1845.

126. *Western Washingtonian*, October 31, 1845.

127. Cist, *Cincinnati in 1851*, 158–159.

128. Dannenbaum, *Drink and Disorder*, 60, 86.

129. *Journal of the American Temperance Union* 2, no. 11 (November 1838): 178.

130. *Journal of the American Temperance Union* 1, no. 10 (October 1837): 146.

131. *Western Washingtonian*, November 1851.

132. Daniel Drake, "Breweries vs. Foundries: Address Given at Louisville, Kentucky, December 25, 1841, and Chillicothe, Ohio, July 4, 1842," MSS qD761RM, Cincinnati History Library and Archives.

133. Dannenbaum, *Drink and Disorder*, 152n50.

134. Alison Clark Efford, *German Immigrants, Race, and Citizenship in the Civil War Era* (New York: Cambridge University Press, 2013), 195.

135. Fortin, *Faith and Action*, 127.

136. John F. Quinn, "Father Mathew's Disciples: American Catholic Support for Temperance, 1840–1920," *Church History* vol. 65, no. 4 (December 1996), 626.

137. *Catholic Telegraph*, June 18, 1842.

138. Charles Dickens, *American Notes for General Circulation*, vol. 2 (London: Chapman & Hall, 1842), 86.

139. *Cincinnati Enquirer*, December 20, 1849; and *Western Christian Advocate*, May 19, 1843.

140. John F. Quinn, *Father Mathew's Crusade: Temperance in Nineteenth-Century Ireland and Irish America* (Amherst: University of Massachusetts Press, 2002), 231.

141. Frank J. Mathew, *Father Mathew: His Life and Times* (London: Cassell, 1890), 199.

142. Tyler Anbinder, *Nativism and Slavery: The Northern Know Nothings and the Politics of the 1850s* (New York: Oxford University Press, 1992), 142, 145.

143. *Cincinnati Commercial*, January 22, 1847.

144. *Cincinnati Daily Gazette*, July 30, 1849.

145. *The Ohio Gazetteer and Travelers' Guide* of 1839, in a list of communities with post offices in Hamilton County, uses the name Mount Healthy. Warren Jenkins, *The*

Ohio Gazetteer and Travelers' Guide (Columbus, Ohio: Isaac N. Whiting, 1839), 216. I am grateful to Dr. Julie Turner of the Mount Healthy Historical Society for sharing this history.

CHAPTER 3

1. *Cincinnati Journal*, March 2, 1832.

2. Lyman Beecher to Catharine Beecher, July 8, 1830, in: Beecher, *Autobiography*, 2:67.

3. John R. Bodo, *The Protestant Clergy and Public Issues, 1812–1848* (Princeton, New Jersey: Princeton University Press, 1954), 22.

4. Steven Mintz, *Moralists and Modernizers: America's Pre-Civil War Reformers* (Baltimore: Johns Hopkins University Press, 1995), 52.

5. Calvin Colton, *Protestant Jesuitism* (New York: Harper & Brothers, 1836), iv, 24.

6. Daniel Walker Howe, "Religion and Politics in the Antebellum North," in *Religion and American Politics: From the Colonial Period to the Present*, ed. Mark A. Noll and Luke E. Harlow (New York: Oxford University Press, 2007), 130.

7. On the Benevolent Empire in New York, see: Edwin G. Burrows and Mike Wallace, *Gotham: A History of New York City to 1898* (New York: Oxford University Press, 2000), 493–508.

8. *The First Report of the American Home Missionary Society* (New York: D. Fanshaw, 1827), 3.

9. Congregationalist minister Samuel Goodrich's parody of Methodist Lorenzo Dow, in: Hatch, *Democratization*, 20.

10. Cartwright, quoted in: William Warren Sweet, *Religion on the American Frontier, 1783–1850*, vol. 3, *The Congregationalists* (Chicago: University of Chicago Press, 1939), 257n34.

11. Presbyterianism placed distant second with 18.7 percent of the Ohio population; Congregationalists amounted to just 2.9 percent. Philip Barlow and Mark Silk, eds., *Religion and Public Life in the Midwest: America's Common Denominator?* (Walnut Creek, California: Altamira Press, 2004), 69.

12. Cist, *Cincinnati in 1851*, 83.

13. Timothy Flint (Cincinnati) to Abel Flint (Hartford, Connecticut), March 20, 1816, MSS VF 4270, Cincinnati History Library and Archives.

14. Beecher, *Autobiography*, 1:253.

15. Michael P. Young, *Bearing Witness against Sin: The Evangelical Birth of the American Social Movement* (Chicago: University of Chicago Press, 2006), 67.

16. Tocqueville, *Democracy in America*, 306.

17. Pierson, *Tocqueville and Beaumont in America*, 553.

18. The A.H.M.S. classified Kentucky, Tennessee, and Arkansas as "Western" rather than "Southern," although none of these states were especially significant to its operations. Eventually, its "Western" operations stretched to the Pacific, though the Midwest remained within the same jurisdiction.

19. *The Tenth Report of the American Home Missionary Society* (New York: James van Norden, 1836), 32.

20. *The Twenty-Fifth Report of the American Home Missionary Society* (New York: J. F. Trow, 1851), 59, 64, 67–72, 76–84.

21. David G. Horvath, ed., *Guide to the Microfilm Edition of the Papers of the American Home Missionary Society, 1816–1894* (Woodbridge, Connecticut: Scholarly Resources, 2005), 24.

22. *Home Missionary* 3, no. 2 (June 1830).

23. Colin B. Goodykoontz, *Home Missions on the American Frontier: With Particular Reference to the American Home Missionary Society* (Caldwell, Idaho: Caxton Printers, 1939), 290.

24. Absalom Peters to John Sargent, February 22, 1830, box 501, folder 7, A.H.M.S. records, Amistad Research Center, Tulane University, New Orleans, Louisiana.

25. Taylor, *Frontiers of Freedom*, 20–21.

26. Benjamin P. Thomas, *Theodore Weld: Crusader for Freedom* (New Brunswick, New Hampshire: Rutgers University Press, 1950), 76.

27. Beecher, *Autobiography*, 2:244.

28. Beecher, *Autobiography*, 2:242.

29. On the Lane debates, see: Thomas, *Theodore Weld*, 100–111.

30. *Cincinnati Journal*, December 14, 1832.

31. *The Fifteenth Report of the American Home Missionary Society* (New York: William Osborn, 1841), 71.

32. David H. Riddle, *Our Country for the Sake of the World: A Sermon on Behalf of the American Home Missionary Society* (New York: Baker, Godwin, & Co., 1851), 14, 19, 8.

33. *Home Missionary* 12, no. 8 (December 1839).

34. *Report of the First Annual Fair of the Ohio Mechanics Institute* (Cincinnati, 1838), quoted in: Aaron, *Cincinnati*, 36.

35. G. C. Judson (Grafton, Ohio) to Milton Badger, February 16, 1849, box 302, folder 3, A.H.M.S. records, Amistad Research Center, Tulane University, New Orleans, Louisiana.

36. Ellery Bascom (Wilkesville, Ohio) to Milton Badger, January 8, 1858, box 299, folder 6, A.H.M.S. records, Amistad Research Center, Tulane University, New Orleans, Louisiana.

37. Charles Hall to Horace Hooker, July 22, 1832, box 503, folder 1, A.H.M.S. records, Amistad Research Center, Tulane University, New Orleans, Louisiana.

38. "Lane became definitely a school for educating young Yankees in the West. Of the forty members of the first theological class listed . . . the antecedents of thirty-seven are known, and thirty-one of these were Yankees from New England or upstate New York." Robert Samuel Fletcher, *A History of Oberlin College from Its Foundation through the Civil War*, vol. 1 (Oberlin, Ohio: Oberlin College, 1943) 54–55.

39. James W. Fraser, *Pedagogue for God's Kingdom: Lyman Beecher and the Second Great Awakening* (Lanham, Maryland: University Press of America, 1985), 114.

40. Beecher, *Autobiography*, 2:183.

41. *Home Missionary* 6, no. 12 (April 1834).

42. Absalom Peters to Horace Hooker, July 23, 1828, in: Sweet, *Religion on the American Frontier*, 3:104.

43. *Home Missionary* 12, no. 5 (October 1830).

44. *The Eleventh Report of the American Home Missionary Society* (New York: William Osborn, 1837), 84.

45. *Home Missionary* 13, no. 1 (May 1840).

46. *First Report of the American Home Missionary Society*, 51.

47. *The Tenth Report of the American Home Missionary Society* (New York: James van Norden, 1836), 63.

48. *Eleventh Report of the American Home Missionary Society*, 58.

49. Thornton Mills to Milton Badger, December 2, 1839, box 299, folder 7, A.H.M.S. records, Amistad Research Center, Tulane University, New Orleans.

50. Henry Le Duc and John Follett (Johnstown, Ohio) to the Executive Committee of the A.H.M.S., January 1, 1840, box 300, folder 1, A.H.M.S. records, Amistad Research Center, Tulane University, New Orleans.

51. See: Francis Murray (Portage, Ohio) to Charles Hall, September 6, 1849, box 304, folder 3, and Chester Colton (New Carlisle, Ohio) to Milton Badger, January 24, 1849, box 302, folder 4, A.H.M.S. records, Amistad Research Center, Tulane University, New Orleans, Louisiana.

52. *The Seventeenth Report of the American Home Missionary Society* (New York: William Osborn, 1842), 78.

53. *Home Missionary* 1, no. 1 (May 1828).

54. *Cincinnati Journal*, November 5, 1831, and May 11, 1832.

55. *Catholic Telegraph*, October 22, 1831.

56. One historian noted: "early issues of *The Home Missionary* . . . lack any reference to Rome." Bodo, *The Protestant Clergy*, 65n13.

57. *Home Missionary* 2, no. 1 (May 1830).

58. *Home Missionary* 8, no. 1 (May 1835).

59. Thomas Adams, ed., *Germany and the Americas: Culture, Politics, and History* (Santa Barbara, California: ABC-CLIO, 2005), 240

60. Max Oertel (1851), in: Joseph M. White, "Cincinnati's German Catholic Life: A Heritage of Lay Participation," *U.S. Catholic Historian* 12, no. 3 (Summer 1994): 1.

61. *Home Missionary* 7, no. 4 (August 1834).

62. *Home Missionary* 11, no. 9 (January 1839).

63. Robert C. Rau, "History of the German Evangelical Churches in Cincinnati," in *Das Ohiotal—The Ohio Valley: The German Dimension*, ed. Don Heinrich Tolzmann (New York: Peter Lang, 1993), 160–161.

64. Arthur M. Schlesinger, quoted in: John Tracy Ellis, *American Catholicism* (Chicago: University of Chicago Press, 1969), 151.

65. Ray Allen Billington, *The Protestant Crusade, 1800–1860: A Study of the Origins of American Nativism* (New York: MacMillan, 1963), 108.

66. *Home Missionary* 16, no. 4 (August 1843).

67. *Home Missionary* 12, no. 4 (August 1839).

68. On violence in Louisville, see, for example: Charles E. Deusner, "The Know Nothing Riots in Louisville," *Register of the Kentucky Historical Society* 61, no. 2 (April 1963): 122–147.

69. Francis Murry (Portage, Ohio) to Charles Hall, November 22, 1849, box 300, folder 3, A.H.M.S. records, Amistad Research Center, Tulane University, New Orleans, Louisiana.

70. John T. Sherwin (Berlin, Ohio) to Milton Badger and Charles Hall, May 1, 1839, box 299, folder 6, A.H.M.S. records, Amistad Research Center, Tulane University, New Orleans, Louisiana.

71. David Smith (Maumee, Ohio) to Absalom Peters, January 3, 1832, box 297, folder 3, A.H.M.S. records, Amistad Research Center, Tulane University, New Orleans, Louisiana.

72. Richard L. Bushman, *The Refinement of America: Persons, Houses, Cities* (New York: Alfred A. Knopf, 1992), 330.

73. Horace Bushnell, *Barbarism the First Danger: A Discourse for Home Missions* (New York: William Osborn, 1847), 5–6, 20, 28.

74. *Cincinnati Journal*, June 22, 1832.

75. George H. Holland (Columbus, Ohio) to Milton Badger, January 13th, 1853, box 306, folder 7, A.H.M.S. records, Amistad Research Center, Tulane University, New Orleans, Louisiana.

76. Thornton Mills (Cincinnati, Ohio) to Milton Badger, February 9, 1853, box 307, folder 1, A.H.M.S. records, Amistad Research Center, Tulane University, New Orleans, Louisiana.

77. D. W. McClung, *The Centennial Anniversary of the City of Hamilton, Ohio* (Cincinnati: Laurence Printing & Publishing, 1891), 174.

78. George Gompert and Charles Gustavus Muller (Hamilton, Ohio) to the Executive Committee of the American Home Missionary Society, October 26, 1853, box 307, folder 2, A.H.M.S. records, Amistad Research Center, Tulane University, New Orleans, Louisiana.

79. Ralph Cushman to Absalom Peters, December 17, 1830, in: Sweet, *Religion on the American Frontier*, 2:104.

80. Joshua Lacy Wilson, *Four Propositions Sustained against the Claims of the American Home Missionary Society* (Cincinnati: Robinson & Fairbank, 1831), 3, 4.

81. Joshua Lacy Wilson to Thomas Hopkins Gallaudet, March 23, 1818, Joshua Lacy Wilson Papers, Reuben T. Durrett Collection, Special Collections, University of Chicago Library.

82. Wilson, *Four Propositions*, 8.

83. James B. Morrow (Columbus, Ohio) to Absalom Peters, January 21, 1830, box 295, folder 5, A.H.M.S. records, Amistad Research Center, Tulane University, New Orleans, Louisiana.

84. Absalom Peters to Henry Little (Oxford, Ohio), April 9, 1832, box 503, folder 1, A.H.M.S. records, Amistad Research Center, Tulane University, New Orleans, Louisiana.

85. J. W. Douglass (Cincinnati, Ohio) to Absalom Peters, October 8, 1832, box 297, folder 1, A.H.M.S. records, Amistad Research Center, Tulane University, New Orleans, Louisiana.

86. Vincent Harding, *A Certain Magnificence: Lyman Beecher and the Transformation of American Religion* (New York: Carlson Publishing, 1991), 381.

87. Stansbury, *Trial of the Rev. Lyman Beecher*, 3.

88. Joshua Lacy Wilson to John H. Groesbeck, March 9, 1835, in: Harding, *A Certain Magnificence*, 378.

89. Beecher, *Autobiography*, 2:344.

90. Bertram Wyatt-Brown, *Lewis Tappan and the Evangelical War against Slavery* (Cleveland: Press of Case Western Reserve University, 1969), 293.

91. Thornton A. Mills (Cincinnati, Ohio) to Milton Badger, February 9, 1853, box 307, folder 1, A.H.M.S. records, Amistad Research Center, Tulane University, New Orleans, Louisiana.

92. Marcus Hicks (Columbus, Ohio) to Milton Badger, June 10, 1853, box 306, folder 7, A.H.M.S. records, Amistad Research Center, Tulane University, New Orleans, Louisiana.

93. Cronon, *Nature's Metropolis.*

94. Steven J. Ross, *Workers on the Edge: Work, Leisure, and Politics in Industrializing Cincinnati, 1788–1890* (New York: Columbia University Press, 1985), 6.

95. John Locke's *A Letter Concerning Toleration* (1689) was the textbook of pluralism in the early American republic. Locke's advocacy of toleration influenced separation of church and state, but many Protestants and nativists reiterated Locke's exclusion of atheists and Catholics from public life.

96. *Western Spy*, December 7, 1811.

97. Michael Scott, John M. Mahon, John White, and P. Walsh to John Carrere, November 23, 1818, in: *Catholic Historical Review* 5 (1920): 431.

98. Fortin, *Faith and Action*, 15–17. For Catholic-Protestant cooperation in early Cincinnati, see: DePalma, *Dialogue on the Frontier*, especially chapter 2.

99. *Liberty Hall and Cincinnati Gazette*, March 30, 1822.

100. DePalma, *Dialogue on the Frontier*, 51–52.

101. DePalma, *Dialogue on the Frontier*, 54–55.

102. Hatch, *Democratization*, 46.

103. Jay P. Dolan, *Catholic Revivalism: The American Experience, 1830–1900* (Notre Dame, Indiana: University of Notre Dame Press, 1978), 7.

104. Fortin, *Faith and Action*, 26–27.

105. John H. Lamott, *History of the Archdiocese of Cincinnati, 1821–1921* (New York and Cincinnati: Frederick Pustet, 1921), 121.

106. Francis X. Weininger's revival at Lancaster, Ohio, was described as a folk-mission, an Anglicization of *Volks-Mission. Catholic Telegraph*, October 29, 1850.

107. "Second Letter from Rev. Mr Hill" (1824), in: *American Catholic Historical Researches* 10, no. 4 (October 1893): 148.

108. Orestes Brownson "Protestant Revivals and Catholic Retreats," *Brownson's Quarterly Review* 3, no. 3 (July 1858): 312, 303, 289.

109. "Extract of a Letter of Rev. Mr. Montgomery, at Cincinnati, to Dr. Fenwick, Bishop of Cincinnati," in: *American Catholic Historical Researches* 10, no. 4 (October 1893): 148.

110. *Catholic Telegraph*, October 29, 1831.

111. Jenny Franchot, *Roads to Rome: The Antebellum Protestant Encounter with Catholicism* (Berkeley: University of California Press, 1994), 281n10.

112. Buggeln, "A Marketplace for Religion," 361.

113. Brownson, "Protestant Revivals," *Brownson's Quarterly Review* 3, no. 3 (July 1858): 299.

114. Edward Fenwick to P. Pallavicini, March 29, 1825, in: DePalma, *Dialogue on the Frontier*, 167n39.

115. James M. O'Toole, *The Faithful: A History of Catholics in America* (Cambridge, Massachusetts: Harvard University Press, 2008), 27; and Fortin, *Faith and Action*, 45.

116. Fortin, *Faith and Action*, 57. A total of 1,156 Cincinnati Catholics were baptized in 1843 alone.

117. *Catholic Telegraph*, May 16, 1840.

118. While the United States Census Bureau collected some information on religious institutions beginning in 1850, it collected no data on private religious affiliation. According to church estimates, however, Cincinnati's Catholic population reached fifty thousand in 1846. Lamott, *History of the Archdiocese of Cincinnati*, 78.

119. Fortin, *Faith and Action*, xi.

120. The Lyon-based Society for the Propagation of the Faith was especially beneficial, contributing some 175,000 francs to the Diocese of Cincinnati between 1823 and 1836. William Baughin, "Nativism in Cincinnati Before 1860" (master's thesis, University of Cincinnati, 1963), 34.

121. Ohio's Catholic clergy in 1844 included native-born Americans, Germans, French, Irish, Italians, Belgians, and one Spaniard. Fortin, *Faith and Action*, 57.

122. Nathan Bangs, *A History of the Methodist Episcopal Church*, vol. 2 (New York: Carlton & Phillips, 1853), 399–400.

123. Edward Fenwick to J. B. Clicteur, July 13, 1829, Ii-4-D, Archdiocese of Cincinnati Collection, University of Notre Dame Archives. While Fenwick's letter to Clicteur was mostly in French, he lapsed into English to express personal frustrations with Badin's quirks.

124. Stephen Badin to Edward Fenwick, April 7, 1825, and August 12, 1825, Ii-4-d, Archdiocese of Cincinnati Collection, University of Notre Dame Archives.

125. Stephen Badin to Edward Fenwick, August 12, 1825, Ii-4-d, Archdiocese of Cincinnati Collection, University of Notre Dame Archives.

126. DePalma, *Dialogue on the Frontier*, 64.

127. Peter Leo Johnson, *Crosier on the Frontier: A Life of John Martin Henni* (Madison: State Historical Society of Wisconsin, 1959), 42.

128. Fortin, *Faith and Action*, 22.

129. Francis P. Kenrick to Edward Fenwick, April 29, 1832, Ii-4-e, Archdiocese of Cincinnati Collection, University of Notre Dame Archives.

130. DePalma, *Dialogue on the Frontier*, 166n38.

131. Johnson, *Crosier on the Frontier*, 33–34

132. Lamott, *History of the Archdiocese of Cincinnati*, 135.

133. See: Peter Williams, "German-American Catholicism in Cincinnati" (unpublished MSS), MSS VP 903, Cincinnati History Library and Archives.

134. Johnson, *Crosier on the Frontier*, 39–48.

135. Baptismal records from 1840 show Cincinnati's 8,800-strong German Catholic population at 65.9 percent of the city's Catholic total. Fortin, *Faith and Action*, 78.

136. Fortin, *Faith and Action*, 51–52.

137. In order of foundation, Cincinnati's earliest German parishes were: Holy Trinity (1834), St. Mary's (1845), St. John the Baptist (1845), St. Joseph's (1845), St. Philomena (1846), St. Paul's (1847), St. Michael's (1847), St. Augustine's (1852), St. Francis Seraph (1859), Immaculate Conception (1859), St. Anthony's (1859), and St. Louis (1859). See: Williams, "German-American Catholicism in Cincinnati."

138. E. T. Collins to John Baptist Purcell, January 27, 1834, Ii-4-e, Archdiocese of Cincinnati Collection, University of Notre Dame Archives.

139. John Neumann to John Baptist Purcell, May 31, 1839, in: Jeffrey G. Herbert, *Old St. Mary's Church, Cincinnati: A History of the First 160 Years of Catholic Faith* (Milford, Ohio: Little Miami, 2006), 3–4.

140. Anthony Blanc to John Baptist Purcell, March 15, 1859, Ii-4-O, Archdiocese of Cincinnati Collection, University of Notre Dame Archives.

141. John Brunner to John Baptist Purcell, May 18, 1854, Ii-4-m, Archdiocese of Cincinnati Collection, University of Notre Dame Archives.

142. A.H.M.S. recorded $4,013,198.08 in receipts, 1826–1861. Frederick Kuhns, "A Glimpse of Home Missionary Activities in the Old Northwest, 1826–1861," *Journal of the Presbyterian Historical Society* 27, no. 2 (June 1949): 104.

143. Horvath, *Papers of the American Home Missionary Society*, x–xi.

144. Colton, *Protestant Jesuitism*, 35.

145. Friedrich C. D. Wyneken, "The Distress of German Lutherans in North America" (1843), in *Antirevivalism in Antebellum America: A Collection of Religious Voices*, ed. James D. Bratt (Piscataway, New Jersey: Rutgers University Press, 2006), 117.

146. Calvin Colton, "Thoughts on the Religious State of the Country" (1836), in: Bratt, *Antirevivalism*, 97, 102, 103.

147. Tocqueville, *Democracy in America*, 300–301.

148. Hugh Brogan, *Alexis de Tocqueville: A Biography* (New Haven, Connecticut: Yale University Press, 2007), 178.

149. Samuel F. B. Morse, *Foreign Conspiracy against the Liberties of the United States* (New York: Leavitt, Lord, & Co., 1835), 96.

CHAPTER 4

1. New School African Presbyterian Church (between Main and Walnut Streets) and Bethel African Methodist Episcopal Church were among several houses of worship identified by Charles Cist's 1841 city directory but omitted in Doolittle & Munson's influential Cincinnati map that same year. The other omitted houses of worship were: the United German Protestant Church; the German Lutheran Church (housed in a basement on Walnut Street); the United Brethren in Christ; the Disciples of Christ; the First Restorationist meetinghouse; the Bethel Union Chapel; the Welsh Congregational Chapel; the Welsh Calvinistic Methodist Chapel; Asbury Chapel; and the 2nd and 3rd Societies of the New Jerusalem Church (Swedenborgian). Such omissions suggest how race and ethnicity, as well as visibility, marked recognition. Cist, *Cincinnati in 1841*, 96–99; and Curtis Doolittle and James Munson, *Topographical Map of the City of Cincinnati, from Actual Survey* (Cincinnati: Doolittle & Munson, 1841).

2. Hugh Kirkland, *Narratives of Scenes and Events Which Occurred Lately in Cincinnati, Entitled Freedom of Speech Vindicated, Defended, and Maintained* (Cincinnati: H. Kirkland, 1853), 16–17.

3. James Brown Scouller, *A Manual of the United Presbyterian Church of North America, 1751–1887* (Pittsburgh: United Presbyterian Church of North America, 1887), 411. Scouller's biographical note alludes to "the remaining twenty-five or thirty

years of [Kirkland's] life," following his 1834 break with the Associate Presbyterians, thus estimating the year of his death c. 1859–1864.

4. Kirkland, *Narratives*, 7, 2.
5. Kirkland, *Narratives*, 4.
6. Kirkland, *Narratives*, 1, 18–19, 20, 25–26.
7. Kirkland, *Narratives*, 9, 12.
8. Ezra 1:2 (King James Bible).
9. William Manchester, *A World Lit Only by Fire: The Medieval Mind and the Renaissance* (Boston: Little, Brown, 1993), 10.
10. John Locke, *An Essay Concerning Toleration*, vol. 1 (London: Awnsham Churchill, 1689), 47–48.
11. *Cincinnati Journal*, December 14, 1832.
12. Morse, *Foreign Conspiracy*, 60.
13. Harding, *A Certain Magnificence*, 234–235.
14. Beecher, *Autobiography*, 1:252, 253n.
15. Franklin Y. Vail, in: Beecher, *Autobiography*, 2:181.
16. Howe, *What Hath God Wrought*, 2–3. Morse was allegedly besotted with Annie Ellsworth, the daughter of United States patent commissioner Goodrich Ellsworth.
17. Beecher, *A Plea for the West*, 31.
18. In its twelfth year of operation, the A.T.S. claimed to have 125,682,000 pages of religious literature and to have distributed 96,851,174 pages. *Twelfth Annual Report of the American Tract Society* (New York: D. Fanshaw, 1837), 13.
19. Wyatt-Brown, *Lewis Tappan*, 50–51.
20. "From the Rev. DR. LYMAN BEECHER," in *McGuffey's Newly Revised Fourth Eclectic Reader* (Cincinnati: Winthrop B. Smith, 1848), 6.
21. "Memorandum of the Executive Committee," Lane Theological Seminary, 1834, 286-1-30, folder 15, Lane Theological Seminary Records, Presbyterian Historical Society, Philadelphia.
22. Cincinnati's major industry was meatpacking. Some four hundred thousand pigs per annum were processed from its slaughterhouses in the 1850s, feeding millions of slaves. Roger Horowitz, *Putting Meat on the American Table: Taste, Technology, Transformation* (Baltimore: Johns Hopkins University Press, 2006), 47.
23. *Cincinnati Whig*, December 21, quoted in: *The Philanthropist*, January 1, 1836.
24. *The Philanthropist*, January 8, 1836.
25. *The Philanthropist*, January 29, 1836.
26. "Judge Jay to Oliver Wetmore, New York, November 17, 1835," *The Philanthropist*, February 19, 1836.
27. *The Philanthropist*, March 11, 1836.
28. *The Philanthropist*, February 12, 1836.
29. "The right of governing society, which the majority supposes to derive from its superior intelligence, was introduced into the United States by the first settlers." Tocqueville, *Democracy in America*, 255.
30. Many historians have seen the antigovernment Regulator Rebellion of 1765–1771 as a forerunner of the American Revolution. See: Marjolene Kars, *Breaking Loose Together: The Regulator Rebellion in Pre-Revolutionary North Carolina* (Chapel Hill: University of North Carolina Press, 2002).

31. David Grimsted, *American Mobbing, 1828–1861: Toward Civil War* (New York: Oxford University Press, 1998), viii.

32. According to Stowe, the two honorable exceptions in the local press were the *Cincinnati Journal* and *Hammond's Gazette*. Isabella Beecher Hooker, "A Brief Sketch of the Life of Harriet Beecher Stowe," in *Stowe in Her Own Time: A Biographical Chronicle of Her Life, Drawn from Recollections, Interviews, and Memoirs by Family, Friends, and Associates*, ed. Susan Belasco (Iowa City: University of Iowa Press, 2009), 257.

33. Taylor, *Frontiers of Faith*, 151. The Ohio Supreme Court eventually overturned Birney's 1837 conviction for harboring a female fugitive slave in his household.

34. *The Philanthropist*, February 12, 1836.

35. Ernst Trice Thompson, *Presbyterianism in the South*, vol. 1 (Richmond, Virginia: John Knox Press, 1963), 345.

36. Thomas J. Biggs to Lyman Beecher, August 18, 1834, quoted in: Harding, *A Certain Magnificence*, 361–362.

37. *Nile's Weekly Register* 69 (September 1835).

38. Charles Beecher, ed., *The Autobiography of Lyman Beecher, D. D.* (New York: Harper & Bros., 1865), 2:333.

39. *Historical Records and Studies*, vol. 4 (New York: United States Catholic Historical Society, 1906), 221.

40. Edward Wakin, *Enter the Irish-American* (Lincoln, Nebraska: Author's Guild, 2002), 75.

41. Daniel A. Cohen, "The Respectability of Rebecca Reed: Genteel Womanhood and Sectarian Conflict in Antebellum America," *Journal of the Early Republic* 16, no. 3 (Autumn 1996): 426.

42. Billington, *The Protestant Crusade*, 73.

43. Billington, *The Protestant Crusade*, 61.

44. "Report of the Committee, Relating to the Destruction of the Ursuline Convent, August 11, 1834," in *Documents Relating to the Ursuline Convent in Charlestown* (Boston: Samuel N. Dickinson, 1842), 6.

45. "Report of the Committee," in *Documents Relating to the Ursuline Convent*, 8.

46. *Catholic Telegraph*, August 29, 1834.

47. Beecher, *Autobiography*, 2:335.

48. "A body of native citizens is excited to indignation," Morse wrote, "(whether true or false alters not the case,) that an act of foul play . . . had occurred in the Charlestown nunnery." Though Morse claimed to "know of no one who justifies the illegal violence," he insisted that "the feeling of indignation which animated the populace, was a just and proper feeling." The "secret tyrannical punishment" allegedly inflicted on young novices thus reinforced perceptions of corruption at the heart of American Catholicism, regardless of any particulars in nativist minds. Morse, *Foreign Conspiracy*, 182–183.

49. Novices endured a diet of plain vegetables and bitter herbal tea, "in imitation of the Holy Fathers of the Desert, to mortify our appetites." Rebecca Reed, *Six Months in a Convent* (Boston: Russell, Odiorne, & Metcalf, 1835), 83. Reed's best-selling book sold fifty thousand copies in its first year. Cohen, "The Respectability of Rebecca Reed," 451.

50. Richard Hofstadter, *The Paranoid Style in American Politics and Other Essays* (New York: Knopf Doubleday, 2012), 21.

51. Anbinder, *Nativism and Slavery*, 9.

52. Slocum admitted fabricating Monk's narrative following a series of lawsuits. Sandra Frink, "Women, the Family, and the Fate of the Nation in American Anti-Catholic Narratives, 1830–1860," *Journal of the History of Sexuality* 18, no. 2 (May 2009): 238; *Thirty-Ninth Annual Report of the American Board of Commissioners for Foreign Missions* (Boston: T. R. Marvin, 1848), 54.

53. Bridget Ford, *Bonds of Union: Religion, Race, and Politics in a Civil War Borderland* (Chapel Hill: University of North Carolina Press, 2016), 24.

54. Isaac Kelso, *Danger in the Dark: A Tale of Intrigue and Priestcraft* (Cincinnati: Moore, Anderson, Wilstach, & Keys, 1854), v, 21.

55. Charles Elliott, *Delineation of Roman Catholicism, Drawn from the Authentic and Acknowledged Standards of the Church of Rome* (New York: Lane & Scott, 1851), 5.

56. Emil Klauprecht, *Cincinnati, or the Mysteries of the West*, trans. Steven Rowan, ed. Don Heinrich Tolzman (New York: Peter Lang, 1996), 4.

57. George C. Schoolfield, "The Great Cincinnati Novel," *Bulletin of the Historical and Philosophical Society of Ohio* 20, no. 1 (January 1962): 54.

58. Klauprecht, *Cincinnati*, 632, 638, 643.

59. John Baptist Purcell recruited the first Jesuits for Cincinnati on a visit to Rome in 1839. He appreciated their reputation, noting: "The Jesuits have come to Cincinnati. There is a growling indistinctly heard among the dens of bigots, like that of a distant and unfeared menagerie." Lamott, *History of the Archdiocese of Cincinnati*, 228.

60. Klauprecht, *Cincinnati*, 657.

61. Cist, *Cincinnati in 1851*, 83.

62. Tocqueville, *Democracy in America*, 300–301.

63. Beecher, *A Plea for the West*, 52–53.

64. Beecher, *A Plea for the West*, 49.

65. One historian described Kossuth's 1852 Cincinnati visit as "the greatest single reception of his entire American trip," notwithstanding stopovers in cities such as New York and Philadelphia. John W. Oliver, "Louis Kossuth's Appeal to the Middle West—1852," *Mississippi Valley Historical Review* 14, no. 4 (March 1928): 491. Quote by Kossuth's traveling companion Francis Pulszky in: Ford and Ford, *History of Cincinnati*, 100.

66. *Home Missionary* 15, no. 7 (November 1842): 147.

67. *Home Missionary* 15, no. 7 (November 1842).

68. Buggeln, "A Marketplace for Religion," 262.

69. Cist, *Cincinnati in 1851*, 78–82.

70. Wyneken, "The Distress of the German Lutherans," in: Bratt, *Antirevivalism in Antebellum America*, 103. Wyneken served in this period as an itinerant preacher for the Lutheran Church; his circuit included southern Ohio and large parts of the Midwest.

71. *Western Christian Advocate*, November 13, 1850.

72. Franz Von Löhner, "The Landscape and People of Cincinnati, 1846–47," trans. Frederic Trautmann, in *Ethnic Diversity and Civic Identity: Patterns of Conflict and Cohesion in Cincinnati since 1820*, ed. Henry D. Shapiro and Jonathan Sarna (Urbana: University of Illinois Press, 1992), 42.

73. Fortin, *Faith and Action*, 52.

74. Wilhelm Unterthiner to Provincial Arbogast Schoepf, July 23–26, 1844, in: Pat McCloskey, *God Gives His Grace: A Short History of the John the Baptist Provinces, 1844–2001* (Cincinnati: The Province, 2001), 9.

75. Williams, "German-American Catholicism," 25.

76. Orestes Brownson, "The Mission of America," *Brownson's Quarterly Review* 1 (July 1856): 417, 414.

77. F. X. Weininger to Orestes Brownson, September 1, 1854, I-3-1 ALS, Archdiocese of Cincinnati Collection, University of Notre Dame Archives.

78. Orestes Brownson, "Protestant Revivals and Catholic Retreats," *Brownson's Quarterly Review* 3, no. 3 (July 1858): 299, 312, 317–318.

79. Fortin, *Faith and Action*, 95.

80. James H. Campbell, "New Parochialism: Change and Conflict in the Archdiocese of Cincinnati, 1878–1925," in *Ethnic Diversity and Civic Identity: Patterns of Conflict and Cohesion in Cincinnati since 1820*, ed. Henry D. Shapiro and Jonathan Sarna (Urbana: University of Illinois Press, 1992), 125–126.

81. *Catholic Telegraph*, December 3, 1831.

82. *Cincinnati Journal*, November 5, 1831.

83. *Cincinnati Journal*, January 14, 1837.

84. *Catholic Telegraph*, February 20, 1835.

85. Richard W. Van Alstyne, *The Rising American Empire* (New York: W. W. Norton, 1960), 142.

86. *Catholic Telegraph*, May 21, 1846.

87. Tyler V. Johnson, *Devotion to the Adopted Country: Immigrant Volunteers in the Mexican War* (Columbia: University of Missouri Press, 2012), 59.

88. *Der Wahrheitsfreund*, July 1, 1847, trans. Andrew Thomas, in: Johnson, *Devotion to the Adopted Country*, 51.

89. *Catholic Telegraph*, November 5, 1846.

90. *Cincinnati Gazette*, October 6, 1852.

91. *Catholic Telegraph*, November 25, 1847.

92. *The Anti-Papist*, January 30, 1847. The longevity of this journal appears to have been limited. Only one issue survives extant.

93. *Cincinnati Daily Times*, September 4, 1848.

94. James L. O'Sullivan, "Annexation," *United States Magazine and Democratic Review* 17, no. 1 (July–August 1845).

95. Anbinder, *Nativism and Slavery*, 45.

96. *Cincinnati Daily Gazette*, February 7, 1853.

97. Maura Jane Farrelly, *Anti-Catholicism in America, 1620–1860* (Cambridge: Cambridge University Press, 2017), 181.

98. *Catholic Telegraph*, April 8, 1863.

99. *New York Tribune*, November 10, 16, 1853, in: Anbinder, *Nativism and Slavery*, 21.

100. Edward Fenwick to Anthony Blanc, March 22, 1853, vi-1-e, Archdiocese of New Orleans Collection, University of Notre Dame Archives.

101. Anbinder, *Nativism and Slavery*, 167.

102. *Cincinnati Daily Times*, April 13, 1855.

103. *Cincinnati Enquirer*, July 23, 1845.

104. *Cincinnati Enquirer*, November 18, 1845.

105. *Cincinnati Enquirer*, October 13, 1854.

106. *Cincinnati Enquirer*, June 15, 1854.

107. Baughin, "Nativism in Cincinnati," 125.

108. Peter Kenrick to John Baptist Purcell, November 9, 1853, II-4-1, Archdiocese of Cincinnati Collection, University of Notre Dame Archives.

109. J. W. King, *Alessandro Gavazzi: A Biography* (London: Partridge, 1857), 67–69.

110. *Hartford Daily Courant*, January 2, 1854, in: James F. Connelly, *The Visit of Archbishop Gaetano Bedini to the United States (June, 1853–February, 1854)* (Rome: Analecta Gregoriana, 1960), 132.

111. Frink, "Women, the Family, and the Fate of the Nation," 257.

112. Quoted in: Connelly, *The Visit of Archbishop Gaetano Bedini*, 99.

113. John Baptist Purcell to Anthony Blanc, December 30, 1853, vi-1-f, Archdiocese of New Orleans Collection, University of Notre Dame Archives.

114. Klauprecht, *German Chronicle*, 186.

115. *Catholic Telegraph*, December 31, 1853.

116. Anthony Blanc to John Baptist Purcell, January 12, 1854, II-4-m ALS, Archdiocese of Cincinnati Collection, University of Notre Dame Archives.

117. DePalma, *Dialogue on the Frontier*, 107.

118. *Cincinnati Enquirer*, January 25, 1854.

119. Agnes McCann, *Nativism in Kentucky to 1860* (Washington, DC: Catholic University of America Press, 1944), 55.

120. Edward Purcell to Anthony Blanc, January 19, 1854, vi-1-g, Archdiocese of New Orleans Collection, University of Notre Dame Archives.

121. Grimsted, *American Mobbing*, 228.

122. *Cincinnati Daily Gazette*, January 10, 1854.

123. *Cincinnati Enquirer*, January 19, 1854.

124. *Cincinnati Daily Gazette*, January 16, 1854.

125. *Cincinnati Enquirer*, March 18, 1855.

126. *Cincinnati Daily Times*, March 31, 1855.

127. John Baptist Purcell to Anthony Blanc, March 20, 1854, vi-1-g, Archdiocese of New Orleans Collection, University of Notre Dame Archives.

128. *Boston Bee*, June 15, 1855, in: Anbinder, *Nation and Slavery*, 117.

129. J. Mudd to Orestes Brownson, August 31, 1854, i-3-1, Orestes Brownson Collection, University of Notre Dame Archives.

130. *Cincinnati Daily Times*, March 31, 1855.

131. *Cincinnati Daily Times*, April 5, 1855.

132. Billington, *Protestant Crusade*, 421.

133. Grimsted, *American Mobbing*, 236.

134. Martin Weitz to "Dear devoted father, brother, sister-in-law, and children," July 29, 1855, in: Ronald H. Baylor, ed., *The Columbia Documentary History of Race and Ethnicity in America* (New York: Columbia University Press, 2004), 252.

135. Ernst Stille (1847), in: Walter D. Kamphoener, Wolfgang Johannes Helbich, and Ulrike Sommer, eds., *News from the Land of Freedom: German Immigrants Write Home* (Cornell, New York: Cornell University Press, 1991), 85–86.

136. *Cincinnati Daily Gazette*, January 30, 1854.

137. Thomas Spooner, *Resolutions of the Executive Council of Ohio*, June 5, 1855 (s.l., 1855), 1–2.

138. Anbinder, *Nativism and Slavery*, 46.

139. Anbinder, *Nativism and Slavery*, 174.

140. Eric Foner, *The Fiery Trial: Abraham Lincoln and American Slavery* (New York: W. W. Norton, 2010), 78.

141. Donald Bruce Johnson, ed., *National Party Platforms*, vol. 1, *1840–1956* (Champaign: University of Illinois Press, 1956), 27.

142. Anbinder, *Nativism and Slavery*, 175–176.

143. Billington, *The Protestant Crusade*, 417.

144. James Hennessey, *American Catholics: A History of the Roman Catholic Community in the United States* (New York: Oxford University Press, 1981), 170.

145. Fortin, *Faith and Action*, 105.

146. *Catholic Telegraph*, October 20, 1836.

CHAPTER 5

1. *The Bible in the Public Schools: Proceedings and Addresses at the Mass Meeting, Pike's Music Hall, Cincinnati, Tuesday Evening, September 28, 1869* (Cincinnati: The Committee in Charge of the Meeting, 1869), 8–9. Confusingly, a longer, but similarly titled book was published in Cincinnati the following year, recounting the arguments in the superior court trial that followed on the use of the Bible in the public schools. See *The Bible in the Public Schools: Arguments in the Case of John D. Minor et al., Versus the Board of Education of the City of Cincinnati et al: Superior Court of Cincinnati* (Cincinnati: Robert Clarke, 1870). To minimize confusion, the former will be referred to below as *The Bible in the Public Schools: Proceedings and Addresses*; the latter as *The Bible in the Public Schools: Arguments*.

2. "The Northwest Ordinance of 1807," in: Shriver and Wunderlin, *The Documentary Heritage of Ohio*, 60.

3. See article VIII, sections 3 and 25, at "Ohio Constitution of 1803 (Transcript)," Ohio History Central, accessed April 11, 2017, http://www.ohiohistorycentral.org/w/Ohio_Constitution_of_1803_(Transcript)#ARTICLE_VII._OFFICIAL_OATHS.

4. See, for example: Don H. Tolzmann, ed., *The First Description of Cincinnati and Other Settlements: The Travel Report of Johann Heckewelder (1792)*, trans. H. A. Ratterman (Lanham, Maryland: University Press of America, 1988), 43.

5. Goss, *Cincinnati: The Queen City*, 63.

6. *Western Spy and Hamilton Gazette*, October 31, 1801.

7. *Western Spy and Hamilton Gazette*, March 26, 1800.

8. James E. Klotter, *Our Kentucky: A History of the Bluegrass State*, 2nd ed. (Lexington: University Press of Kentucky, 2015), 100.

9. Aaron, *Cincinnati*, 205.

10. Farnsworth, *The Cincinnati Directory*, 37–39.

11. Aaron, *Cincinnati*, 190.

12. Virginia E. McCormick and Robert W. McCormick, *New Englanders on the Ohio Frontier: Migration and Settlement of Worthington, Ohio* (Kent, Ohio: Kent State University Press, 1998), 249.

13. John B. Shotwell, *A History of the Public Schools of Cincinnati* (Cincinnati: School Life, 1902), 38.

14. Shotwell, *Public Schools of Cincinnati*, 6–7, 123–124.

15. Isaac Martin, *History of the Schools of Cincinnati and Other Educational Institutions, Public and Private* (Cincinnati, 1900), 33.

16. *Fourth Annual Report of the Trustees and Visitors of Common Schools to the City Council of Cincinnati* (Cincinnati: The School Board, 1833), 7.

17. Fortin, *Faith and Action*, 36–39.

18. Fortin, *Faith and Action*, 37.

19. James Aloysius Burns, *The Growth and Development of the Catholic School System in the United States* (New York: Benziger Brothers, 1912), 182.

20. Hugh J. Nolan, ed., *Pastoral Letters of the American Hierarchy, 1792–1970* (Huntingdon, Indiana: Our Sunday Visitor, 1971), 138.

21. Pastoral Letter of 1861: F. Michael Perko, in: *A Time to Favor Zion: The Ecology of Religion and School Development on the Urban Frontier in Cincinnati, 1830–1870* (Chicago: Educational Studies, 1988), 158.

22. *Historical Sketches of Public Schools in Cities, Villages, and Townships of the State of Ohio* (s.l., 1876), n.p.

23. Steven K. Green, *The Bible, the School, and the Constitution: The Clash That Shaped Modern Church-State Doctrine* (New York: Oxford University Press, 2012), 96–97.

24. Beecher, *A Plea for the West*, 52.

25. *Western Christian Advocate*, February 18, 1848.

26. DePalma, *Dialogue on the Frontier*, 127.

27. William E. Smith and Ophia D. Smith, eds., "The Diary of Charles Peabody," *Bulletin of the Historical and Philosophical Society of Ohio* 11, no. 4 (October 1953): 285.

28. DePalma, *Dialogue on the Frontier*, 124.

29. *Catholic Telegraph*, March 15, 1851.

30. The Board of Education included two members for each city ward. Their religious affiliations in the year 1868–1869 were listed as: two "Jews," eighteen "Protestants," ten "Roman Catholics," and ten "Others." *The Bible in the Public Schools: Proceedings and Addresses*, 1.

31. Beecher, *A Plea for the West*, 140.

32. Calvin Stowe, "Professor Stowe's Report on the Education of Emigrants," in *Transactions of the Fifth Annual Meeting of the Western Literary Institute and College of Professional Teachers* (Cincinnati: The Executive Committee, 1836), 66.

33. On McGuffey's career, see: David Stradling, *In Service to the City: A History of the University of Cincinnati* (Cincinnati: University of Cincinnati Press, 2018), 30–32.

34. "Characters of the Puritan Fathers," in *McGuffey's Fourth Eclectic Reader*, 303.

35. John H. Westerhoff III, *McGuffey and His Readers: Piety, Morality, and Education in Nineteenth-Century America* (Nashville: Abingdon, 1978), 55. In spite of Smith's legal worries, his fortune reflected Cincinnati's economic growth and national demand. Among America's largest publishers of religious literature, Truman & Smith produced not only the *Eclectic Readers* but also the works of Lyman Beecher. McGuffey received a modest $1,000 plus limited royalties for his first edition; Winthrop Smith became a millionaire. See: Walter Havighurst, *The Miami Years, 1809–1869* (New York: G. P. Putnam & Sons, 1969), 65.

36. In 2019, the Texas State Board of Education revised curriculum standards in history. Among other complaints, critics alleged these standards minimized the impact of slavery. More broadly, concerns arose that these revisions would be reflected nationally, given the large public system in Texas.

37. Beecher, *A Plea for the West*, 11–12, 90–91.

38. Beecher, *A Plea for the West*, 63.

39. "From the Rev. DR. LYMAN BEECHER," in *McGuffey's Fourth Eclectic Reader*, 6.

40. Aaron, *Cincinnati*, 214.

41. *Transactions of the Eight Annual Meeting of the Western Literary Institute and College of Professional Teachers* (Cincinnati: James R. Allbach, 1839), v, 20–21. The W.L.I.C.P.T. aimed to establish "normal schools" under the patronage of every western state legislature and to promote uniform standards of teaching excellence. In 1838, for example, the W.L.I.C.P.T. approved eleven core competencies for graduate teacher trainees in fields ranging from pedagogy, science, and modern languages to "the history of education, including an outline of the educational systems of different ages and nations." The resolution also approved the "religious obligations of teachers in respect to benevolent devotedness to the moral and intellectual welfare of society, habits of entire self-control, purity of mind, elevation of character, etc."

42. Almira H. Lincoln Phelps, "An Essay on Female Education," in *Transactions of the Eight Annual Meeting of the Western Literary Institute and College of Professional Teachers* (Cincinnati: James R. Allbach, 1839), 174, 178.

43. David Root to George Beckwith, July 14, 1830, 286-1-5, folder 18, Lane Theological Seminary Records, Presbyterian Historical Society, Philadelphia.

44. Trollope, *Domestic Manners*, 62–63.

45. Fully two-thirds of converts during the Second Great Awakening were women. This feminization was evident in Cincinnati, prompting Fanny Trollope to observe in 1832 that nowhere else "religion has so strong a hold upon the women, or a lighter hold upon men." Donald C. Swift, *Religion and the American Experience: A Social and Cultural History, 1765–1997* (Armonk, New York: M. E. Sharpe, 1998), 106.

46. *Cincinnati Journal*, February 9, 1836.

47. Stuart C. Henry, *Unvanquished Puritan: A Portrait of Lyman Beecher* (Grand Rapids, MI: William B. Eerdmans, 1973), 171.

48. Fortin, *Faith and Action*, 129–140.

49. The Cincinnati School Act (1853) specified: "The common schools in the several districts of the city, shall at all times be equally free and accessible to all white children not less than six years of age." *The Bible in the Public Schools: Arguments*, 399.

50. Abdy, *Journal of a Residence*, 394.

51. Trollope, *Domestic Manners*, 30.

52. John-Baptist Purcell to Samuel Eccleston, February 9, 1837, 25Q7, Archdiocese of Baltimore Archives, St. Mary's Seminary and University, Baltimore.

53. Doolittle & Munson's 1841 map omitted several churches referenced in Charles Cist's directory of the Queen City that same year, including the African Presbyterian Church between Symmes and Fourth Streets and Bethel A.M.E. on Sixth Street and Broadway. Doolittle and Munson, *Topographical Map of the City*, 96–97.

54. See, for example: *Catholic Telegraph*, May 20, 1847; September 22, 1860; and July 15, 1863. In 1866, Francis Weininger led Cincinnati Jesuits to organize St. Ann's Colored Church and School, the city's first Catholic school serving the black community. By the beginning of the twentieth century, St. Ann's remained Cincinnati's only black Catholic school. Fortin, *Faith and Action*, 145–146; Perko, *A Time to Favor Zion*, 221.

55. Cincinnati's black population grew from 1,087 (1830) to 1,500 (1840), an increase of 37.9 percent. Cincinnati's total population grew from 24,831 (1830) to 46,338 (1840), up 86.6 percent. Richard W. Pih, "The Negro in Cincinnati, 1802–1841" (M.A. thesis, Miami University, Ohio, 1968), 68.

56. Pih, "The Negro in Cincinnati," 75.

57. Shotwell, *A History of the Public Schools of Cincinnati*, 450–451.

58. Nancy Bertaux and Michael Washington, "The 'Colored Schools' of Cincinnati and African American Community in Nineteenth-Century Cincinnati, 1849–1890," *Journal of Negro Education* 74, no. 1 (Winter 2005): 45.

59. Taylor, *Frontiers of Freedom*, 48–49.

60. Counted separately from the general male and female population, 738 "Blacks" were recorded across four of five urban wards. The totals for Cincinnati's third ward included no black citizens, presumably a deliberate omission. The directory's editor, Elizur Deming, noted that this unofficial census had been taken in December 1833 and he could not "vouch for its entire accuracy. It no doubt approximated to the truth, but there is reason to believe that the number given is something below the actual population." Deming, *The Cincinnati Directory for the Year 1834*, 266.

61. Calvin E. Stowe, "On the Education of Immigrants," in *Transactions of the Fifth Annual Meeting of the Western Literary Institute and College of Professional Teachers* (Cincinnati: The Executive Committee, 1836), 62, 63, 64, 68.

62. Martin, *History of the Schools of Cincinnati*, 85.

63. Martin, *History of the Schools of Cincinnati*, 84, 85, 88, 90–91.

64. Historian Zane L. Miller wrote: "So far as I know, no Cincinnatian in the mid-nineteenth century, during the heyday of German migration to this city, talked about the need for or the utility of constructing in Cincinnati a German community, that is, an organized group or groups dedicated to enlisting as many Germans as possible in the preservation of German ideals or customs or the genius of the race." Zane L. Miller, "Cincinnati Germans and the Invention of an Ethnic Group," in *Ethnic Diversity and Civic Identity: Patterns of Conflict and Cohesion in Cincinnati since 1820*, ed. Henry D. Shapiro and Jonathan Sarna (Urbana: University of Illinois Press, 1992), 165.

65. *A Debate on the Roman Catholic Religion: Held in the Sycamore-Street Meeting House, Cincinnati, from the 13th to the 21st of January, 1837* (Cincinnati: J. A. James, 1837), 10.

66. *A Debate on the Roman Catholic Religion*, viii, 333.

67. *A Debate on the Roman Catholic Religion*, 174.

68. DePalma, *Dialogue on the Frontier*, 113.

69. Perko, *A Time to Favor Zion*, 122–123.

70. John-Baptist Purcell to Samuel Eccleston, October 8, 1836, 25Q6, Archdiocese of Baltimore Archives, St. Mary's Seminary and University, Baltimore.

71. Roger A. Fortin, "Queen City Catholicism: Catholic Education in Cincinnati," in *Urban Catholic Education: Tales of Twelve American Cities*, ed. Thomas C.

Hunt and Timothy Walch (Notre Dame, Indiana: Alliance for Catholic Education Press, 2010), 122.

72. John-Baptist Purcell to Martin J. Spalding, December 18, 1839, 35Q1, Archdiocese of Baltimore Archives, St. Mary's Seminary and University, Baltimore.

73. *Eleventh Annual Report of the Board of School Trustees and Visitors* (Cincinnati: E. Graham, 1840), 4.

74. *The Bible in the Public Schools: Arguments*, 8.

75. *Western Christian Advocate*, October 27, 1852.

76. "Free Schools in Ohio: Address of the Catholic Archbishop," *New York Times*, March 31, 1853, in: James A. Gutowski, "Politics and Parochial Schools in Archbishop John Purcell's Ohio" (Ph.D. diss., Cleveland State University, May 2009), 90.

77. In 1840, for example, Archbishop Hughes petitioned the New York City school board demanding a share of the common schools fund for parochial education. He also addressed rallies, denouncing anti-Catholic bias in the public school system. Billington, *The Protestant Crusade*, 146–149.

78. Gutowski, "Politics and Parochial Schools," 90.

79. Anbinder, *Nativism and Slavery*, 1853; and William E. Gienapp, *The Origins of the Republican Party, 1852–1856* (New York: Oxford University Press, 1987), 163.

80. *The Bible in the Public Schools: Proceedings and Addresses*, 12, 20–21.

81. *The Bible in the Public Schools: Arguments,* 8–10, 108.

82. Nancy R. Hamant, "Religion in the Cincinnati Schools, 1830–1900," *Bulletin of the Historical and Philosophical Society of Ohio* 21, no. 4 (October 1963): 239.

83. As Tracy Fessenden noted, public school teachers in Cincinnati "thenceforward focused their efforts on supplying a 'moral' education in lieu of a specifically religious one." The use of *McGuffey Readers* (containing biblical excerpts) notably withstood the ban on the King James Bible. Tracy Fessenden, *Culture and Redemption: Religion, the Secular, and American Literature* (Princeton, New Jersey: Princeton University Press, 2007), 80.

84. United States Supreme Court, *Abington School District vs. Schemmp*, FindLaw, accessed January 30, 2017, http://caselaw.findlaw.com/us-supreme-court/374/203.html.

85. Jay P. Dolan, *The American Catholic Experience: A History from Colonial Times to the Present* (Garden City, New York: Doubleday, 1985), 262.

86. J. F. Maclear, ed., *Church and State in the Modern Age: A Documentary History* (New York: Oxford University Press, 1995), 208.

87. *Catholic Telegraph*, May 16, 1834.

88. *Twelfth Annual Report of the Board of Education* (Boston: Dutton & Wentworth, 1849), 117.

89. *Catholic Telegraph*, April 20, 1861.

90. Stradling, *In Service to the City*, 46–49.

91. *Cincinnati Gazette*, November 2, 1869, in: Fessenden, *Culture and Redemption*, 76.

92. *Catholic Telegraph*, September 1,1869.

93. See, for example: F. W. Rauch, *Lincoln Grand March* (Cincinnati: F. W. Rauch, 1860).

94. *The Bible in the Public Schools: Arguments*, 50.

95. *The Bible in the Public Schools: Proceedings and Addresses*, 16.

96. *Cincinnati Daily Gazette*, September 14, 1869.

97. DePalma, *Dialogue on the Frontier*, 133–134.

98. *Cincinnati Daily Gazette*, September 14, 1869.

99. *The Bible in the Public Schools: Proceedings and Addresses*, 16–17, 37.

100. Dolan, *The American Catholic Experience*, 222.

101. "No enlightened Catholic," Purcell told Alexander Campbell in 1837, "holds the Pope's infallibility to a matter of faith." Fortin, *Faith and Action*, 105.

102. *Common Schools of Cincinnati, Forty-First Annual Report for the School Year Ending June 30, 1870* (Cincinnati: Board of Common Schools, 1870), 19.

103. Shotwell, *Public Schools of Cincinnati*, 444–445.

104. *The Bible in the Public Schools: Arguments*, 9.

105. *The Bible in the Public Schools: Arguments*, 70–71.

106. *The Bible in the Public Schools: Arguments*, 105.

107. *The Bible in the Public Schools: Arguments*, 66.

108. *The Bible in the Public Schools: Arguments*, 66.

109. *The Bible in the Public Schools: Arguments*, 207.

110. *The Bible in the Public Schools: Arguments*, 221.

111. *The Bible in the Public Schools: Arguments*, 224.

112. *The Bible in the Public Schools: Arguments*, 226.

113. *The Bible in the Public Schools: Arguments*, 228.

114. *The Bible in the Public Schools: Arguments*, 232, 284.

115. *The Bible in the Public Schools: Arguments*, 323, 26.

116. "Jefferson's Letter to the Danbury Baptists," January 1, 1802, Library of Congress, accessed September 15, 2020, https://www.loc.gov/loc/lcib/9806/danpre.html.

117. *The Bible in the Public Schools: Arguments*, 390, 406.

118. *The Bible in the Public Schools: Arguments*, 370.

119. *The Bible in the Public Schools: Arguments*, 395, 404.

120. Robert Michaelsen, "Common School, Common Religion? A Case Study in Church-State Relations, Cincinnati, 1869–70," *Church History* 38, no. 2 (June 1969): 202–203.

121. Jonathan D. Sarna, "'A Sort of Paradise for the Hebrews': The Lofty Vision of Cincinnati Jews," in *Ethnic Diversity and Civic Identity: Patterns of Conflict and Cohesion in Cincinnati since 1820*, ed. Henry D. Shapiro and Jonathan D. Sarna (Urbana: University of Illinois Press, 1992), 157, 131, 133, 134.

122. Sarna, "A Sort of Paradise," 134, 141, 144, 147.

123. *The Israelite*, October 15, 1869. The longest-running English-language American Jewish newspaper still published, *The Israelite* (1854) was renamed the *American Israelite* in 1874, reflecting Wise's patriotic Reformed Judaism.

124. Sarna, "A Sort of Paradise," 152.

125. *Catholic Telegraph*, February 17, 1870.

126. "Board of Education v. Minor et al. 23 Ohio St. 211," in: John Bouvier, ed., *Bouvier's Law Dictionary: A Concise Encyclopedia of the Law*, vol. 2 (Boston: Boston Book, 1897), 958.

127. Donald E. Boles, *The Bible, Religion, and the Public Schools* (Ames: Iowa State University Press, 1965), 111.

128. Boles, *The Bible, Religion, and the Public Schools*, 203.

129. *The Bible in the Public Schools: Proceedings and Addresses*, 24.

130. The *Telegraph* criticized one anti–King James Bible Catholic board member, Joseph Carberry, for implying that public schools were superior to their parochial equivalents in the eyes of many parents. *Catholic Telegraph*, September 15, 1869.

131. Fessenden, *Culture and Redemption*, 78.

132. Perko, *A Time to Favor Zion*, 188.

133. Stephan F. Brumberg, "The Cincinnati Bible War (1869–1873) and Its Impact on the Education of the City's Protestants, Catholics, and Jews," *American Jewish Archives Journal* 54, no. 2 (2002): 30.

134. Sarna, "A Sort of Paradise," 147.

135. Brumberg, "The Cincinnati Bible War," 32–33.

136. *The Israelite*, January 8, 1869.

137. Brumberg, "The Cincinnati Bible War," 31–32.

138. DePalma, *Dialogue on the Frontier*, 135.

139. *The Bible in the Public Schools: Arguments*, 395.

140. Perko, *A Time to Favor Zion*, 209. The Arnett Act (1887) barred Ohio schools from refusing to accept students on the basis of color.

EPILOGUE

1. Don Heinrich Tolzmann, *Cincinnati's German Heritage* (Bowie, Maryland: Heritage Books, 1994), 128–135.

2. Douglas Carl Fricke, *Genealogy of the Mangold Family from Bavaria to Cincinnati, 1800 to 1930s* (Martinsville, Indiana: Allodium Chase, 2017), 51. Today, I-75 is notorious for poor maintenance and congestion.

3. The Association of Statisticians of American Religious Bodies counted 205,094 Catholics in Hamilton County (where Cincinnati is located) in its *2010 U.S. Religion Census*. This amounted to 25.6 percent of the Hamilton County population and 48.7 percent of all 421,006 religious adherents counted in Hamilton County that year. Clifford Grammich et al., eds., *2010 U.S. Religion Census: Religious Congregations and Membership Study* (Kansas City, Missouri: Nazarene Publishing House, 2012), 447.

4. "The American Values Atlas," PRRI, accessed July 27, 2020, http://ava.prri.org /#religious/2019/MetroAreas/religion. Of the thirty metro areas highlighted in PRRI's 2019 survey, the number of Catholics as a percentage of total population was as follows: Los Angeles (33 percent), Boston (30 percent), Miami (30 percent), San Francisco (27 percent), Chicago (25 percent), Philadelphia (25 percent), Pittsburgh (25 percent), Detroit (24 percent), Phoenix (24 percent), Cleveland (23 percent), Denver (23 percent), Houston (23 percent) Dallas (22 percent), Las Vegas (22 percent), Orlando (22 percent), Washington, DC (22 percent), Indianapolis (21 percent), Milwaukee (21 percent), Minneapolis–St. Paul (21 percent), St. Louis (21 percent), Cincinnati (19 percent), Columbus (19 percent), Kansas City (19 percent), New York City (19 percent), Portland (19 percent), Tampa–St. Petersburg (19 percent), Seattle (18 percent), Charlotte (17 percent), Atlanta (16 percent), and Nashville (14 percent).

In 1854, when Isaac Mayer Wise arrived, Cincinnati's population was 155,000, including 4,000 Jews (2.58 percent total population). Max B. May, *Isaac Mayer Wise: The Founder of American Judaism* (New York: G. P. Putnam's Sons, 1916), 153.

5. Archdiocese of Cincinnati, accessed July 27, 2020, http://www.catholiccincinnati .org/education/mycatholicschool/fast-facts-about-our-catholic-schools/.

6. Archdiocese of Cincinnati, accessed July 27, 2020, http://www.catholiccincinnati .org/ministries-offices/cise-catholic-inner-city-schools-education-fund/frequently -asked-questions/.

7. Higher education institutions under the Archdiocese of Cincinnati are: Mount St. Joseph University and Xavier University (both in Cincinnati), the Ursuline-administered Chatfield College (Brown County), and the University of Dayton. The *Catholic Telegraph* was founded in 1831.

8. Nutt, *Contending for the Faith*, 112.

9. Goodykoontz, *Home Missions*, 301, 342.

10. "QuickFacts: Cincinnati City, Ohio," United States Census Bureau, accessed August 18, 2021, https://www.census.gov/quickfacts/cincinnaticityohio.

Bibliographic Essay

·

This essay identifies the most valuable sources relating to this book. While not every source is cited, the bibliographic description is designed for utility, enabling readers to identify useful and relevant material according to the general scope of the book and each chapter.

GENERAL SOURCES

Archival Sources

Although this book was written in Cincinnati, its research led further afield. My doctoral research on Kentucky revivalism helped describe the frontier landscape in Chapter 1. The diary of Baptist preacher David Barrow is a rich source on the Ohio Valley, as is Robert Breckinridge McAfee's "The History of the Rise and Progress of the First Settlements on Salt River & Establishment of the New Providence Church." Both manuscripts are at the Filson Historical Society in Louisville, Kentucky. John Lyle's "Journal of a Missionary Tour within the Bounds of the Cumberland Presbytery Performed in the Year 1805," held in manuscript at the Kentucky Historical Society in Frankfort, is another key source on the Great Revival. In addition, the Reuben T. Durrett Collection, University of Chicago Library Special Collections, is one of the most extensive collections of Ohio Valley manuscripts curated in the nineteenth century.

The Archdiocese of Cincinnati Collection (1815–1963) at the University of Notre Dame archives in South Bend, Indiana, includes a wealth of correspondence from Cincinnati's Catholic clergy, including Edward Fenwick, Stephen Badin, and John Baptist Purcell. The Archdiocese of Baltimore Archives at St. Mary's Seminary and University, Baltimore, includes useful correspondence between Cincinnati's Catholic clergy and Baltimore, the first Catholic archdiocese of the United States. The Lane Theological Seminary Records at the Presbyterian Historical Society, Philadelphia, include essential material on the founding of the seminary, as well as archives relating to the Lane rebels.

A remarkable research collection was the records of the American Home Missionary Society (1816–1907). This archive, consisting of volumes of incoming and outgoing correspondence, has been at the Amistad Research Center at Tulane University, New Orleans, since 1969. Although the detailed quarterly reports field missionaries proved to the A.H.M.S. are invaluable, they remain overlooked by historians. A systematic study of the records, while valuable, would be daunting, given the size of the collection (294 linear feet) and its unindexed status.

The Cincinnati Historical Library was home base for the initial research of this book. Archival resources include Caleb Swann Walker's manuscript, "Diary," MSS VP 2307, which provides one of the fullest descriptions of early Cincinnati's religious landscape, and the Lytle Family Papers, MSS L996p, an extensive archive from one of Cincinnati's leading families.

Newspapers

Cincinnati's many newspapers catered to both English and German readers. William Maxwell, an apprentice of Kentucky printer John Bradford, founded Ohio's first newspaper, the *Centinel of the Northwest Territory*, in 1793. In 1796, publisher Edmund Freeman purchased the *Centinel*, which ran as *Freeman's Journal* until 1800. Other pioneering newspapers included the *Western Spy and Hamilton Gazette* (founded 1799) and *Liberty Hall* (1815–1857). See: V. C. Stump, "Early Newspapers of Cincinnati," *Ohio History* 34, no. 2 (April 1925).

The proliferation of nineteenth-century newspapers reflected population growth. Steam printing and the telegraph enabled the shift from weekly to daily publication of many titles. The *Cincinnati Daily Enquirer* (1841–present) became the leading Democratic-affiliated paper in the city, surviving as the *Cincinnati Enquirer*. Other leading newspapers of the mid-nineteenth century included the *Cincinnati Daily Gazette* (1827–1881), edited by urban reformer Louis Wright, and the *Cincinnati Commercial* (1843–1884), which, as its name suggested, specialized in the business concerns of the city.

Other unique newspapers include the *Western Christian Advocate* (1834–1929), the influential Cincinnati organ of the Methodist Episcopal Church. The *Cincinnati Journal* (1829–1841), noted for its Presbyterian perspective, was the newspaper of choice for the Beecher-Stowe family. Under the aegis of publisher James D. "Pap" Taylor, the *Cincinnati Daily Times* (1841–1879) served as the mouthpiece for the anti-immigrant American Party in the 1850s and is a key source on Cincinnati nativism. Influenced by William Lloyd Garrison's abolitionism, James G. Birney's newspaper *The Philanthropist* (1836–1843) became a political lightning rod in the Queen City. The *Catholic Telegraph* (1831–present) remains the oldest surviving Catholic newspaper in the nation, although its German-language sister publication, *Der Wahrheitsfreund* (1837–1907), is long since defunct. Other German-language newspapers included *Der Republikaner* (1842–1858), edited by Emil Klauprecht, and Friedrich Hausaurek's *Die Hochwaechter* (1845–1849).

Other Primary Sources

Together, Daniel Drake's *Natural and Statistical View, or Picture of Cincinnati and the Miami Country* (Cincinnati: Looker & Wallace, 1815) and Frances Trollope's *Domestic*

Manners of the Americans (New York: Penguin Classics, 1832, 1997) provide an invaluable synopsis, combining the enthusiasm of the former classic account with the skepticism of the latter. A brace of studies by Cincinnati booster Charles Cist—*Cincinnati in 1841: Its Early Annals and Future Prospects* (Cincinnati, 1841) and *Sketches and Statistics of Cincinnati in 1851* (Cincinnati: William H. Moore, 1851)—furnish a wealth of statistical and anecdotal evidence found nowhere else. Business directories provide a wealth of insight into early life in the city. Notable examples include: Oliver Farnsworth, *The Cincinnati Directory* (Cincinnati: Oliver Farnsworth, 1819); and Edward Deming, *The Cincinnati Directory for the Year 1834* (Cincinnati: E. Deming, 1834).

The Queen City was a magnet for visitors, both foreign and domestic. Notable travel writers included Alexis de Tocqueville, who with his friend Gustave de Beaumont journeyed through the city and its region in 1831. See: George Wilson Pierson, ed., *Tocqueville and Beaumont in America* (Baltimore: Johns Hopkins University Press, 1996). The following decade, novelist Charles Dickens visited the region on a literary tour, described in his *American Notes for General Circulation*, vol. 2 (London: Chapman & Hall, 1842). In addition to household names such as Dickens and Tocqueville, significant descriptions of Cincinnati can be found in such travelogues as: Edward S. Abdy, *Journal of a Residence and Tour of the United States of North America, from April 1833, to October, 1834*, vol. 2 (London: John Murray, 1835); Isabella Lucy Bird, *The Englishwoman in America* (London: John Murray, 1856); and Charles Fenno Hoffman, *A Winter in the West* (New York: Harper & Brothers, 1835).

Secondary Sources

Despite several excellent histories on the Queen City, there has been no comprehensive monograph on Cincinnati's antebellum religious landscape. At the denominational level, useful studies of religion include: Roger Fortin, *Faith and Action: A History of the Archdiocese of Cincinnati, 1821–1996* (Columbus: Ohio State University Press, 2002); John H. Lamott, *History of the Archdiocese of Cincinnati, 1821–1921* (New York and Cincinnati: Frederick Pustet, 1921); Rick Nutt, *Contending for the Faith: The First Two Centuries of the Presbyterian Church in the Cincinnati Area* (Cincinnati: Presbytery of Cincinnati, 1991); and Jonathan D. Sarna and Nancy H. Klein, *The Jews of Cincinnati* (Cincinnati: Center for the Study of American Jewish Experience, Hebrew Union College–Jewish Institute of Religion, 1989).

Margaret DePalma's study of sectarian identity in the Ohio Valley, *Dialogue on the Frontier: Catholic and Protestant Relations, 1793–1883* (Kent, Ohio: Kent State University Press, 2004), explores Catholic-Protestant relations under the tenures of Edward Fenwick, the first Catholic bishop of Cincinnati, and his successor, John Baptist Purcell. While acknowledging sectarian tensions, DePalma shows how pluralism evolved amid Protestant-Catholic dialogue, exchange, and debate.

F. Michael Perko's *A Time to Favor Zion: The Ecology of Religion and School Development on the Urban Frontier in Cincinnati, 1830–1870* (Chicago: Educational Studies Press, 1988) explores Cincinnati's public schools alongside their parochial equivalent. Perko identified conflict between Catholicism and mainstream Protestantism as crucial to both systems in the antebellum era. Written as a dissertation in 1942 but published as a book five decades later, Daniel Aron's *Cincinnati: Queen City of the West, 1819–1838* (Columbus: Ohio State University Press, 1992) remains valuable on early Cincinnati, including its chapter on religion. Like Perko, Aaron emphasized controversies between Catholic and Presbyterian clergy. Though less concerned with religion, Alan I. Marcus's *Plague of Strangers: Social Groups and the Origins of City Services in Cincinnati, 1819–1870* (Columbus: Ohio State University Press, 1991) focused on Catholic immigrants in the context of social groups and city services. Another useful study, Nikki Taylor's *Frontiers of Freedom: Cincinnati's Black Community, 1802–1868* (Athens: Ohio University Press, 2005), discusses Cincinnati's black population in relation to the city's religious and educational landscape. Walter Stix Glazer's *Cincinnati in 1840: The Social and Functional Organization of an Urban Community during the Pre-Civil War Period* (Columbus: Ohio State University Press, 1999) focuses on labor relations while recognizing the role of religious institutions in building community. Other significant studies of nineteenth-century Cincinnati include: Henry C. Binford, *From Improvement to City Planning: Spatial Management in Cincinnati from the Early Republic through the Civil War Decade* (Philadelphia: Temple University Press, 2021); and Steven J. Ross, *Workers on the Edge: Work, Leisure, and Politics in Industrializing Cincinnati, 1788–1890* (New York: Columbia University Press, 1985).

CHAPTER 1: BEYOND THE FRONTIER: THE RELIGIOUS LANDSCAPE

Primary

Early accounts of the Ohio Valley reveal settler fascination with the ancient mounds that punctuated the landscape. Among the most notable accounts are: Caleb Atwater, *A History of the State of Ohio, Natural and Civil* (Cincinnati: Glazen & Shepard, 1838); and William Henry Harrison's *A Discourse of the Aborigines of the Ohio Valley* (Chicago: Fergus, 1883). General accounts by itinerant preachers illustrating the religious landscape include: Francis Asbury, *Journal of the Rev. Francis Asbury, Bishop of the Methodist Episcopal Church* (New York: Lane & Scott, 1852); Timothy Flint, *Recollections of the Last Ten Years, Passed in Occasional Residences and Journeyings in the Valley of the Mississippi* (Boston: Cummings, Hilliard, & Co., 1826); and Johann Heckewelder, *The First Description of Cincinnati and Other Ohio Settlements (1792)*, trans. Don Heinrich Tolzmann (Lanham, Maryland: University Press of America, 1990). Martin John Spalding, *Sketches of the Early Catholic Missions of Kentucky, from Their Commencement in 1787, to the Jubilee of 1826–7* (Louisville, Kentucky: J. Webb & Brothers, 1844) includes numerous accounts by Catholic preachers in Kentucky, most of whom itinerated in Ohio.

Notable primary sources on the Great Revival of the West include: James B. Finley, *Autobiography of James B. Finley; or, Pioneer Life in the West* (Cincinnati, 1853); James McGready, *The Posthumous Works of the Reverend and Pious James M'Gready* (Nashville: J. Smith, 1837); Richard McNemar, *The Kentucky Revival; or, a Short History of the Late Extraordinary Out-Pouring of the Spirit of God, in the Western States of America* (Pittsfield, Massachusetts, 1808); Levi Purviance, *The Biography of Elder David Purviance* (Dayton, Ohio: B. F. & G. W. Ells, 1848); Adam Rankin, *Review of the Noted Revival in Kentucky, Commenced in the Year of Our Lord, 1801* (Lexington, Kentucky: John Bradford, 1803); and Barton Stone, *The Biography of Eld. Barton Warren Stone* (Cincinnati: J. A. & U. P. James, 1847). In addition to the aforementioned relatively well-known titles (written by clergymen), the collected letters of Charlotte Chambers

Ludlow Riske, curated in the form of a memoir, provide a fascinating perspective on Cincinnati evangelical culture: Lewis H. Garrard, *Memoir of Charlotte Chambers, by Her Grandson, Lewis H. Garrard* (Philadelphia: T. K. & P. G. Collins, 1856).

William Warren Sweet's magisterial *Religion on the American Frontier*, 4 vols. (New York: Harper & Row, 1936) contains much material still otherwise unavailable, with volumes dedicated to the Presbyterian, Congregationalist, Baptist, and Methodist clergy of the Ohio Valley frontier. Reuben Gold Thwaites's thirty-two-volume edited collection, *Early Western Travels, 1748–1846* (Cleveland: Arthur H. Clark, 1904–1907), remains a treasure trove for the old Northwest. A more recent curation of eyewitness accounts, Ellen Eslinger, ed., *Running Mad for Kentucky: Frontier Travel Accounts* (Lexington: University Press of Kentucky, 2004), presents a vivid panorama of frontier Kentucky, prefaced with an excellent introductory essay.

Secondary

Though his American exceptionalism is now dated, Frederick Jackson Turner anticipated a more holistic history of the United States with his emphasis on physical geography and environment. His "frontier thesis" remains a seminal document and is essential for understanding later developments of frontier historiography. See: Frederick Jackson Turner, "The Significance of the Frontier in American History," in *Frontier and Section: Selected Essays of Frederick Jackson Turner*, ed. Ray Allen Billington (Englewood Cliffs, New Jersey: Prentice Hall, 1961).

In describing the American frontier, Richard C. Wade was arguably the first modern urban historian. His *The Urban Frontier: The Rise of Western Cities, 1790–1830* (Cambridge, Massachusetts: Harvard University Press, 1959) emphasized the vitality of commercial river cities—notably Cincinnati, Louisville, and St. Louis—in the development of the Midwest. Rather than passively evolving in response to agrarian growth, as Turner implied, Wade asserted that these cities spearheaded the cultural, political, and democratic emergence of their hinterlands. Timothy L. Smith's *Revivalism and Social Reform: American Protestantism on the Eve of the Civil War* (New York: Harper & Row, 1957) offered a strikingly similar challenge to Turner's frontier thesis, describing how the beating heart of American Protestantism lay in urban, not rural, society. In so doing, Smith complicated the prevailing historical identification of the cities with Catholicism versus agrarian Protestant communities.

Useful accounts of the Ohio Valley frontier include: Andrew R. L. Cayton, *Ohio: The History of a People* (Columbus: Ohio State University Press, 2002); Craig Thompson Friend, *Along the Maysville Road: The Early American Republic in the Trans-Appalachian West* (Knoxville: University of Tennessee Press, 2005); Patrick Griffin, *American Leviathan: Empire, Nation, and Revolutionary Frontier* (New York: Hill & Wang, 2007); R. Douglas Hurt, *The Ohio Frontier: Crucible of the Old Northwest, 1720–1830* (Bloomington: Indiana University Press, 1998); and Mary Stockwell, *Unlikely General: "Mad" Anthony Wayne and the Battle for America* (New Haven, Connecticut: Yale University Press, 2018).

Among the best histories of the Great Revival, although mostly neglecting its urban dimensions, are: John B. Boles, *The Great Revival, 1787–1805: The Origins of the Southern Evangelical Mind* (Lexington: University Press of Kentucky, 1972); and Paul Conkin, *Cane Ridge: America's Pentecost* (Madison: University of Wisconsin Press, 1990).

CHAPTER 2: ATHENS OF THE WEST? IMMIGRATION, CHOLERA, AND ALCOHOL

Primary

Cincinnati newspapers reporting on the cholera epidemic of 1849 included the *Catholic Telegraph*, the *Cincinnati Daily Gazette*, the *Cincinnati Daily Times*, the *Cincinnati Enquirer*, the *Cincinnati Volksblatt*, the *Daily Atlas*, the *Daily Dispatch*, *Der Wahrheits-freund*, *Liberty Hall*, and the *Western Christian Advocate*.

John Lea's epidemiological survey of Cincinnati in 1849, a landmark investigative study of epidemic disease in the nineteenth century, was recently reprinted: John Lea, "Reprints and Reflections: 'Cholera, With Reference to the Geological Theory: A Proximate Cause—a Law by Which It Is Governed—a Prophylactic,'" *International Journal of Epidemiology* 42 (2013). Other noteworthy sources on the pandemic include: Thomas C. Carroll, "Observations on the Asiatic Cholera, As It Appeared in Cincinnati during the Years 1849 and 1850," *Western Lancet* 15 (1854); J. P. Harrison, "Letter on the Sanitary Conditions of Cincinnati," in *The Transactions of the American Medical Association*, vol. 2 (1849); S. A. Latta, *The Cholera in Cincinnati: or, A Connected View of the Controversy between the Homeopathists and the Methodist Expositor* (Cincinnati: Morgan & Overend, 1850); L. M. Lawson, *Cholera: Its Nature and Treatment* (Cincinnati: Robinson & Jones, 1848); and Orin E. Newton, *Asiatic Cholera as It Appeared in Cincinnati, O., in the Years 1849, 1850 and 1866* (Cincinnati: American Eclectic Review, 1867).

Daniel Drake's civic leadership and medical influence transcended Cincinnati and the Ohio Valley. See: Edward D. Mansfield, *Memoirs of the Life and Services of Daniel Drake: With Notices of the Early Settlement of Cincinnati, and Some of Its Pioneer Citizens* (Cincinnati: Applegate, 1860); and Henry D. Shapiro and Zane L. Miller, eds., *Physician to the West: Selected Writings of Daniel Drake on Science and Society* (Lexington: University Press of Kentucky, 1970).

The *Western Washingtonian and Sons of Temperance Record* (1845–?) provides fascinating insight into the culture of Cincinnati temperance radicals. The *Journal of the American Temperance Union* (1837–1857) provides a national overview of early temperance reform, rooted in middle-class evangelicalism.

Secondary

Cholera in the United States has not enjoyed the scholarly attention recently afforded other pandemics, including yellow fever, smallpox, or even influenza, but Owen Whooley's *Knowledge in the Time of Cholera* (Chicago: University of Chicago Press, 2013) showed how cholera's urban impact spurred the professionalization and national growth of American medicine. Charles Rosenberg's classic reprint, *The Cholera Years: The United States in 1832, 1849, and 1866* (Chicago: University of Chicago Press, 2009), is another standard work. J. S. Chambers, *The Conquest of Cholera: America's Greatest Scourge* (New York: MacMillan, 1938) remains valuable, despite its age. In addition to these works, Martin V. Melosi's *The Sanitary City: Infrastructure in America from Colonial Times to the Present* (Baltimore: Johns Hopkins University Press, 2000) showed how the "sanitary idea" developed in Victorian Britain, entering the mainstream of American urban reform, city planning, and public infrastructure.

There is no monographic treatment of cholera in Cincinnati, but several scholarly articles address its impact in the Queen City and the Ohio Valley, notably: Ruth C. Carter, "Cincinnatians and Cholera: Attitudes toward the Epidemics of 1832 and 1849," *Queen City Heritage* 50 (1993); Donald A. Hutslar, "God's Scourge: The Cholera Years in Ohio," *Ohio History Journal* 105 (Summer–Autumn 1996); and Joan E. Marshall, "Cholera in an Indiana Market Town: 'Boosters' and Public Health Policy in Lafayette, 1849," *Indiana Magazine of History* 98, no. 3 (September 2002).

Jed Dannenbaum's *Drink and Disorder: Temperance Reform in Cincinnati from the Washingtonian Revival to the WCTU* (Urbana and Chicago: University of Illinois Press, 1984) established the Queen City's mainstream importance amid the currents of urban reform in nineteenth-century America. See also: Jed Dannenbaum, "The Crusader: Samuel Cary and Cincinnati Temperance," *Cincinnati Historical Society Bulletin* 33, no. 2 (Summer 1975); and Jed Dannenbaum, "Immigrants and Temperance: Ethnocultural Conflict in Cincinnati, 1845–1860," *Ohio History* 87, no. 2 (Spring 1978).

For broader discussion of drink and temperance, the following studies were especially valuable: William J. Rorabaugh, *The Alcoholic Republic: An American Tradition* (New York: Oxford University Press, 1979); and John F. Quinn, *Father Mathew's Crusade: Temperance in Nineteenth-Century Ireland and Irish America* (Amherst: University of Massachusetts Press, 2002).

CHAPTER 3: "THE DESTINY OF OUR NATION": MISSIONARY COMPETITION IN THE OHIO VALLEY

Primary

The American Home Missionary Society produced much literary propaganda, but perhaps the most consequential sermon by an A.H.M.S. minister is Horace Bushnell's *Barbarism the First Danger: A Discourse for Home Missions* (New York: William Osborn, 1847). In addition to its annual reports and correspondence, the society's *Home Missionary and American Pastor's Journal* (1828–1908) furnishes a rich array of correspondence, reports, and editorials, with much material on Cincinnati and the Ohio Valley. The society's huge archives, now housed at the Amistad Research Center at Tulane University, are dauntingly underresearched. A useful starting point is: David G. Horvath, ed., *Guide to the Microfilm Edition of the Papers of the American Home Missionary Society, 1816–1894* (Woodbridge, Connecticut: Scholarly Resources, 2005).

On the leading representative of evangelical Presbyterianism in Cincinnati, see: Lyman Beecher, *Autobiography of Lyman Beecher*, 2 vols., ed. Barbara Cross (Cambridge. Massachusetts: Belknap Press, 1961). On Beecher's feud with Joshua Lacy Wilson, see: Arthur J. Stansbury, *Trial of the Rev. Lyman Beecher, D.D. Before the Presbytery of Cincinnati on the Charge of Heresy* (New York: New York Observer, 1835); and Joshua Lacy Wilson, *Four Propositions Sustained against the Claims of the American Home Missionary Society* (Cincinnati: Robinson & Fairbank, 1831).

For the anti-revivalist perspective of American Protestantism, see: Calvin Colton, *Protestant Jesuitism* (New York: Harper & Brothers, 1836); and James D. Bratt, ed., *Antirevivalism in Antebellum America: A Collection of Religious Voices* (Piscataway, New Jersey: Rutgers University Press, 2006). *Brownson's Quarterly Review* (1844–1864) likewise offers a contrarian perspective, colored by the eccentric Catholicism of its editor, Orestes Brownson.

Secondary

Despite several recent historical studies of American foreign missions, the domestic missionary movement remains neglected. The only comprehensive monograph on the A.H.M.S. is now over eighty years old: Colin B. Goodykoontz, *Home Missions on the American Frontier: With Particular Reference to the American Home Missionary Society* (Caldwell, Idaho: Caxton Printers, 1939).

For general reading on religion and reform in nineteenth-century America, see: John R. Bodo, *The Protestant Clergy and Public Issues, 1812–1848* (Princeton, New Jersey: Princeton University Press, 1954); Jay P. Dolan, *Catholic Revivalism: The American Experience, 1830–1900* (Notre Dame, Indiana: University of Notre Dame Press, 1978); Jenny Franchot, *Roads to Rome: The Antebellum Protestant Encounter with Catholicism* (Berkeley: University of California Press, 1994); Vincent Harding, *A Certain Magnificence: Lyman Beecher and the Transformation of American Religion* (New York: Carlson Publishing, 1991); Nathan O. Hatch, *The Democratization of American Christianity* (New Haven, Connecticut: Yale University Press, 1989); Steven Mintz, *Moralists and Modernizers: America's Pre-Civil War Reformers* (Baltimore: Johns Hopkins University Press, 1995); Bertram Wyatt-Brown, *Lewis Tappan and the Evangelical War against Slavery* (Cleveland: Press of Case Western Reserve University, 1969); and Michael P. Young, *Bearing Witness against Sin: The Evangelical Birth of the American Social Movement* (Chicago: University of Chicago Press, 2006).

CHAPTER 4: "THE CAUSE OF AMERICA": NATIVISM, TOLERATION, AND FREEDOM

Primary

The two most influential antebellum nativist tracts were Lyman Beecher's *A Plea for the West* (Cincinnati: Truman & Smith, 1835) and Samuel F. B. Morse's *Foreign Conspiracy against the Liberties of the United States* (New York: Leavitt, Lord, & Co., 1835). For James L. O'Sullivan's editorial "Annexation," which popularized the term "Manifest Destiny," see: *United States Magazine and Democratic Review* 17, no. 1 (July–August 1845). Other notable nativist sources include: Charles Elliott, *Delineation of Roman Catholicism, Drawn from the Authentic and Acknowledged Standards of the Church of Rome* (New York: Lane & Scott, 1851); Isaac Kelso, *Danger in the Dark: A Tale of Intrigue and Priestcraft* (Cincinnati: Moore, Anderson, Wilstach, & Keys, 1854); Rebecca Reed, *Six Months in a Convent* (Boston: Russell, Odiorne, & Metcalf, 1835); and *Documents Relating to the Ursuline Convent in Charlestown* (Boston: Samuel N. Dickinson, 1842).

In its modern English translation, Emil Klauprecht's mystery novel, *Cincinnati, or the Mysteries of the West*, trans. Steven Rowan, ed. Don Heinrich Tolzman (New York: Peter Lang, 1996), provides an imaginative dive into the Queen City's antebellum backstreets.

The Cincinnati Historical Library houses a copy of Hugh Kirkland's self-published *Narratives of Scenes and Events Which Occurred Lately in Cincinnati, Entitled Freedom of Speech Vindicated, Defended, and Maintained* (Cincinnati: H. Kirkland, 1853).

Secondary

Among the most useful studies of Know-Nothingism is: Tyler Anbinder, *Nativism and Slavery: The Northern Know Nothings and the Politics of the 1850s* (New York: Oxford University Press, 1992). Other studies of nativism and anti-Catholicism include: Ray Allen Billington, *The Protestant Crusade, 1800–1860: A Study of the Origins of American Nativism* (New York: MacMillan, 1963); Maura Jane Farrelly, *Anti-Catholicism in America, 1620–1860* (Cambridge: Cambridge University Press, 2017); Bridget Ford, *Bonds of Union: Religion, Race, and Politics in a Civil War Borderland* (Chapel Hill: University of North Carolina Press, 2016); David Grimsted, *American Mobbing, 1828–1861: Toward Civil War* (New York: Oxford University Press, 1998); and Tyler V. Johnson, *Devotion to the Adopted Country: Immigrant Volunteers in the Mexican War* (Columbia: University of Missouri Press, 2012). An indispensable collection of essays, Henry D. Shapiro and Jonathan Sarna, eds., *Ethnic Diversity and Civic Identity: Patterns of Conflict and Cohesion in Cincinnati since 1820* (Urbana: University of Illinois Press, 1992), illustrates the breadth and depth of diversity in the antebellum city. In addition, William Baughin's well-researched 1963 University of Cincinnati master's thesis, "Nativism in Cincinnati before 1860," contains much valuable detail on ethnic and sectarian history.

CHAPTER 5: "A YOUNG EMPIRE OF MIND": EDUCATION AND THE BIBLE WAR

Primary

Key primary sources for the Cincinnati Bible War include: *The Bible in the Public Schools: Proceedings and Addresses at the Mass Meeting, Pike's Music Hall, Cincinnati, Tuesday Evening, September 28, 1869* (Cincinnati: The Committee in Charge of the Meeting, 1869); *The Bible in the Public Schools: Arguments in the Case of John D. Minor et al., Versus the Board of Education of the City of Cincinnati et al: Superior Court of Cincinnati* (Cincinnati: Robert Clarke, 1870); and "Board of Education v. Minor et al. 23 Ohio St. 211," in: John Bouvier, ed., *Bouvier's Law Dictionary: A Concise Encyclopedia of the Law*, vol. 2 (Boston: Boston Book, 1897). Also indispensable are the *Annual Reports* of Cincinnati's Board of Education ("Board of Trustees and Visitors") established in 1829.

More than a textbook, William Holmes McGuffey's *Eclectic Readers* series shaped American public education for over a century in numerous editions. See, for example: William H. McGuffey, *McGuffey's New First through Sixth Eclectic Reader* (Cincinnati: Winthrop B. Smith, 1836–1857).

The famous debate between Alexander Campbell and John Baptist Purcell is recorded in: *A Debate on the Roman Catholic Religion: Held in the Sycamore-Street Meeting House, Cincinnati, from the 13th to the 21st of January, 1837* (Cincinnati: J. A. James, 1837).

On Reform Judaism in Cincinnati, see: *The Israelite* (founded 1854). Renamed the *American Israelite* in 1874, this oldest Jewish newspaper in America remains in print to this day.

Secondary

On Cincinnati's Bible War, see: Donald E. Boles, *The Bible, Religion, and the Public Schools* (Ames: Iowa State University Press, 1965); Stephan F. Brumberg, "The Cincinnati Bible War (1869–1873) and Its Impact on the Education of the City's Protestants,

Catholics, and Jews," *American Jewish Archives Journal* 54, no. 2 (2002); Steven K. Green, *The Bible, The School, and the Constitution: The Clash That Shaped Modern Church-State Doctrine* (New York: Oxford University Press, 2012); James A. Gutowski, "Politics and Parochial Schools in Archbishop John Purcell's Ohio" (Ph.D. diss., Cleveland State University, May 2009); Nancy R. Hamant, "Religion in the Cincinnati Schools, 1830–1900," *Bulletin of the Historical and Philosophical Society of Ohio* 21, no. 4 (October 1963); and Robert Michaelsen, "Common School, Common Religion? A Case Study in Church-State Relations, Cincinnati, 1869–70," *Church History* 38, no. 2 (June 1969).

The following early histories chronicle Cincinnati's public schools: Isaac Martin, *History of the Schools of Cincinnati and Other Educational Institutions, Public and Private* (Cincinnati, 1900); John B. Shotwell, *A History of the Public Schools of Cincinnati* (Cincinnati: School Life, 1902); and *Historical Sketches of Public Schools in Cities, Villages, and Townships of the State of Ohio* (1876).

James Aloysius Burns, *The Growth and Development of the Catholic School System in the United States* (New York: Benziger Brothers, 1912) remains useful on the growth of the parochial system. For a more up-to-date history of Catholic schooling and culture, see: Jay P. Dolan, *The American Catholic Experience: A History from Colonial Times to the Present* (Garden City, New York: Doubleday, 1985); and Tracy Fessenden, *Culture and Redemption: Religion, the Secular, and American Literature* (Princeton, New Jersey: Princeton University Press, 2007).

On William Holmes McGuffey and the culture of higher education, see: Walter Havighurst, *The Miami Years, 1809–1869* (New York: G. P. Putnam & Sons, 1969); David Stradling, *In Service to the City: A History of the University of Cincinnati* (Cincinnati: University of Cincinnati Press, 2018); and John H. Westerhoff III, *McGuffey and His Readers: Piety, Morality, and Education in Nineteenth-Century America* (Nashville: Abingdon, 1978).

The epigraphs in this book are from the following sources: Introduction: Isaiah 59:19 (Authorized King James Bible); Chapter 1: "The Northwest Ordinance of 1787," in Phillip R. Shriver and Clarence E. Wunderlin, Jr., eds., *The Documentary Heritage of Ohio* (Athens: Ohio University Press, 2000), 60; Caleb Atwater, *A History of the State of Ohio: Natural and Civil* (Cincinnati: Glezen & Shepard, 1838), 11; Chapter 2: Karl Marx and Friedrich Engels, *The Communist Manifesto*, trans. Samuel Moore, at www.marxists.org, accessed May 20, 2022, https://www.marxists.org/archive/marx/works/1848/communist-manifesto/ch01.htm#007; Chapter 3: Frederick Jackson Turner, "The Significance of the Frontier in American History," *Frontier and Section: Selected Essays of Frederick Jackson Turner*, Ray Allen Billington, ed. (Englewood Cliffs: Prentice Hall, 1961), 37; Chapter 4: George Washington, "Address to the Inhabitants of Canada, 14 September, 1775," at https://founders.archives.gov, accessed May 20, 2022, https://founders.archives.gov/documents/Washington/03-01-02-0358; Chapter 5: "The Northwest Ordinance of 1787," in Shriver and, Jr., eds., *The Documentary Heritage of Ohio*, 60; Epilogue: John B. Stallo, quoted in *The Bible in the Public Schools: Arguments in the Case of John D. Minor et al., Versus the Board of Education of the City of Cincinnati et al: Superior Court of Cincinnati* (Cincinnati: Robert Clarke, 1870), 105.

Index

Matthew Smith is a Visiting Professor of History at Miami University.